Jule Carr

JULE

General without an Army

by Mena Webb

The University of North Carolina Press

Chapel Hill and London

CARR

Manufactured in the United States of America

Library of Congress Cataloging-in-Publication Data

Webb, Mena.

  Jule Carr: general without an army.

  Includes index.

  1. Carr, Julian Shakespeare. 2. Durham (N.C.)—
Biography. I. Title.

F264.D9W43 1987   975.6′563   86-1422

ISBN 0-8078-1705-8

General Julian S. Carr (courtesy of Mary Walker Pyne)

For Mack, with love

Only those whose lives are deep-rooted in the past are capable of leading the way to better things for the future.

—JEROME DOWD

Contents

Preface

AROUND 1975, I decided to write my recollections of growing up in Durham during the Roaring Twenties and leave them, as a legacy of sorts, to my grandchildren, who know a great deal about video games and Star Wars and rock-and-roll, but nothing about silent movies, the Depression, or the Charleston. I wanted to tell them about my interesting, eccentric family and some of the equally interesting and eccentric people who lived in our neighborhood, where the tree-lined streets were named Main and Dillard and Queen and Liberty and Cleveland. A fabulous Victorian mansion at the corner of Main and Dillard towered above the other houses in that sedate section of Durham. Many of those houses were quite handsome, but none was so grand as Somerset Villa, where I was allowed to play with the youngest grandchildren of the owner, a short, stout, pink-cheeked, snowy-haired gentleman whom everybody called General Carr. I had no idea, when I started my project, that the little general would take it over completely, and that what had begun as a personal memoir would end as a record of the life and times of Julian Shakespeare Carr.

Facts about Carr began to appear in print as early as 1884, and by 1927 many more appeared in *The Story of Durham: The City of the New South*, by William Kenneth Boyd. One look at the index of Boyd's history convinced me that Julian S. Carr did more for the town of Durham than any other man in the last quarter of the nineteenth century. I set out to discover how he managed to accomplish all that, and just what sort of man he really was.

Almost every person I asked for assistance gave it graciously, cheerfully, and enthusiastically. Librarians are among the nicest people in the world, I believe, and I am especially indebted to those in the University of North Carolina Library at Chapel Hill, where I did most of my research. Carolyn Wallace, Richard Schrader, and Michael Martin, of the Southern Historical Collection, and H. G. Jones, Alice Cotten, Jeffrey Hicks, and Robert Anthony, of the North Carolina Collection, have my sincere thanks. So does William S. Powell, of the University's history department, who answered all my questions with the prompt courtesy that is, to me, his hallmark. Without the help of these people, I never would have discovered so many things about Jule Carr.

I am also grateful to Mattie Russell, William King, the Reverend Albert Nelius, Robert Byrd, Patricia Webb, Samuel Boone, and Doris Shockley, of the Duke University Library; and to George Linder, former director of the Durham County Library, and Betty Clark, Peter Neal, and Ann Berkeley, current staff members of that institution. All of them extended helping hands to this novice researcher not once, but many times.

Others who supplied me with valuable information include the late Aycock Brown of Manteo, J. Claiborne Carr and Clarence Walker of Hillsborough, Mary Claire Engstrom and the late Manly Wade Wellman of Chapel Hill, Beth S. Taylor of Edenton, Catherine Bishir and Robert Dalton of Raleigh, O. L. "Bugs" Barringer of Rocky Mount, Mary Skinner Standell of Glendale, Calif., James G. Kenan of Atlanta, and Lola Williams, Betty Hodges, Julia Manning Wily, Mary Blackwell Pridgen Martin, Kate Lee Hundley Harris, Mary Leigh Webb, Ethel Lipscomb Girvin, Mary Walker Pyne, Mary Toms Cameron, Jessie M. Blount, Nita Brock, Katherine Guthrie, Bacon Fuller, George Cralle, Dr. Keith Brodie, Dr. Lenox Baker, the late Arthur M. Harris, the late Arnold Briggs, and the late Wyatt Dixon, all of Durham.

From other cities, members of the Carr clan came forward with invaluable letters, diaries, clippings, artifacts, and their own special memories of their unforgettable kinsman. The late Laura Noell Carr Chapman of Spartanburg, S.C., the late Henry C. and Betty Flower of Greenwich, Conn., Ruth Flower Lester and Ruth Patton Kline of Kansas City, Mo., Julian and Anne Carr of Atlanta, Mary Evelyn Carr Quisenberry of Wetumpka, Ala., J. Carr Dorman of Charlottesville, Va., A. Marvin Carr, Jr. of Miami, Claiborn McDowell Carr, Jr. of Watch Hill, R.I., Rufus Tucker Carr of Lawrence, N.Y., Austin and Millie Carr of Winston-Salem, Albert and Katherine Carr of Durham, Ann Sanger English of Bronxville, N.Y., Paul Sanger, Jr. of Atlanta, and the late Mary Ann Carr Sanger of Charlotte all supplied me not only with tangible aids to my research, but also with much needed encouragement. My debt to them is one I shall never be able to repay.

Most of all, I thank my husband and my two daughters for their moral support during the past ten years, and my grandchildren for inspiring me to begin what has at last become a book. Mack Webb, especially, kept me going with his belief in me and his insistence that I ignore all aspects of housekeeping and get on with what was really important—my research on the life and times of one of North Carolina's most outstanding citizens.

Much more could—and should—be written about Julian Shakespeare Carr, who deserves far more recognition for his services to Durham, the state, and the nation than he has yet received.

Jule Carr

1. Forebears, Franklin Street, and the University

JULIAN SHAKESPEARE CARR of Chapel Hill, North Carolina, was at Appomattox, Virginia, on 9 April 1865. In all probability he was one of the soldiers who wept when he learned that General Lee had surrendered to General Grant and that the Confederate States of America had ceased to exist. The nineteen-year-old Private Carr, half-starved, exhausted, and grief stricken over the South's defeat, faced at least two hundred miles of walking before he reached home. With no money, no provisions, and no prospects for the future, he had every reason to weep.

In 1884, less than twenty years after Appomattox, Julian Carr was a millionaire manufacturer of smoking tobacco, a man with a brilliant future. Not only was he happy, and perhaps a bit too well fed; he also was on his way to becoming famous. He had just launched the world's first international advertising campaign. The next sixteen years would see him involved in the establishment of railroads, utilities, banks, newspapers, hotels, and textile mills. By the end of the nineteenth century he would be North Carolina's leading business-man and one of the most successful entrepreneurs in the South.[1]

Carr's father propelled him into the career that led him from Little Rock, Arkansas, to Durham, a shabby little settlement twelve miles northeast of Chapel Hill. John Wesley Carr, who had been a prosperous merchant before the Civil War, was looking for a way to recoup his losses; when he learned that two Durham men were seeking capital for their burgeoning tobacco business, he saw a chance to become part of a venture that seemed bound to succeed. If John Carr had not believed that the manufacture and sale of bright leaf tobacco could mean economic salvation for himself and his son Julian, he never would have bought a partnership in the W. T. Blackwell Company.[2]

Nor would that partnership have been available had not William Thomas Blackwell and his associate, James R. Day, been in dire need of funds. There was a growing demand for their "Genuine Durham

Smoking Tobacco," which had become popular with both Union and Confederate soldiers during the closing days of the war; but in order to stay ahead of the fierce competition that was beginning to threaten them, they had to buy more raw leaf, hire more hands to process it, and enlarge their factory, a small frame building that looked more like a shed than a place of business. All that would cost money, and Blackwell and Day had only $210.63 between them, plus a debt of $509.63 that demanded repayment.[3]

John Carr had $4,000 to exchange for a one-third interest in the business and a job for his son, a short, square-jawed "college man" with light gray eyes, a ruddy complexion, and a large head. Jule, as his father called him, might come in handy at that. Jule Carr could manage the office. He could take over all the boring paperwork, handle the advertising, and leave "Buck" Blackwell and Jim Day free to buy and sell tobacco, which was what they did best.

So the four men agreed, money changed hands, and a contract was signed on 12 October 1870, which happened to be Jule Carr's twenty-fifth birthday. It was a significant milestone in his extraordinary life, which had begun in "the remotest town of the quietest county of the most backward old state in the Union" and would end fifty-four years later in a Chicago hotel room.[4]

Family records do not explain why John Wesley and Eliza Bullock Carr named their third son and fourth child for England's famous playwright. Those records state only that Julian Shakespeare was preceded into the world and the Carr household by William Green, Joseph Deems, and Mary Ella; he was followed, at two-year intervals, by Albert Gallatin, John Thomas, Emma, Eliza, and Robert Emmett. Neither Joseph nor John survived his first year, and William died at twenty, so Julian inherited the role of elder son when he was fifteen.[5]

The mother of these nine children was of English descent, and her family coat-of-arms, inscribed *Nil consciri sibi*, proclaims that to be a Bullock is "to be conscious of no fault." Being a sensible woman and a good Methodist, Eliza probably never took that inscription literally, but she was proud of her heritage and no doubt happy to be able to supply her son Julian with an ancestor who paved the way for his membership in the prestigious Society of the Cincinnati, formed in 1783 by officers of the Continental Army, who persuaded George Washington to join their group and become its president.[6]

This ancestor was Eliza's maternal grandfather, Solomon Walker, a lieutenant in the Sixth Regiment of the North Carolina Continental Infantry who fought with Washington at Valley Forge. Solomon Walker was not Eliza's only illustrious forebear. On her father's side was Captain Hugh Bullock, an Englishman who was born in 1580, became a member of the King's Council in 1631, and subsequently decided to emigrate to America, where some of his kinsmen already were living. Hugh Bullock took his family to York County, Virginia, where he became a planter, merchant, member of the colonial assembly, and a man of considerable importance. Apparently he also became homesick, for he eventually returned to England and died there in 1650.[7]

One of the captain's grandsons, Richard Bullock, "sold out on account of Indian trouble" and moved to Nutbush Creek in Granville County, North Carolina. He acquired land, slaves, and a number of children, one of whom he christened Joshua. Joshua Bullock married Ann Cook and subsequently had a son named Richard, after his father; this Richard Bullock married Solomon Walker's daughter, Mildred, "at Pop Castle, Granville County, N.C. in 1804." They were a prolific couple, and their youngest child, Eliza Panill, was born on 6 April 1815 at Tally Ho, a few miles south of Oxford, the county seat.[8] Nothing is known about her life until she moved with her widowed mother to Chapel Hill, where she met and married John Wesley Carr, a handsome young storekeeper with an expressive, thin-lipped mouth, deep-set blue eyes, and "a fine natural red in his cheeks."[9]

Unlike Eliza Bullock, John Carr did not grow up on a plantation. His father was a yeoman farmer without wealth or influence, but with an impressive lineage. According to a genealogist later hired by his son Julian to explore the family tree, two thirteenth-century Scottish border chieftains, Ralph and John Karre, were the progenitors of everyone named Carr, as well as of everyone named Karre, Kerre, Kerr, and Ker. That genealogical surmise forged a link between John Wesley Carr of Orange County, North Carolina, and Robert Carr, earl of Somerset and the Scottish favorite of King James I of England. It is almost certain that John Carr grew up not knowing he was kin to the man who became lord chamberlain to England's king in 1614, but the fact did surface in 1888, when his son built a palatial mansion in Durham and called it Somerset Villa.[10]

Other facts concerning John Carr's paternal ancestry indicate that his forebears frequently intermarried and often changed the spelling of their name. His great-great-great-grandfather, Mark Kerr of Roxburghshire, Scotland, had a son, John, who changed his surname to Carr before he married an Irish girl named Margaret Kerr. A few years later, John and Margaret Carr and their infant sons, John and Peter, were forced to leave Scotland for political reasons; Parish Aghnamullen, County Monoghan, Ireland, became their new home. The older boy, John, took a wife named Sarah Kerr and lived on a farm in County Down from 1732 until 1741, when he emigrated to America and settled within a few miles of Philadelphia. After nine years in Pennsylvania, he moved his family to a site near Leesburg, Virginia, and became "a very important person" who lived to be 110 years old.[11]

The second son of this patriarch, also named John, became a soldier and a father during the same week, at the age of fifty-three. On 10 February 1781, he was commissioned an ensign in the First Virginia Regiment of the Revolutionary Army; five days later his only son and namesake was born in Loudon County, Virginia. That son, the fourth John Carr, migrated to North Carolina in 1810 and married Martha Cheek before the year was out. He was a man of great energy and the first Carr to embrace the teachings of John Wesley. Like so many zealous converts, he named one of his sons for the founder of Methodism. Martha Cheek Carr bore her husband six children: James Madison, John Wesley, Susan, Anderson Beaufort, Thomas Estridge, and Burroughs Cheek. Burroughs's birth, in 1832, led to her death.[12]

John Wesley Carr, often called "Wes," was eighteen at that time, and for the better part of a year he looked after the younger children while his brother James helped their father run the farm. His sister Susan having died in her third year, John had no female companionship, nor did he have any instruction in mothering except what he occasionally picked up from neighboring farm wives. (One taught him to use a spinning wheel and to sew well enough to make a few garments for the baby out of the cloth he wove.) His role as a substitute mother ended in 1833, when his father married a young woman named Martha Baldwin. By the time John was nineteen, his stepmother was expecting the first of the seven children that she would bear in little more than a decade, and it was then that he decided to make some changes in his life.[13]

Soon after his half-brother, William, was born in 1834, John Carr left the farm on Orange Grove Road and moved to Chapel Hill, about ten miles away. There he found work with N. J. King, "one of the largest and most influential merchants in Orange County" and the owner of a general store on Franklin Street, the main traffic artery that had grown up around the University of North Carolina. It may have been Carr's eagerness to learn the business and his ready acceptance of whatever wage King offered that won him the job, but King soon discovered that his new clerk was no ordinary young man. Carr was hardworking, shrewd, thrifty, and always pleasant to customers.

In 1836 John Carr and N. J. King became partners.[14] Carr must have lived very frugally in order to buy what apparently was a controlling interest in the store. Carr and King offered the public men's hats, ladies' bonnets, suiting and dress goods, buttons, ribbon, lace, salt, sugar, flour, molasses, confectionery, paint, hardware, oil, turpentine, medicines, candles, stationery, and whiskey. Some villagers, as well as farmers from the surrounding countryside, supplied the store with eggs, butter, meat, tobacco, fruit, and vegetables, but most of the merchandise came by wagon train from Wilmington and New Bern, North Carolina, and from Petersburg, Virginia.[15]

Carr and King accepted cash, negotiable paper, beeswax, tallow, flax seed, and farm produce in exchange for the goods on their shelves. Cash, however, was what they preferred, and by 1837 John Carr had apparently acquired enough of it to make marriage a possibility. It was Eliza Bullock, recently of Granville County, who caused him to start giving the idea serious thought. Miss Bullock was a stylish, energetic young woman whose square, determined jaw rescued her face from mere prettiness and stamped it with a look of quality; that look must have intrigued John Carr, who began to call on her soon after their first meeting. In the 1830s, courtships were brief, and theirs was no exception. They were married on Christmas Day in 1838 by the Reverend William Mercer Green, a professor of English and one of three acting chaplains at the University of North Carolina. When their first child was born in 1840, they named him William Green Carr, after this minister.[16]

Matrimony being the only respectable field of endeavor open to women in the early nineteenth century, it can be assumed that Eliza Bullock, the daughter of a planter, was brought up to be a dutiful wife and mother and the competent mistress of a household that required the use of slaves to keep it functioning properly. Her instruction in genteel manners, domestic accomplishments, and family duties probably began when she was very young and increased each year until, by the time she married John Carr, she was as much at home in the kitchen, the garden, the smokehouse, and the dairy as she was in the parlor or in the dining room.

Running a household and raising children was not easy, however, even with slaves to help. With the exception of men's coats and hats, and the more elaborate ladies' bonnets, all garments were made, washed, ironed, and mended by hand. Cooking was done in a fireplace; stews, dried beans, "poke salet," and cornmeal mush were simmered in pots that hung from a backbar, and bread dough and cake batter were baked in heavy iron pans that could be thrust into beds of hot coals.[17] Meat was boiled or roasted on a spit, and careful housewives inspected each piece before it was prepared. With no refrigeration except an ice pit, which was supplied during the winter when the ponds froze, they knew that only vigilance in the kitchen would keep their families healthy, especially in the summertime.

Spiritual health was even more important than physical well-being. As John and Eliza's family grew, they regarded each child as a sacred responsibility, to be brought up as a good citizen and a good Christian. In their eyes, to spoil children was weak minded, and to withhold punishment for lying, stealing, disobedience, and impertinence was a sin. People in the village said "they raised their children well, a hard thing to do in Chapel Hill"; hard or not, John Carr saw to it that his sons and daughters said their prayers, regularly attended church, and finished their chores and their lessons before they did any playing.[18] Believing that success in this world and salvation in the next came only through concerted effort and sustained piety, he also saw to it that his children never forgot that everything they had resulted from their father's unending dedication to hard work.

After N. J. King moved to Tennessee, John Carr was associated briefly with several Chapel Hill merchants during the 1840s, among them J. F. Freeland, W. M. Davis, and Jones Watson. Business was good despite prices that were high for the times. Beef, pork, and mutton retailed at five cents a pound, butter at twelve cents a pound, and eggs at eight cents a dozen. Turkeys were fifty cents each, crushed corn twenty-five cents a bushel, and whiskey seventy-five cents a gallon. Tallow was really expensive, more than the wool and broadcloth and French calico that came in on the wagons from Petersburg. In 1840, a year's supply of candles for an average family cost from sixty to seventy-five dollars; nevertheless, candles were a necessity, as were tools for farming and hardware for building.[19]

So John Carr prospered. In 1843 he owned a house and an acre of land on Franklin Street; by 1851 he had acquired additional property on Franklin, Columbia, and Rosemary streets and also on Morgan Creek and Bolin's Creek.[20] His one business venture outside of Chapel Hill was an attempt, with Dr. Bartlett Durham and James Mathews, to establish a store in Durhamville, a depot named for the doctor after he gave four acres of land to the North Carolina Railroad in 1853. Carr had a feeling that Durhamville (which later became Durham) might grow to a respectable size and that a general store there might be profitable, but after a few years he decided to withdraw from the partnership and to confine his efforts to Chapel Hill, where he had become a successful and highly respected citizen.[21]

Politically, Carr was a strong Whig who became a strong Democrat after the Whig party's demise in 1852. When the Whigs asked him to represent them in the state legislature, he refused; but he performed his public duty as a county commissioner, a magistrate, and a member of the Orange County Court of Wardens, an organization that helped to care for the indigent. He often said he was sorry for the poor because he had been poor himself, and he gave to every charitable cause in the village.[22]

Carr was popular with both town and gown. He could count among his friends the president of the university and many of its faculty, men whom he had admired from a distance when he first came to the village. David Lowry Swain, James Phillips, Elisha Mitchell, Manuel Fetter, William Horn Battle, and others similarly engaged in promoting the prestige of the University of North Carolina did not remain strangers to John Carr. He came to exchange opinions, swap pleasantries, and share laughter with them, and they were largely responsible for his strong support of the university.

Although he never amassed anything like a fortune, he did manage to accumulate a sizable estate. The fact that he was able to buy into the W. T. Blackwell Company five years after the Civil War indicates that he may not have converted all of his holdings into Confederate bonds and currency. Even if he had had to borrow part or even all of the $4,000 he put into Blackwell and Day's business, it turned out to be a risk well worth taking, for within a relatively short time he was realizing a highly satisfactory return on his investment. But John Carr never obtained what he considered his rightful share of the profits from Genuine Durham Smoking Tobacco, a commodity that

John Wesley Carr (courtesy of Laura Noell Carr Chapman)

Eliza Panill Bullock Carr (courtesy of Austin Heaton Carr, Jr.)

made his son a millionaire and turned a crossroads into a town "re-nowned the world around."[23]

Although little is known of Julian Carr's childhood, some writers and speakers (not altogether unbiased) have said that he was strongly influenced by the spirit of liberty and freedom that emanated from the University of North Carolina; that his independence and self-reliance were evident at an early age; and that, when he was not attending school, he usually could be found working in his father's store or on the family farm. It is extremely doubtful, however, that his boyhood was all work and no play. On the contrary, reliable accounts of life in Chapel Hill before the Civil War indicate that his early years may have been very pleasant years indeed.[24]

Home was next to his father's store on Franklin Street, in a roomy house sheltered by a grove of handsome oak trees and protected from wandering pigs and cattle by an iron picket fence. There Julian Carr learned who he was and what was expected of him, and there he was taught that the God of the Methodists was One to be feared as well as loved. In that house, where he perceived much that was never put into words, he discovered that there could be open affection as well as barely concealed hatred between white people and black people, but that there could never be true equality.

Beyond the fence, other houses and a few stores were scattered along Franklin Street, with its horse troughs and hitching posts, its blacksmith shop, and its small hotel whose owner, Miss Nancy Hilliard, had earned a statewide reputation for hospitality, kindness, and good food.[25] Like the few lanes that crossed or paralleled it, Franklin Street was either red mud or red dust, depending on the weather. In winter it sometimes was a criss-cross of frozen, treacherous ruts, but every spring it was transformed by the flowers that bloomed in the front yards on either side. Then it was bordered with the jewel-like colors of violets, jonquils, crocuses, narcissus, hyacinths, wild honeysuckle, camellias, and phlox; roses bloomed all summer long, sometimes into November.

On the south side of Franklin Street and in the approximate center of the village was the University of North Carolina, the oldest state-supported institution of higher learning in America and a place of great importance—so Julian Carr had been told many times, by many people. The quadrangle, formed by three small buildings and an old well covered with a wooden belfry, was not a very impressive sight; he was impressed by it, nevertheless, because he had been told that some of the boys who had lived and studied in those buildings and drawn water from that well had later become senators, lawyers, doctors, congressmen, ambassadors, and governors. One student, James Knox Polk, had even become president of the United States.

In 1847, President Polk had accepted an invitation to attend commencement at his alma mater, and Miss Nancy Hilliard added a sizable wing to the Eagle Hotel in order to accommodate the great man's entourage. Improvements were also made at the university—all of the buildings were washed with hydraulic cement, and a fresh coat of paint was applied to every door, window, post, and sill.[26] Because every female in Chapel Hill wanted a new frock for the occasion, John Carr probably sold more dress goods and thread and buttons and ribbon and lace than ever during a single season. Julian, being only twenty months old, could not remember that exciting time; nor did he enjoy learning later that his brother William and his sister Mary had seen the president while he had not, simply because he was too young.

When he was old enough to leave the yard and explore the village, young Julian discovered the forest that stretched away in every direction as far as his eyes could see. In autumn the hardwoods flamed scarlet and gold and wine and copper and rust; in spring the pale green of new leaves was laced with white where the dogwood bloomed and splashed with red by the Judas tree. After the first Thursday in June, when the university students went home for a six-week summer holiday, the paths that wound through the woods reverted to the villagers, and expeditions to the forest increased. Young boys especially made the most of that perfect place to build forts, dam creeks, trap muskrats, climb trees, and stalk make-believe Indians, and Julian Carr must often have been among them.

Entertainment for village children was simple. They played ball, mumbledy-peg, and marbles, and rolled hoops, if they were boys; they searched the woods for chinquapins and nuts and picked blackberries wherever they found them. During the coldest months, when the ponds froze, both boys and girls, as well as many adults, went ice skating. Once or twice during most winters, snow transformed the familiar landscape of Chapel Hill into a vast white playground, and the village took on a holiday air. When Julian Carr was twelve, a blizzard piled eighteen inches of snow and ice on the town; for three days the pursuit of education was abandoned and all business ceased.

The storm brought "serious inconvenience and some suffering" to many, but it also brought the necessary ingredients for snowball fights, sledding parties, and snow cream made with milk and sugar. During the weeks of intense cold that followed, the snowmen that had appeared on both sides of Franklin Street thrived long past their usual prime.[27]

But life was not all pleasure for children, and Julian Carr did his share of hauling wood, raking leaves, running errands, and helping out in the store. He also spent a considerable amount of time studying, first under his mother's supervision and later in the "pay schools" that were run by itinerant teachers for a few months each year. When he had progressed sufficiently in reading, writing, spelling, and arithmetic, his father hired a tutor to prepare him for college. While Julian was under the jurisdiction of Mr. J. L. Stewart, a second United States president came to Chapel Hill.[28]

Commencement was the highlight of the year for young and old; it was a celebration that required months of preparation and lasted almost a week. Rounds of parties and receptions were climaxed by a grand ball honoring the seniors, a gala that often went on all night. Visitors with sufficient stamina to make the trip to Chapel Hill by train, stagecoach, buggy, or wagon came from all parts of North Carolina, as well as from many other states. Julian Carr had been too young to enjoy the 1847 presidential visit, but he was exactly the right age to take in every detail of the one that occurred in 1859, when President James Buchanan and Secretary of the Interior Jacob Thompson, an alumnus of the university, were the honored guests at commencement.[29]

North Carolina newspapers, as well as others in New York, Washington, Richmond, Petersburg, and Columbia, South Carolina, covered the event, but their correspondents had great difficulty in reaching Chapel Hill. Many arrived late and grumbling about the fact that no transportation from the railroad station in Durham, twelve miles away, had been provided for them. They continued to complain loudly as they discovered that they had no accommodations for eating or sleeping, and no reserved seats or tables at any of the scheduled functions.

University officials may have been too absorbed in preparations for President Buchanan's visit to remember the needs of the press. By the time reporters reached the village, over 2,500 visitors, more than had ever before been seen at commencement, already filled the hotel, all the boarding houses, and every private home that could accommodate them; some people were happy to sleep on couches and even on floors. Eliza Carr, who was renowned for hospitality, probably had as many guests as the house on Franklin Street would hold. She also may have been one of many Chapel Hill housewives who stretched their dining tables to capacity and served as many as nine meals a day.

Like the newspaper reporters, President Buchanan had trouble reaching the village. He arrived two days late, "all covered with the dust of travel"—and probably greatly relieved to discover that he had missed the opening sermon to the senior class, the declamations of ten freshmen, and an address to the Dialectic and Philanthropic Societies. There was still much more to come. After hearing and responding to several speeches of welcome, he and Jacob Thompson accompanied the university's president, David Swain, to his home on Franklin Street, where they were joined by the trustees, the faculty, the seniors, and a number of prominent visitors for a three o'clock dinner on the lawn. Long tables had been set up under the trees, and "luscious eatables" were served by "blooming young ladies" of the village. Because the John Carrs were on friendly terms with the David Swains, fifteen-year-old Mary Ella Carr may have been one of those volunteer waitresses. It is also very likely that Julian Carr was near enough to observe the proceedings, along with other youngsters bent on catching a glimpse of President Buchanan.

Following the meal, guests trooped back to Gerrard Hall to hear an address by the Reverend William Hooper, who combined a humorous reminiscence of the university as it had been in the first decade of the nineteenth century with an impassioned plea for temperance to the young men in the audience. The minister's appeal was echoed later that evening by the chief executive, who declared that strong drink caused more damage than yellow fever or any other pestilence. His dire warnings against intoxicating beverages were well received by some in the audience, who described his speech as "peculiarly felicitous."

Early the next morning, President Buchanan, Jacob Thompson, and David Lowry Swain led the military company, the band, the faculty, the students, and many villagers from Swain's home to the university chapel, where they heard opening prayers, a Latin salutatory, and ten sophomore declamations. Newspaper correspondents were impressed by the "gorgeous splendor" of the ladies' gowns; later, at an informal reception on the campus, a reporter noted that although the president shook many hands, he gave a kiss to only "one pretty girl, and deputized her to impart it to others."

Prayers, sermons, and speeches occurred prior to the presentation of diplomas and the awarding of prizes and honors, and at the end of the long day President Buchanan declared that he was too tired to attend the grand ball for the seniors. Apparently offended by what they considered to be a snub, some whispered that it was not fatigue, but the president's strong Presbyterian principles that kept him away from the culmination of all the festivities, which featured a midnight supper and dancing until dawn. The *New York Herald* reporter praised the ball and the "magnificent" supper: "the costly array of dress and glittering trinkets there exhibited vastly surpassed any idea I had hitherto conceived of the taste of the people of North Carolina."

If a metropolitan newspaperman was impressed by what came to be known in Chapel Hill as "the Buchanan Commencement," thirteen-year-old Julian Carr must have been dazzled by the affair. Unfortunately, that memorable event marked the end of an era of prosperity and growth for the University of North Carolina. Ten months later Julian Carr's dream of spending four happy years there as a student was shattered by far-away guns at Fort Sumter, South Carolina.

2. Student and Soldier

NORTH CAROLINA, as a whole, was opposed to leaving the Union, but students at the state university began to clamor for secession as soon as they learned that the newly formed Confederacy had fired on the federal garrison at Fort Sumter. The attack took place on 12 April 1861, and two weeks later a majority of the junior, sophomore, and freshman classes petitioned the trustees for a suspension of exercises until fall. Saying that it was "impossible to attend to duty on account of the excitement," they urged the board to "see the necessity of every arm being wielded in the coming contest and every son's participating in defense of our homes and firesides." President David Swain took a different view of the matter. Issuing a circular to parents and patrons of the university, Swain asked for support in "restraining the young and inexperienced from rushing prematurely into the army." Because he won that support, the petition failed, and the result was "general gloom over the Commencement of 1861."[1]

Like other Chapel Hill boys, Julian Carr was caught up in the wave of patriotism that swept the campus and spilled over into the town. In the spring of 1862, when North Carolina had been in the Confederacy for a year, he was still only seventeen and too young to serve in the Confederate Army. Commencement that year was gloomier still, and heavy thunderstorms further dampened everyone's spirits. Not a mother, sister, brother, or cousin of any of the twenty-four seniors was on hand to watch the awarding of diplomas, but people who had traveled for refuge to Chapel Hill from the coastal cities of Wilmington, New Bern, and Edenton helped swell the gathering of spectators to a respectable size. A group of village ladies decorated the chapel with spring flowers, and the Right Reverend Thomas Atkinson, a bishop of the Episcopal church, preached the baccalaureate sermon. There was no music, there were no marshals, and for the first time there was no grand ball honoring the seniors.[2]

Six weeks after that bleak occasion, Julian Carr entered the university as a freshman. Because he was no stranger to the faculty and knew the campus well, he was spared much of the trauma of orientation; and, being naturally gregarious, he probably had less trouble than most when it came to making new friends.

One of those friends was Eugene Morehead of Greensboro, whose father, John Motley Morehead, had been an alumnus and trustee of the university and a two-term governor of the state. "Gene" Morehead was born in 1845, the year his father left office; he was exactly one month older than Jule Carr and not unlike him. Both were high spirited, generous, and eager for new experiences, even in war; both had a taste for stylish clothes, pretty girls, and "high society." Jule never forgot his years with Gene at Carolina, where, as fellow members of the Dialectic Society and the Zeta Psi fraternity, they "often sang together while strolling through the campus at night, after our recitation had been prepared and our society had adjourned."[3]

Carr's first grades in history, mathematics, Latin, and Greek were deemed respectable (R) by his professors, and in French and Bible they were deemed very respectable (VR). Until he left college to join the Confederate Army in 1864, he received only four tolerable (T) grades; one each in history and mathematics, and two in Greek.[4] As one of the freshman declaimers at the 1863 commencement, his youthful eloquence failed to "win most praise," but despite that inauspicious beginning, he later developed a talent for oratory that put him in frequent demand as a public speaker.

Although he was short, Carr was a good-looking young man, slim but sturdily built, with dark hair, light gray eyes, his mother's determined jaw, and his father's ruddy skin. His disposition was sanguine, and he adapted to most situations with apparent ease; even so, he may have had some difficulty in adjusting to wartime changes in the university. The student body was reduced to boys under eighteen, like himself, and those exempt from military service because of physical disability. The army also had claimed every eligible faculty member. With only ministers and older men teaching, the atmosphere in the classrooms, as well as on campus, was vastly different from what he had envisioned.

It was different for the faculty, too. Because war had reduced the student body to "a mere handful," tuition fees, a major source of revenue for the school, also were reduced. Faculty salaries had to be cut, and maintenance of the grounds and buildings became difficult at best, and often impossible.[5] With a decrease in the value of Confederate currency, by 1863 President Swain's annual salary of $2,000 was worth only $133 in gold, and a professor drawing $1,500 actually received no more than $100. Assistant professors who had earned $1,100 in 1860 were realizing about $87 in 1863, but some of those who were still on the university payroll were faring worse. The gold value of the bursar's wages amounted to approximately $33 in United States currency, and the librarian's stipend came to only a little over $6.[6]

General Robert E. Lee's victory at Fredericksburg in December 1862 warmed hearts in Chapel Hill, but it did little to warm cold bodies. The university, in an attempt to look after its own, granted faculty members permission to cut firewood from the surrounding forest, provided the trees were first marked by Professor Manuel Fetter, who also was the bursar. The villagers, highly indignant at being excluded from this arrangement, took matters in their own hands, and neither Fetter nor President Swain could stop them from pillaging. They stripped several nearby acres of many fine oaks, elms, and hickories, but there were no reprisals.[7] How could there be, when General Lee himself had ordered James Longstreet to steal provisions from the vicinity of Suffolk, Virginia, in order to feed his hungry Confederate troops? War was hell, not only at Vicksburg and Chancellorsville and Chattanooga, but also in Chapel Hill.

Times were difficult also for people whose existence depended upon the university, and whose way of life was altered drastically as more and more students left Chapel Hill to take up arms. As a merchant, John Carr was one of the first to feel the pinch. Who could buy flour that cost one hundred and fifty dollars a barrel, or coffee that sold for fifteen dollars a pound? People ate cornbread, and instead of coffee they drank a brew made of parched sweet potatoes and grains of rye, or tea steeped from yaupon leaves. Beef, mutton, and pork had sold for five cents a pound in 1845, when Julian Carr was born; by the time he was eighteen, beef had jumped to three dollars a pound and bacon to five dollars and fifty cents a pound. No one in Chapel Hill could afford that kind of meat. As for sugar to sweeten the ersatz coffee and tea, it was definitely out of the question at thirty dollars per pound.[8]

In spite of hard times, the villagers were cheerful, for the most part. According to one who kept a journal during the war years, morale did drop each time they learned that a university student had been killed or wounded. Cornelia Phillips Spencer, a keen-eyed observer of human nature in general and of the people of Chapel Hill in particular, recorded that "the bonds of common sympathy became stronger as the pangs of common suffering became more intense."[9] Of the 1,062 university students and alumni who entered the army, 312 died. Mrs. Spencer, whose bitterness about the war was evident in what she wrote, probably spoke for all the women in Chapel Hill when she said, "There they lie, rolled in their blankets, in their bloody Confederate uniforms, and for what . . . that the negroes might be freed with every circumstance of insolence and violence, that southern property might be confiscated, southern people cowed, insulted, oppressed, robbed, all southern rights ignored. For this our boys have died—for this."[10]

Sentiment against Yankees and their sympathizers ran high in Chapel Hill, especially among students, many of whom became highly indignant when President Swain petitioned Confederate President Jefferson Davis to exempt those liable for conscription until they had finished school. Davis complied, saying, "I will not grind up the seed corn."[11] The edict applied only to juniors and seniors, however, and when Julian Carr became eighteen during his sophomore year, he decided to enlist—no doubt because he knew that those who joined voluntarily usually were allowed to choose their own companies and stay with their friends.

In the spring of 1864 Carr became a member of Company K in the Third North Carolina Cavalry, which was a unit of General Rufus Clay Barringer's brigade and part of General W. H. F. "Rooney" Lee's division of Hampton's Corps, in the Army of Northern Virginia. Assigned to the Conscript Bureau, Carr served as a clerk under Captain W. M. Swain until early fall, when he became an enrolling officer of the Fifth Congressional District of North Carolina. He saw action toward the end of October 1864 at Hatcher's Run, and again in February 1865. Lieutenant Colonel Walter Clark, who later became a chief justice of the North Carolina Supreme Court,[12] recalled Warren's Raid on Belfield and the Battle of Weldon Railroad:

> The Third Cavalry (41st N.C.) now was passed to the front and the pursuit vigorously pressed. About nine o'clock that night Captain Harding of Company K got the enemy's rear guard fairly started, and charging them over two miles, forced them back precipitously into their camps. His zeal led him too far, and into a furious fire from the enemy's interior guards. But the brave and skillful captain still pressed forward, and

after some hairbreadth escapes, succeeded in extricating his command with a loss of only about a dozen men.

Our comrade, Julian S. Carr, was in this charge to my personal knowledge. That "interior guard" formed an ambuscade for Captain Harding's troopers. They fired from each side of the road into each flank of those charging Carolinians. I know that Julian S. Carr was in that charge and went as far in it as any man, because I saw and spoke to him then and there, and congratulated him on his safety.[13]

Other Confederates, both soldiers and civilians, had not been so lucky back in November 1864. Three months before Julian Carr miraculously escaped the "furious fire" of the enemy in Virginia, Union General William Tecumseh Sherman captured Atlanta; on 14 November he left that city in flames and began his march to Savannah, looting, burning, and foraging as he went. In an effort to break the will of the South, he destroyed roads, bridges, factories, homes, public buildings, railroads, and cotton gins. By his own admission he demolished, in the state of Georgia alone, $100,000,000 worth of property. General Sherman, a man with a practiced eye for pretty women and an almost pathological aversion to Negroes, took a realistic approach to battle. "If the people of Georgia raise a howl against my barbarity and cruelty," he said, "I will answer that war is war, and not popularity-seeking."[14]

Sherman's advance northward through the Carolinas took an even greater toll. While General Joseph E. Johnston and his army of starving Confederates were unable to stop it, they did manage to slow the invasion and to hold out until late April 1865—one of the most momentous months in America's history, a time of endings and beginnings, of despair and elation, and often of utter confusion throughout the South. It gave the people in Julian Carr's home town "three weeks of such excitement as a century may fail to reproduce."[15]

Miles from the nearest railroad and lacking telegraph wires, Chapel Hill was virtually isolated. Although rumors about the war surfaced daily, the verification of any event was slow in coming. Lee's surrender to Grant, which took place at Appomattox on Palm Sunday, 9 April 1865, was not known in Chapel Hill until President Swain announced it to the citizenry five days later, on Good Friday.

General Sherman had captured Raleigh the day before the surrender. President Swain, accompanied by a former governor of the state, William A. Graham, had gone to the Union general and begged him not to destroy North Carolina's capitol city and its state university. Sherman, as weary of war as any man, had promised to spare both places, but the joy that this announcement occasioned in Chapel Hill was followed by shock and sadness when Swain reported the South's surrender. He had learned about it, he said, at Union headquarters just outside Raleigh, when he and Graham were allowed to see correspondence concerning the terms of surrender that had passed between Lee and Grant.[16]

It is easy to imagine the effect of such news on John and Eliza Carr, whose son Julian was a soldier in Lee's army. As it happened, however, neither of them had much time to worry about Julian or to mourn Lee's defeat. Before the day was over, Confederate General Joseph Wheeler's cavalry, retreating from Sherman's advancing army, moved into the village and began making preparations to defend it against possible attack by digging rifle pits at a location known as Point Prospect, which overlooked the road to Raleigh. After Wheeler set up headquarters at the home of Kendal Waitt, across the street from the Episcopal church on Franklin Street, Cornelia Spencer wrote that "the whole town was busy night and day cooking and feeding the men," who ate potatoes, cabbage, collard greens, fatback, corn pone, milk, and sorghum. This was all anyone had to give them, and to those hungry soldiers that plain fare must have been a feast. Eliza and John Carr, being involved in that community effort, were at least temporarily distracted from anxiety about their own son.

On Easter Sunday, two days after General Wheeler's arrival, Confederate scouts brought word that Union troops far outnumbering their own were approaching Chapel Hill, whereupon Wheeler abandoned his plan of defense and withdrew, taking along as many horses and mules as his men had time to confiscate. For a few hours the village was quiet and the citizens waited, many of them sitting on their porches, not knowing what to do. Then, according to Mrs. Spencer, toward evening the quiet was broken by the sound of marching feet, and in a matter of minutes "a dozen bluejackets dashed in from the Raleigh road and we were captured."[17]

At eight o'clock the next morning, four thousand Union cavalrymen rode into Chapel Hill. One colonel from Michigan remembered for the rest of his life "the beauty of the day, the brilliant sunshine in the young leaves, the pink and white flowers in the woods, the perfume and peace after our long, rough ride from Raleigh."[18]

Against that colorful spring background the conquerors advanced, led by the thirty-year-old General Smith B. Atkins, a man who, for a variety of reasons, would never be forgotten by his captives. The young general, who was extremely handsome and exquisitely polite, lost no time in obeying William Tecumseh Sherman's orders to protect the university and its immediate environs. After stationing guards in the buildings and at every house in the village, he and some of his officers called first on President Swain and then on several members of the faculty, where they "chatted pleasantly and petted the children." Meanwhile, the guards outside "lounged in and out of yards, and appeared in all respects like human beings."[19]

This favorable first impression did not apply to all of Atkins's troops, however. People soon learned that some of the enlisted men were foraging in the surrounding countryside, "ransacking houses, plundering fields, stealing whatever they could and then wasting much of it, giving it to negroes and prostitutes around the town." Because plundering was condoned by the military for ten days after Lee's surrender, General Atkins made no attempt to stop what was going on so close to the village he was pledged to protect. He did apologize, after a fashion, saying that he "deplored all this as one of the inevitable accompaniments of war."[20]

Another consequence of war that the people of Chapel Hill resented was watching Union cavalrymen stable their mounts in the university library. Still another was seeing those same horses grazing on the campus, eating and trampling the grass, dropping ordure, and chewing the bark from many fine old trees. But the worst consequence by far was learning that General Atkins and President Swain's daughter Eleanor had fallen in love on the very day when Atkins had paid his first call at the president's home. Rumor said that Eleanor's parents were worried about the situation but powerless to control it; this caused no surprise, as it was common knowledge that the Swains had always spoiled their children and their slaves. The love affair progressed rapidly, and as it did, respect for the Swains declined. General Atkins presented Ellie with a fine riding horse, which she accepted; and each evening at sunset he sent his regimental band to Swain's front yard to serenade her, in a spectacle that set tongues wagging all over town.[21]

It was into this highly charged emotional climate that Julian Carr returned from the war. He may have arrived in the company of other soldiers from Lee's army who passed through the village after the surrender at Appomattox, men described by Cornelia Spencer as "straggling homeward . . . footsore, penniless, despondent."[22] The details of his homecoming are not known, but in a letter many years later he wrote, "I was in the Confederate Army and went home from Appomattox in '65. I was in the Cavalry branch of the service, which was not paroled at Appomattox, but disbanded. On my return to Chapel Hill, N. C., a week or ten days after the surrender, there was a large force of Federal troops there, and I was paroled by the officer of the command, whom I have an idea was a Michigan colonel."[23]

Carr's homecoming within ten days of the surrender at Appomattox would have coincided with General Atkins's highly visible courtship of Ellie Swain, and it is possible that Carr heard the regimental band playing love songs on Franklin Street and wondered, as did so many, if Ellie had taken leave of her senses. Despite his good looks and gentlemanly facade, General Atkins was still the enemy, and to see one of their own consorting with a "damn Yankee" engendered considerable anger among both townspeople and students. That anger increased to fury when it was learned that the new horse President Swain had begun to drive was a gift from the arch enemy himself, William Tecumseh Sherman.[24]

Having fallen in love "at first sight," so they said, Eleanor Swain and Smith Atkins were determined to marry in spite of what people thought, and their wedding took place on 23 August 1865, three months after they met. Although many guests were invited and "a grand supper prepared," very few villagers attended. Cornelia Spencer's journal recorded the sad fact that "invitations were spit upon in one or two houses." University students, eager to demonstrate their opinion of traitors, rang the bell in South Building for three hours, in order to disturb the peace of the wedding day. After the ceremony was over, they hanged General Atkins and President Swain in effigy.[25]

Julian Carr, who undoubtedly shared the feelings of those angry young men, may have been part of that noisy demonstration. To return from war defeated and to find the conquerors policing his home town, guarding his father's house, and stabling their horses in the halls of his alma mater was bad enough; but to see one of his childhood friends marry "a Yankee whose sword is yet reeking with the blood of its victims, her own relations or at least her own countrymen,"[26] must have been a bitter pill. It is to his credit that he did not carry such bitterness with him to the grave, as did many of his fellow North Carolinians.

Throughout the state there was a great deal of anger at President Swain. Some felt that he should have been hanged literally, not merely in effigy, for fraternizing with the enemy and for accepting horses that could have been stolen from Confederate owners. Nevertheless, David Swain was mainly responsible for the fact that Chapel Hill and the university were spared the terrible damage that was inflicted elsewhere in North Carolina. Millions in railroad property, factories, bridges, military supplies, and food were destroyed at Wilkesboro, Salem, Salisbury, Greensboro, Statesville, Lincolnton, Shelby, Morganton, Rutherfordton, Hendersonville, Asheville, and Waynesville by General George Stoneman during the last days of the war. "Stoneman's Raid" cost the state four cotton factories, 7,000 bales of cotton, 35,000 bushels of corn, 56,000 bushels of wheat, 160,000 pounds of bacon, 100,000 suits of clothing, 250,000 blankets, 20,000 pounds of leather, 10,000 pounds of saltpeter, drugs worth $100,000, all the machine shops at Salisbury that manufactured arms and ammunition, and much rice, sugar, and salt.[27] The people of Chapel Hill had much to be thankful for, by comparison—but worse times were coming.

The university, described by one poetic villager as "the source of all life, like the sun that blazed on the hoary trees of the campus," had been on a downhill course since 1861 and was declining rapidly. Although it was the only institution of rank in the South to hold graduation exercises in 1865, what took place on the first Thursday in June was a mockery, with only one graduate and four trustees present. No juniors and only five sophomores and two freshmen attended, but Julian Carr did see his brother Albert serve as assistant marshal and speak as a sophomore declaimer. Moreover, he noticed among the small audience the thirty-five Union soldiers who had been detailed by General Atkins to protect university property. The rest of the cavalry, which had numbered over four hundred men, had left by that time; but the place where they had camped, at the western edge of the village, was a bleak reminder of their presence during the last three weeks of April. "Not a blade of grass, nor leaf of any kind is to be found there," Cornelia Spencer wrote. "The ground is stamped as smooth as a floor."[28]

In August, after the usual six-week vacation, the university opened with no endowment and only twenty-two students. It has been said that Julian Carr was among them for a while, but no student records document that statment. Like most young Confederate veterans, Carr probably was at loose ends during the first desolate months after Appomattox. During his childhood, North Carolina had been a prosperous, progressive state, full of opportunity; now it was worn out from war, with over 40,000 of its best men dead from battle or disease and thousands more disabled. It was a sad, depressing time. Chapel Hill, like the rest of the South, was bankrupt. Worse still, it was in a state of turmoil because of the Emancipation Proclamation and the Freedmen's Bureau.

After the Confederate surrender at the Bennett farmhouse near Durham, many Negroes left Chapel Hill to seek a new life of freedom. Because many were considered ignorant and lacking in initiative, they were seen as wanderers who "stole everything they could get their hands on," and many whites thought their servants "were inclined to do as little, and to get as much as they possibly could."[29] Reconstruction intensified racist feelings among blacks and whites, and in August, soon after the university opened, a fight broke out between a group of freedmen and some village boys and students. Many came out of that fight "with heads and arms broken," so Cornelia Spencer said. Years later, Julian Carr publicly admitted that he took part in the fracas and whipped a black woman who, on a quiet village street, had "maligned a Southern lady." It is obvious that the unfortunate incident may have influenced his thinking about the black race and the Republican party, as did certain other events that occurred in Chapel Hill during Reconstruction.[30]

In many parts of the South, and especially in Chapel Hill, Reconstruction was worse than the war. Under Republican Governor William Holden, appointed by President Andrew Johnson in 1865, the university received no assistance from the legislature. Although the commencement of 1866 was a slight improvement over the previous year (there were three graduates, instead of one), the institution's future looked hopeless. It owned 2,000 shares of worthless bank stock, had $25,000 invested in worthless Confederate securities, and was over $100,000 in debt. Needless to say, there was no money with which to pay the faculty, to whom it already owed $7,000 in back salaries. With no endowment, its survival depended entirely on tuition fees, and when only fifty students enrolled in 1867, the faculty agreed that they could not hang on beyond the end of the school year.[31]

Matters were taken out of their hands, however, when the Republican party, with Negroes constituting half of its membership, took control of the legislature in the spring of 1868. Governor Holden decided to reorganize the University of North Carolina for the "common people." He began by sending a guard of Negro soldiers to take over the campus and buildings, where they "remained for many months, to the great disgust and indignation of the inhabitants." He then fired the board of trustees, President Swain, and the entire faculty.[32]

Many Carolinians, still angry with Swain because of his involvement with General Sherman and because of his daughter's marriage to General Atkins, were glad to see him deposed. But anger often changed to pity and sorrow when Swain died not long after his forced resignation, apparently from an accident caused by the high-spirited horse he had accepted from General Sherman. Swain's buggy overturned when the horse bolted, but because he seemed to have no injuries other than severe bruises, some thought that his death, on 27 August 1868, was from shock and "a broken heart."[33]

Cornelia Spencer felt that Swain's death brought on "the disintegration of society here and the dispersion of its members with a rapidity and in a degree quite unexampled in the history of any other village in this State. Thirty families went almost immediately," she wrote in her journal. One of those who joined the exodus was Julian Carr, whose ultimate destination was Little Rock, Arkansas.[34] No doubt he chose that city because his father's elder brother, James Madison Carr, lived and worked there, and if he hoped for some assistance from his uncle, he was not disappointed—James Carr was able to help his nephew find a job in a local store. Except for two visits home, Julian remained in Little Rock for about eighteen months.[35] Thus he was spared a firsthand experience of events in Chapel Hill during that time, although letters from his family probably kept him apprised of a steadily worsening situation.

In January 1869, Governor Holden's newly appointed "Reconstruction" board of trustees elected Solomon Pool, a native of Elizabeth City, as the university's new president. A graduate of the class of 1853 and a Methodist minister, Pool had been a teacher of mathematics and secretary of the university faculty until 1866, when he resigned to become an appraiser in the revenue service of the Republican administration. It is not surprising that the people in Chapel Hill considered him a renegade and a traitor.[36]

The university reopened on 3 March 1869, but only a handful of students appeared. When Julian Carr visited his parents the following September, he found "the two or three boys who came here prepared for college disgusted." His father, who obviously shared that disgust, confronted Pool and advised him to resign; Pool replied, with considerable anger, that he would not resign for $50,000. "If no whites will come here," he told John Carr, "I will have Negro students."[37]

If Pool intended to antagonize Carr and his fellow villagers, most of them former slaveowners, he met with instant success, even though he did not carry out his threat. During the first year of his administration, when the entire student body numbered only thirty-five, it was rumored that "now and then a small black face appeared among them"; but because there are no records of Negro attendance at the university until the twentieth century, the allegation no doubt sprang from fear rather than fact. About twenty-five students did have to be placed in a preparatory department because they lacked sufficient education to enter college. In the eyes of one Chapel Hill resident, most of them were "just little barefoot boys from the village and the adjoining country, with their home-made breeches held up by a string across the shoulder, and their dinner in a little tin bucket."[38]

Although 1870 enrollment increased to fifty-three students, many considered college "a grand frolic" and were not inclined to attend classes. Others, openly defiant, refused to study Greek and expressed their displeasure at going to school with "them Yanks." Attempts at discipline were feeble. Faculty morale was extremely low, no doubt because there was not enough money in the state treasury to pay teachers, and also because the people of Chapel Hill were so openly hostile. It is not surprising that the professors all but ignored insubordination, thievery, and vandalism.[39]

Commencement in 1870 was a farce: no students graduated from one of America's foremost antebellum institutions of higher learning. The following November, when it became apparent that Governor Holden's plan to revamp the university along more proletarian lines was not working out, the board of trustees announced that faculty salaries would cease as of 1 February 1871. On that day a disillusioned student or a sorrowful villager wrote on one of the blackboards in an empty classroom, "February 1, 1871. This old University has busted and gone to hell today."[40]

Chapel Hill had now experienced the worst. For the next five years those who stayed there, either by choice or from necessity, experienced the bitter truth of what President Swain had often said: the university and the village were so interdependent that they were bound to either sink or swim together. The sinking was painful, and North Carolina's wartime governor, Zebulon Baird Vance, noted that "an air of melancholy, of ruin, pervades everything where once was so much active and intelligent life." Buildings that had already experienced severe neglect during the war fell into even more pitiful disrepair. Doors sagged open or fell away entirely from rusty hinges; birds flew through broken windows to build nests in empty, rat-infested rooms. The campus, which had been landscaped by a celebrated English gardener during Julian Carr's childhood, became a jungle of weeds and vines.[41]

Thieves stole everything that could be moved from the buildings, and vandals mutilated much of what was left, including expensive mathematical and astronomical equipment. Gangs of Negroes took over South Building and spent noisy nights there drinking and carousing, their laughter often turning into angry shouts and curses. Most villagers were so frightened that they kept to their houses even during the daytime, and Chapel Hill turned into "a desolate, silent wilderness."[42]

But while Reconstruction was slowly strangling the University of North Carolina and the village of Chapel Hill, tobacco addiction was pumping new life into the little hamlet of Durham, where Union and Confederate soldiers had camped during the final days of the Civil War. Their craving for tobacco had prompted them to steal several thousand pounds of it from a local dealer, and that crime, committed in 1865, was beginning to have far-reaching consequences, not only for Durham, but also for Julian Shakespeare Carr.[43]

3. Endings and Beginnings

THE business that Julian Carr entered when he moved to Durham in 1870 had been evolving for twelve years, beginning in 1858, with Robert F. Morris and his two sons, and passing through a number of hands before it became the property of W. T. Blackwell and James R. Day. Two years after the Morrises began manufacturing tobacco in a small house near the train station, they acquired a partner, Wesley A. Wright, of Virginia, whose main contributions to the enterprise were a name for the brand (Best Flavored Spanish Smoking Tobacco) and a flavoring compound to mitigate its "noxious qualities." About a year later, when North Carolina entered the war and Wesley Wright joined the Confederate Army, Dr. Richard Blacknall replaced him, and the company name was changed from Morris and Wright to Blacknall and Morris. During the war three other men (W. H. Bowles, W. A. Ward, and John Ruffin Green) moved in and out of Durham's only tobacco business. Of those three, only Green remained constant, and in 1864 he became the sole owner of the little factory and its stock of Best Flavored Spanish Smoking Tobacco.[1]

By that time the Civil War had greatly enhanced the popularity of tobacco, both as a sedative and as a booster of sagging morale among the troops. For three long years tobacco (as well as whiskey) had eased the pain of soldiering in both the Union and the Confederate armies, and the craving for it did not stop when, seventeen days after Appomattox, General Joseph E. Johnston surrendered to General William T. Sherman a few miles west of Durham.

Ten days earlier, on 16 April 1865, a temporary armistice was declared while the two generals worked out terms of surrender at the Bennett farmhouse in Orange County. During that period Yankee and Rebel soldiers forgot their differences and camped together in Durham, which had been classified as neutral ground. Those who could afford it headed straight for the barrooms and brothels that had given the place an unsavory reputation; others, either less solvent or less sophisticated, pleasured themselves by shooting at targets, running footraces, and swapping horses.[2]

Sooner or later, however, most of the men began to forage, and one of their first victims was John Ruffin Green, whose small factory obviously held something of value. Locks posed no difficulty for men who had become adept at petty thievery, and in a matter of minutes they had the door open and were helping themselves to tobacco already shredded and packed for shipping. Finding it far superior to the tongue-biting rations of their respective armies, these soldiers, along with other "bummers" who straggled into Durham during the next few days, made off with every sack of Green's tobacco. Green, who must have been absent from Durham while these multiple thefts were occurring, loudly proclaimed himself ruined and suffered accordingly—until he began to realize that what he had regarded as a tragedy was giving him a great deal of excellent advertising at absolutely no cost. The men who had robbed him could not forget "that good Durham tobacco."[3] Back home after the surrender, as they faced the difficulties of living in a postwar world, they remembered the fine, mild taste of that stolen leaf; many of them even wrote to the stationmaster in Durham to ask how they could buy more of it. Their letters, which came from all parts of the country, were relayed to Green, who at last began to reap the rewards of having followed "a hunch, so to speak, that there was a future in the manufacturing of tobacco."[4]

That hunch had been strong enough, in 1856, to make Green take on processing and selling tobacco as a sideline to his regular occupation of farming in Person County. Although it was difficult and time consuming to raise and cure the leaf, beat it into granules, pack it in bags, and haul it in a mule-drawn wagon to various parts of the state, he persisted for almost five years and made enough profit to build a new house, which he hoped to follow with a small factory for his growing business. But just as the house was nearing completion, it burned to the ground, and Green, after a period of near despair, decided to sell his farm and move to Durham. With the country at war, his family would be reasonably safe in that obscure hamlet.

Although a preponderance of saloons and sporting houses had given Durham a bad name, it did have some redeeming features. Those included two churches, a log schoolhouse, a private academy for boys, and a Masonic lodge, all of which provided a modicum of respectability for the fewer than one hundred citizens. The population also supported a small hotel, four stores, a blacksmith shop, two cotton gins, and a post office located in the rear of a carpenter's shop. Of prime interest to Green, however, was the modest frame building that stood about a hundred yards from the North Carolina Railroad depot. In that building Robert Morris, who owned the hotel, and Richard Blacknall, the local doctor, were manufacturing Best Flavored Spanish Smoking Tobacco.[5]

When Robert Morris decided to move to Virginia, John Ruffin Green and W. A. Ward, who had moved to Durham from eastern North Carolina, pooled their resources and purchased Blacknall and Morris's business. Their partnership was brief. Within a relatively short time, Green bought Ward's interest and became the sole owner of Durham's original tobacco factory, which resembled a ten-foot-high cow shed and was surrounded by "a dozen small, dingy buildings, a country store or two, a smithy, and, as may be supposed, a whiskey shop."[6]

Apparently prone to hunches, at least where tobacco was concerned, John Ruffin Green began to feel that pipe smoking eventually would supplant chewing, and that he should therefore buy the mildest and best leaf he could find. He also convinced himself that university students passing through Durham on their way to Chapel Hill would be good advertisers of his tobacco, provided he could persuade them to try it. As it happened, the Civil War drastically reduced the number of students en route to the university, but that same war, as it was about to end, gave Green enough marauding soldiers to spread the good word about his product "from Maine to Texas."[7]

When letters from ex-soldiers who had robbed Green began to arrive at the little post office in the carpenter's shop, competition followed immediately, but that competition was of less concern to the manufacturer of Best Flavored Spanish Smoking Tobacco than was the blatant appropriation of the words *Durham*, *Spanish*, and *Flavored* by his unscrupulous rivals. These men evidently hoped some of the magic in those words would rub off on their own products, and Green began to ponder a new name for his brand. It has been rumored, enough to be taken for fact, that the solution came while he was eating fried oysters with John Y. Whitted, a friend from the nearby town of Hillsborough.[8]

As Green fretted aloud, the story goes, Whitted listened carefully and, at the same time, stared fixedly at a jar of Coleman's Mustard that had been placed on the table with the oysters. This mustard, made in Durham, England, and labeled with a Durham bull's head, apparently inspired Whitted to suggest that the entire side view of a bull, combined with the words "Genuine Durham Smoking Tobacco," would be a striking way to catch the public eye. Green accepted the suggestion on the spot, and thus one of the most famous trademarks in advertising history supposedly was conceived.

Within a matter of days, Green located James Berry, a sign painter and buggy maker who had taken refuge in Durham from New Bern; Berry, carrying out Whitted's idea, painted the first Bull Durham sign on a large piece of sheet iron, which Green had mounted on posts in front of his factory. He then applied to the clerk's office of the Southern District of New York for a copyright on "Genuine Durham Smoking Tobacco." After it was granted, on 2 May 1866, he began to use the side view of a Durham bull on his tobacco labels.[9]

Sales increased, and Green was able to hire several local Negroes to process his tobacco for smoking. His health, which had not been good for some time, began to decline steadily, and by 1869 his need for additional help led him to seek out two young men with whom he had enough in common to presuppose an amicable relationship. Like Green, William Thomas Blackwell and James R. Day had been born and raised on farms near Woodsdale, in Person County; also like Green, they had peddled tobacco to both Union and Confederate soldiers during the war. After the surrender, Blackwell and Day opened a jobbing house in Kinston, North Carolina. Because they had watched Green's Genuine Durham Smoking Tobacco become the most popular brand they handled, it was not difficult for them to give up their own business and join Green's, which already had the beginnings of a national reputation.[10]

Green's price for half interest in his company was $1,500. The contract, drawn up on 30 March 1869, stipulated that the full amount was to be used "for manufacturing, exclusively and for no other purpose, for twelve months from date." The contract further stated that Day was expected to give all his personal attention to the management of the business, and that Green would do as much as his health would permit. Although Blackwell's duties were not spelled out, it can be assumed that he took charge of the buying and selling, at which he was widely acknowledged as an expert. Any profits, after allowing Green $1,000 "for the rent of the factory and the advantage of my trade," were to be divided three ways; likewise, any losses were to be borne equally.[11]

That contract was never fulfilled, for Green died of tuberculosis less than four months after he signed it. Blackwell and Day found themselves mourning the death of their senior partner and faced with the prospect of either buying the business or seeing it sold. Having no ready cash, they procrastinated for almost nine months while Mager Green, as administrator of his son's estate, advertised for a buyer in both the *Raleigh Sentinel* and the *Raleigh Standard*. When no buyer materialized and the elder Green decided to sell the factory and fixtures at public auction, Buck Blackwell somehow managed to come up with the necessary money, although "it was exceedingly scarce and hard to procure." On 9 April 1870, Blackwell paid $2,292 to John Ruffin Green's estate "without naming his partner, Mr. Day, although the latter appears to have retained his interest."[12]

Had Buck Blackwell been able to foretell the future, he might have terminated his business relationship with Jim Day, whose growing tendency to put pleasure before business would prove difficult in later years. But Day was an experienced judge of tobacco and a good salesman, and those attributes compensated for the cavalier approach he was beginning to acquire. So the two young men from Person County continued to work together under the name of "W. T. Blackwell, Successor to J. R. Green and Company." When John Carr heard that they were looking for additional capital with which to push their business, he began to smell opportunity. Losing no time, he composed a letter to his son Julian, in Little Rock, and then he hitched up his buggy and drove down the pot-holed, winding road to Durham.

To John Carr, as to most of the people in Chapel Hill, Durham had always been a depressing little place. There were a few flimsy stores and barrooms, a few rickety houses, the blacksmith's shop, the depot with its woodshed and water tank, and Blackwell's factory, sitting square in the middle of a patch of red earth that turned into thick red slime after a hard rain and what looked like brick dust after a dry spell. No streets, only paths leading to stores and barrooms, wells and privies, pigpens and chicken coops, houses and churches. One church for Methodists, another for Baptists. Not many trees, but plenty of unsightly stumps.

But there was an odor of progress mixed in with the smell of tobacco and dust and manure and pigs and horse flesh and human sweat. It was in the air, like spring rain just before the first drops fall, like Christmas just before Christmas comes, and John Carr, breathing it in, may have felt a stab of excitement for the first time since the war. What transpired during his first encounter with Blackwell and Day is not known, but the final results of that meeting, and any others that may have taken place before the contract was signed, are documented in a statement made by his son Julian some years later: "On the 12th day of October, 1870, I joined Mr. W.T. Blackwell and Mr. James R. Day in business at Durham, N.C., my father furnishing $4,000, the amount requisite to buy a ⅓rd interest in the firm, the understanding between my father and myself being that he would furnish the necessary capital, and I would do the work, and we would share ½ each in the ⅓rd interest which we purchased."[13]

That day in October 1870 may have been one of Julian Carr's happiest birthdays, although he would later regret the terms of his father's agreement with Blackwell because it did not include any rights to the company's trademark: "Unfortunately for the interest of my father and myself, as well, when my father contracted to buy an interest of Mr. W.T. Blackwell, he failed to specify that an interest in the trade mark was to be included. I need not say to intelligent folk that the trade mark (the Durham Bull) was the cream of the business and [neither] my father nor I had no interest whatever in this valuable asset."[14]

The contract was to be renewed every three years *only* *if* all the partners agreed. That first contract flatly stated that Blackwell was the sole owner of the trademark, and that Day and the two Carrs had the right to use it only as long as they were in business with him. Julian Carr eventually came to regard this as "a most anomalous position to occupy," but in his early days with the company he was too busy learning his job to worry about the fact that he had no legal right to the trademark. Blackwell and Day were adept at buying and selling tobacco, but because they had little talent for bookkeeping or letterwriting, Carr "superintended and directed their correspondence, managed their finances, lines of credit, etc.," and assumed responsibility for the office.[15]

Julian Carr also took it upon himself to learn everything he did not already know about raising, curing, and processing tobacco. Although his partners and the hands who worked on the second floor of the factory were his primary sources of information, the farmers who sold directly to the company, instead of hauling their crops to markets in Virginia, were not reluctant to answer his questions about their livelihood. Carr was a great talker, but he could also be a good listener, and by listening to farmers he probably learned much about the back-breaking, never-ending work of planting, transplanting, weeding, topping, suckering, harvesting, hanging, stripping, and prizing.

Nevertheless, Carr would have had to supplement and verify verbal information with the written word in order to find out everything a responsible tobacco manufacturer needed to know. If he read the existing literature on the subject, as no doubt he did, he discovered that, from planting to harvesting, tobacco had to be protected from too much rain, not enough rain, hailstorms, worms, and disease, in so far as that was possible. After harvesting it had to be tied in bundles, piled onto wagons, hauled into barns, hung on sticks, and cured.[16]

Curing was a difficult, risky job designed to starve ripe tobacco leaves of their moisture and starch without smoking them dark, for the lemon-yellow color of bright leaf was as important as its mild taste and light consistency. All three of these valuable components could be maintained only by a tricky combination of intense heat and timely ventilation, which required constant vigilance. Heat from stoves, or fireboxes, forced into almost airtight barns by a system of flues, had to be kept at 90 degrees for two to three hours, then advanced to 125 degrees for a shorter time, and finally reduced to 90 degrees for another hour or so before the fires could be allowed to die down. The barn doors were opened at intervals to admit air and prevent the tobacco from "sweating" too much, since excess moisture caused mold and rot.[17]

Tobacco that had been successfully grown and cured by this method was the kind that Blackwell and Day preferred to buy, and long practice had made them shrewd appraisers. They believed (as had John Ruffin Green) that none but the best tobacco should come into their factory, where it was processed by a dozen black men and boys, most of them former slaves who had learned during Reconstruction that any kind of job, no matter how menial, at any kind of pay, no matter how small, was better than no job at all. They worked, more or less steadily, in a kind of loose-jointed assembly line, and sometimes they sang while they transformed bundles of dried leaf into Genuine Durham Smoking Tobacco. The youngest and strongest hoisted the bundles onto long wooden tables, separated the leaves, and beat them into flakes with wooden sticks; others, each wearing a single heavy glove, forced the flakes through sieves. The most intelligent workers weighed the pulverized tobacco and packed it into cloth bags. Whatever had not passed through the sieves the first time was flailed and sifted again.[18]

Thus the W. T. Blackwell Company produced, in 1870, at least 33,000 pounds of smoking tobacco "without any machinery except sticks and one hand bolt," according to Buck Blackwell. Merely transporting that much tobacco into the factory had taken a great deal longer than the actual manufacturing process; and as long as Virginia retained its monopoly on markets in the so-called bright tobacco belt, transporting top-quality leaf to Durham would remain difficult and time consuming. Blackwell was heartily sick of his enervating and seemingly endless trips to Virginia, where he supplemented his uncertain supply of raw tobacco from nearby growers. Because he was convinced that many North Carolina farmers were equally tired of long hauls to Danville, Lynchburg, Petersburg, and Richmond, he began to consider establishing a market in Durham.[19]

After his partners agreed that the idea was worth pursuing, Blackwell approached Henry A. Reams, another Person County native whose experience in buying and selling tobacco qualified him for the position of manager. When Reams accepted a partnership in the new venture, the two men arranged to erect a small two-story building next to Blackwell's factory, and after setting 17 May 1871 as the date of their opening, they began to advertise, not only in newspapers and tobacco journals, but also by word of mouth.

Edward James Parrish, recently married and a newcomer to town from Raleigh, was hired as their auctioneer. The twenty-four-year-old Parrish was the son of a once-prosperous planter and merchant of Round Hill, a small community fifteen miles north of Durham. He had been a student at Trinity College, a mailing clerk, a bookkeeper, a Confederate cavalryman, a salesman in a dry goods store, and an employee of the state government in Raleigh until he decided to move to Durham with his bride, Rosa, in January 1871. His parents, Claiborn and Ruth Parrish, and his youngest unmarried sister, Nannie Graham, had preceded him there in 1869. Claiborn Parrish, once the owner of twelve slaves, many acres of Orange County farmland, a grist mill, and two general stores, had been reduced to near poverty by the Civil War, but at sixty-four he was making a new beginning as a shoemaker, blacksmith, and active participant in Durham politics.

Young Edward, with some experience in merchandising, opened a grocery and confectionery store in Durham, but without much success. In order to supplement his meager income, he turned to auctioneering. Possessed of a powerful voice and a flair for showmanship, he was admirably suited for his avocation, but until 17 May 1871, when he first "cried sales" for Blackwell and Reams, there had been few demands for his services. That day, which changed the direction of Ed Parrish's life and boosted the careers of Buck Blackwell, Jim Day, and Jule Carr, was also of tremendous importance to the state of North Carolina, for it marked the beginning of the end of Virginia's dominance of the tobacco industry.[20]

The day began noisily, with wagons rolling into town long before dawn. Some were drawn by horses and others by mules; some were covered with canvas and others open to the still-dark skies, but all creaked and rumbled and rattled over roads deeply rutted by the spring rains. The racket set up an answering chorus from dogs, chickens, and pigs, and roused people from their beds. By the time the sun was high, most of Durham's inhabitants had congregated at Blackwell's, where men were shouting and horses were stamping and snorting and farmers and factory hands, grunting and sweating with the effort, were struggling to unload 50,000 pounds of tobacco into the warehouse. The little building was filled before all of the wagons were emptied, and the last loads had to be placed on sheets that had been hastily spread on the ground outside.

For the people of Durham, who numbered fewer than three hundred, that May morning was almost like a national holiday. It provided an occasion, a relief from routine, and when the sale began, it was a spectacle worth watching because of Ed Parrish. Wearing a white shirt, white trousers, and a wide-brimmed white hat, he was clearly the most important man on the scene. It was better than a revival, and almost as good as a circus, when Henry Reams gave the signal and Parrish, with his luxuriant brown mustache and neat goatee, his easy smile and deep, persuasive voice, began his spiel.

That spiel was familiar to the farmers and the fifteen buyers who had come to the sale, but it was like a foreign language to those who had never witnessed a tobacco auction. A stream of unintelligible gibberish poured from Parrish's throat as he moved in and out among the round golden piles of bright leaf, pointing to first one, then another, and setting the pace for the buyers with his rapid-fire, sing-song chant. Moving and chanting, never seeming to pause for breath, Parrish's alert brown eyes caught and interpreted the buyers' signals—those barely perceptible body movements and facial twitches, those winks and nods and salutes and shrugs and outthrust tongues that told him they wanted certain piles of tobacco. His performance delighted the farmers and especially pleased Buck Blackwell, an old hand at auctions who recognized quality singing when he heard it.

Blackwell, sensing almost from the beginning that his new venture was destined to succeed, bought not only the first pile of tobacco, but most of the lot. When the last farmer had been paid and the hand-shaking and back-slapping were over and the crowd had wandered off, he and Reams decided to hold weekly sales, with Parrish as their auctioneer. They told Ed Parrish he was every bit as good as Colonel Chiswell Dabney Langhorne from up in Danville, Virginia, supposedly the best crier in the bright belt.[21] Blackwell figured that if the three of them stuck together, they were bound to prosper; if they prospered, so would everyone else in Durham who had something to sell. A farmer with cash in his pocket would stock up on provisions, whatever he couldn't grow or make at home. If any money remained, he might buy a length of dress goods for his woman, or shoes for his "young 'uns," or maybe even a sack of sweets from Ed Parrish's store, something for the whole family. And then, most likely, he'd go to a grog shop for a well-earned drink of whiskey.

By December 1871, Ed Parrish was better off financially than he had been since before the war, when he had sung the auctioneer's song only on rare occasions, to amuse his five sisters at Round Hill or his friends at Trinity College, in Randolph County. His popularity with farmers and buyers was growing steadily; since May he had auctioned off 700,000 pounds of tobacco for Blackwell and Reams. Parrish began to think about going into business for himself, and he may have discussed the matter with Julian Carr.

The two had much in common. Parrish was twenty-five, and Carr was twenty-six. Aside from being college men, which set them apart from the majority of Durham's citizens, they were Confederate veterans who shared a hatred of William Tecumseh Sherman, carpetbaggers, scalawags, Republicans, and anything connected with Reconstruction. They also shared a strong desire to lead rather than to follow, and a year after the tobacco auction that brought them together in business, both were involved in local government. In May 1872, Ed Parrish succeeded Robert F. Morris as magistrate of police, a title later changed to mayor; Julian Carr was elected to the board of aldermen, a five-man body designed to assist the magistrate in governing the three-year-old town of Durham.

Edward James Parrish (courtesy of Laura Noell Carr Chapman)

Julian S. Carr (courtesy of Laura Noell Carr Chapman)

As an alderman, Carr was instrumental in establishing a board of health, in opening several new streets, and in buying land for a graveyard. He also authored a document condemning the Orange County commissioners for granting licenses to sell "spiritous liquors" to a number of Durham men and women whose applications had previously been turned down by the local board. Carr and his fellow aldermen vowed never to support the commissioners in any future bids for "offices of honor and profit," and he saw to it that the resolution was published in the weekly newspaper.[22]

Serving together as town officials strengthened the bond between Carr and Parrish. Their friendship may also have sparked Carr's interest in Parrish's sister, Nannie Graham, who attended Salem College and was "the pet of everybody who came in contact with her magnetic nature."[23] Her forebears, on both sides of the family, were early American settlers, Indian fighters, and Revolutionary War soldiers who emigrated from England well before 1650. A maternal ancestor, Marmaduke Ward, settled in Rhode Island in 1638; two of his descendants, Enoch and Edward Ward, eventually migrated to North Carolina. Edward Ward, Nannie Graham Parrish's great-great-grandfather, lived in Carteret County until he moved to Onslow County in 1743, became commissioner of roads, and was "a large land and slave owner and a prominant man."

The Ward land and slaves passed from father to son, and Ruth Ann Ward, Nannie Parrish's mother, grew up on a plantation near Jacksonville, North Carolina, and attended school in Hillsborough, which was the state's educational center for women in antebellum days. While she was a student there, either at the Burwell School or at the Female Academy, which was run by the Reverend William Mercer Green (the same gentleman who officiated at the marriage of John Wesley and Eliza Carr), Ruth Ann Ward met Doctor Claiborn Parrish, whose first name had been given to him "because of the old superstition that a seventh son has the gift of healing." After a proper courtship they were married on 1 April 1842.

The earliest Parrish known to have emigrated to America was Thomas Parrish, who came from Yorkshire to Virginia on the ship *Charity* in 1622. Other Parrishes followed in 1635, settling in Virginia, Maryland, Pennsylvania, and, later, in North Carolina, where one John Parrish was "appointed in charge of high ways at a court held in Pequemons [sic] Precinct" and, in 1703, purchased land at Little River. The names of several other John Parrishes appear in military

Doctor Claiborn Parrish (courtesy of Laura Noell Carr Chapman)

records in Chowan, Granville, Guilford, and Caswell counties; one of them received, at the end of the Revolutionary War, "army pay of ninety-seven pounds and four shillings."

The first Claiborn Parrish fought the British, too, and in his later years he appeared before the Court of Pleas and Quarter Sessions in Granville County to apply for a pension. He asked Willie P. Mangum, a United States senator from North Carolina to vouch for him, and on 17 August 1832 Mangum obliged by stating to the proper authorities that he had known Claiborn Parrish "from my earliest infancy, as long as I can remember," and that Parrish had lived "in the immediate neighborhood" of the Mangum home in northern Orange County.

This veteran of the American Revolution (whose pension, when he finally received it, amounted to only forty dollars) was the grandfather of Doctor Claiborn Parrish, who married Ruth Ann Ward and was regarded as the leading citizen of Round Hill. A farmer, merchant, miller, magistrate in the Orange County court, and active member of the Mount Bethel Methodist Church, Claiborn Parrish also became a strong proponent of education as soon as he became a parent. In an era when infant deaths were common, he and his wife lost only one of their seven children. Thomas Lowe, their second son and sixth child, died at the age of three after he was kicked by a horse; but Frances Miriam, Anne Eliza, Edward James, Louisa, Emmaline, and Nancy Graham all grew to maturity and had what seem to have been, in retrospect, idyllic childhoods on the plantation at Round Hill.

According to Frances Parrish, who was called Fanny, the big house sat "on a little hill, beautiful and sloping in every direction," and the wheat fields surrounding it were "pastures of emerald green from early fall until the yellow heads bowed with golden grain." There was a stream, Fanny remembered, where she and her four sisters and their brother, "whom Father had dubbed Neddie," often went fishing for minnows "with a retinue of darkies, carrying their fishing tackle consisting of pin hooks fastened to lines made of one strand of thread."

The children had their own horse and buggy and "would drive for miles with little black Joe perched up behind in case anything should happen we did not know how to manage. This was every day fun." For special outings, Fanny said, "there was a closed-in carriage with carpeted steps, and so large we took great pride in calling it the old

Ship of Zion, for it had landed us safe upon our journey many a time."

Describing her siblings, Fanny Parrish recalled that her sister Annie, "like Martha of old, while a very little girl, was encumbered about many things," and that Louisa, "sprightly and given to see the best side to all things, was a veritable mimic." Emma was the beauty of the family, and Nannie Graham, "a dear, lovely child, with deep, dark and beautiful eyes . . . had a little maid whose special duty it was to see that she was never out alone." Brother Neddie was "on hand with spirits overflowing with tantalizing tricks, the victims being his sisters," but in later years, he became "a very enjoyable companion, always acting the genial escort."

When the high-spirited Neddie was three years old, his father took steps to see that he would have a good education by helping to organize a boys' school at a nearby settlement called South Lowell. As a member of the executive committee of the South Lowell Male Academy, Claiborn Parrish had a hand in hiring the Reverend John A. Dean, a graduate of Wesleyan College, in Connecticut. Dean ran the new school with such expertise that it became successful almost immediately and was soon attracting students "from as far west as Salisbury and as far east as New Bern."[24]

Inspired, perhaps, by the public's response to the South Lowell Male Academy, Parrish decided to start a school for girls. With the nucleus of a student body living under his own roof, and with a number of friends and relatives who were the parents of daughters, he had only to erect a building and find a teacher. Fanny Parrish remembered that the first schoolmarm was "a thing unlovely. She came from the Episcopal School in Raleigh, N.C., recommended by Dr. Smeads [sic] who was then President of St. Mary's. One term sufficed both Father and Mother."[25] The second teacher, appropriately named Martha Duty, was a decided improvement, an amiable young woman who lived with the Parrishes and taught the girls "until they began to cherish college ideas."

The South Lowell Male Academy provided beaux for Claiborn Parrish's daughters, who often were invited to the school for "an evening of entertainment to be given by the school boys." Sometimes the girls were allowed to attend, riding in the carriage they called Ship of Zion and chaperoned by their father.

The Civil War closed both schools, and at Round Hill "each and every one began to realize that economy must be studied and practiced along all lines." Ruth Parrish set her daughters to knitting, saying that the soldiers must have socks; later she ordered that the carpets be torn from the floors, cut into blanket size, and forwarded to "the home regiment." As the war dragged on and hunger became a way of life, everyone on the plantation shared what they had. Sometimes the Parrish slaves, who "knew no other home, had no other friends," came up from the fields to the big house "bringing their hat crowns filled to the brim with partridge eggs." Many of them would find it hard to leave Round Hill, once the war was over and they were free.

The saddest day was when Neddie had to leave Trinity College "to take a place in the army, notwithstanding his youthful years." Although nothing was the same on the plantation after that, Fanny Parrish reported that one thing remained constant: her father, who believed that poetry was "a refuge against work and care," insisted that a few hours each day be spent reading.

Soon after Lee's surrender at Appomattox, Wheeler's cavalry, retreating from Sherman's army, could be seen passing Round Hill. During the ten-day armistice that preceded Johnston's surrender to Sherman, "the tramps following the army scouraged the country. We lived in constant fear of depradations at their hands," Fanny recalled. "They would ride out to Round Hill at night, seemingly very friendly with the servants, and would help them shell corn, singing war songs, but the only thing they carried away was the carriage whip."

A few days after the Confederate surrender at the Bennett farmhouse, near Durham, Edward Parrish returned home from Appomattox. Fanny recorded the event: "He had been wandering around the community for several days, evading the Yankee pickets, for he did not want to give over his beautiful war horse, Santa Anna. He was so poorly clad everyone gave way to a flood of tears. It is impossible to forget that old brown, home-made overcoat, the front of which had so many bullet holes in it. It was a day of rejoicing, for brother Neddie had come."

Devotion to this son and brother no doubt drew the Parrishes and their daughters to Durham's first tobacco auction, where they could watch their cherished Neddie perform. There Julian Carr certainly would have approached them to pay his respects. If he was not already enamoured of Nannie Graham Parrish, her "deep, dark and beautiful eyes" may then have met his intense gray gaze and held it just long enough to make his heart beat faster. Not too long, of course—for no lady ever looked straight into a man's eyes for more than a second or two, and Nannie Parrish was in every respect a lady. Nevertheless, at seventeen, she was highly susceptible to masculine charm, and Jule Carr had plenty of charm.

Although Carr was small, his strong, well-proportioned body gave off an aura of great energy, and he carried himself with such assurance that he seemed taller than he actually was. Immaculately clean and fashionably dressed, he preferred frock coats, double-breasted silk waistcoats, and tall beaver hats that he ordered from a hatter in Baltimore, "because my head is of such a peculiar shape an ordinary beaver won't fit my head."[26] An exceptionally broad brow gave his head a square look, and when he doffed these custom-made hats and bowed to ladies, his hair shone smooth and dark. A full, curving mustache partially hid his mouth, which turned down at its outer corners until he smiled or laughed, but he laughed easily and often. And because his light gray eyes invariably mirrored his feelings, Nannie Parrish probably realized that she had made a conquest even before Julian Carr asked her parents for permission to come calling.

Just when Carr made that first call, or how many followed it before he and Nannie were married, is not known; however, their wedding took place in Trinity Methodist Church on 19 February 1873. Barely two weeks later, the bridegroom was appointed mayor of Durham when his brother-in-law, Ed Parrish, resigned the office and opened a tobacco sales house. Carr served until 17 May. After that he gave his full attention to his business, his bride, and the house he was planning to build for her in what would later become Durham's first fashionable residential section.[27]

There is reason to believe that John M. Wilson and John A. Waddell, of Wilson's Mills, designed and built Carr's first home. The two artisans had a reputation for quality workmanship and had constructed several fine homes in Raleigh, among them the Heck mansion, described as "the most pretentious private residence in the State."[28] Julian Carr, who was definitely partial to quality and by no means averse to ostentation, probably hired Wilson and Waddell to build a residence in the Italianate style, with a mansard roof, large bay windows on either side of the front entrance, and a spacious back porch connected to a separate kitchen.

Situated on five acres of land at the eastern end of Durham's principal street (originally called Pratt, and later changed to Main), the Carr estate had ample room for a barn, a stable, a carriage house,

Nancy (Nannie) Graham Parrish Carr
(courtesy of Laura Noell Carr Chapman)

Julian S. Carr (courtesy of Laura Noell Carr Chapman)

and, because both Julian and Nannie Carr loved flowers, a large greenhouse. To ensure their privacy as well as to protect their lawn from wandering cows, pigs, dogs, and children, an iron picket fence surrounded the entire property, which the owner christened Waverly Honor.[29] Carr's choice of names was allegedly inspired by his admiration for Captain Edward Waverley, the hero of Sir Walter Scott's first novel, although no reason for the misspelling has been advanced. Another, perhaps more valid reason for the selection stemmed from the fact that Carr was a distant cousin of Scott via his connection with Robert Carr, the earl of Somerset. The earl's mother, Janet, was an ancestor of Walter Scott—a remote ancestor, but a reliable one nevertheless.[30]

By creating an estate in the raw frontier town of Durham and giving the place a romantic, high-sounding name, Carr raised many eyebrows and caused much gossip. Other Durham men were to follow his example, however, as soon as tobacco brought them riches enough.

4. The Arena

URING Jule Carr's first thirteen years in Durham, he sometimes complained to Buck Blackwell about the "hard work and drudgery" of his job and the fact that it often left him "worn out, and tired out, and frazzled out, and every other out." But good health and a naturally sunny disposition enabled him to recover quickly from fatigue and frustration, and he obviously enjoyed the excitement of the highly competitive tobacco business. "Let buffalo gore buffalo, and the pasture go to the strongest," he said to his rivals. Among those who took up that challenge were Louis L. Armistead, Wesley A. Wright, John H. McElwee, and Washington Duke.[1]

From 1870 until 1883, Carr and his partners were involved in a series of bitter lawsuits, in a national and international advertising campaign, in the construction of what would eventually become the world's largest smoking tobacco factory, and in a constant search for more efficient methods of manufacturing. Working in what looked like an unpretentious wooden barn, Buck Blackwell, Jim Day, and Jule Carr prospered to the extent that, in 1874, they were able to build a new four-story brick-and-granite factory that was to grow to gigantic proportions within a decade. On the walls of the main office they hung larger-than-life-size portraits of themselves; by 1876 they had added several framed certificates of merit and a gold medal bestowed upon Genuine Durham Smoking Tobacco at the Philadelphia Centennial Exposition. Buck Blackwell installed a whistle in the new factory, "an instrument after the style of the Calliope which imitates the bellowing of a bull with all its variations to a dot," and he saw to it that this contraption bellowed at each day's opening, noon, and closing. Every blast could be heard as far away as Chapel Hill and cost the company six dollars, but it was worth the expense. One newspaper reported that "its effect on strangers unaware of the existence of an artificial bellower is remarkable . . . and Blackwell enjoys it."[2]

Blackwell definitely did not enjoy the many legal battles he was compelled to fight in both Virginia and North Carolina courts, beginning early in 1871, when he discovered that his trademark was in jeopardy. Although Blackwell had a patent on it, the widely recognized symbol, picturing a black short-horn bull standing between the words *Genuine* and *Durham*, was becoming irresistible to other manufacturers of tobacco.[3] At that time, laws pertaining to copyrights and trademarks were not clearly defined, and it is conceivable that Blackwell's competitors felt they were within their rights. Nevertheless, Blackwell and his partners were incensed by what they saw as out-and-out thievery. "Bull Durham Tobacco" was far too profitable to share with anyone else, so they decided to fight for it, never dreaming that the conflict would rage for fifteen years and cost them over $100,000.[4]

Their first suit was against Louis L. Armistead, of Lynchburg, Virginia, in January 1871. Armistead claimed he owned the right to sell "Durham Smoking Tobacco," with a bull's head on its label, because in 1862 he had bought the word *Durham* from Wesley Wright, a partner of Durham's first tobacco manufacturer, Robert Morris. Wright had convinced Armistead that the name he coined for the tobacco he and Morris produced was "Best Spanish Flavored Durham Smoking Tobacco." He gave up manufacturing to join the Confederate Army; when he resumed operations after the war and called his brand "Original Durham Tobacco, W. A. Wright, Originator," he claimed he had a legal right to do so. Wright's postwar business at Liberty, Virginia, did not prosper, and in 1870 he approached Louis Armistead with an offer to sell. Armistead at first rejected it, but later agreed to accept after Wright produced affidavits signed by six Durham citizens. They were, Wright said, "gentlemen of high standing who were willing to state that Wright was, indeed, the originator of the brand," and that no other person was entitled to use it.[5]

The W. T. Blackwell Company secured an injunction against Armistead and the case was tried in the U.S. District Court for the Western District of Virginia in March 1872, with Judge Alexander Rives presiding. Judge Rives viewed much of the testimony as "contradictory, irrelevant and impertinent," but his reaction, compared to Armistead's, was mild.[6] Apparently someone had "gotten to" the six Durham men who had signed Wesley Wright's affidavits, and as Armistead's chief witnesses they left a great deal to be desired.

The first to testify was W. Y. Clark, who told the prosecutor that he wasn't sure he understood the paper Wright read to him, and that he didn't mean to convey the idea that Wright had originated the brand, since he never even saw the brand. William Mangum, following Clark on the stand, said he didn't read the paper because he couldn't read handwriting "unless it is very good." Riley Vickers admitted that he held the paper in his hand, but he "did not examine it much," and he didn't really know what the tobacco in question was called. A fourth witness, P. J. Mangum, told the court he was running an engine when Wright came with the paper for him to sign. He read only a few lines because he was too busy to read, and he didn't intend to imply that Wright was "the originator of Durham brand smoking tobacco." Solomon Shepherd, who had been Durham's first postmaster in 1863, remembered that he read only part of Wright's paper because he had been ill and was "very feeble." Nash Booth said he didn't read the paper but signed it "on Mr. Wright's representation," thinking that Wright only wanted to show that he was the first man "to work smoking tobacco at this place."

Attorneys for the W. T. Blackwell Company maintained that all of Armistead's witnesses believed Wright's paper certified only that he and Morris were the first to "put up" smoking tobacco at Durham, not that they were the first to use the word *Durham* on a brand label. They also pointed out that while there had been considerable argument over whether Morris and Wright's product was called Best Spanish Flavored Smoking Tobacco or Best Spanish Flavored Durham Smoking Tobacco, the only witnesses supporting Wright's testimony were his two sons, who obviously had been briefed on what to say, and a man called Pompey Gordon. Gordon stated that he had read the words *Durham, N.C.*, on Morris and Wright's tobacco, but he didn't know what *N.C.* meant at that time "as I was not then educated, but have since found that N.C. meant North Carolina."

Witnesses for the W. T. Blackwell Company included four tobacconists, three farmers, a carpenter, a schoolteacher, and a mail contractor. All of them testified that Wright's original brand name had been Best Spanish Flavored Smoking Tobacco, minus the word *Durham*, and some of them stated that the tobacco Wright sold often was not marked at all.

In his summation, Judge Rives commented on "the vast amount of testimony" and the "wearisome amount of unprofitable reading" it had necessitated before he finally ruled in favor of the W. T. Blackwell Company.[7] The judge's ruling did not stop Wesley Wright, in 1874, from manufacturing Original Durham Smoking Tobacco and using a bull's head on his labels. Blackwell promptly sued Wright. This time the defendant's lawyers were able to convince the Supreme Court of North Carolina that there was a distinct difference between the word *genuine* and the word *original*, and that the bovine in question was not necessarily a bull but might be an ox or a heifer. So Wesley Wright continued to make what Julian Carr called "spurious Durham," and many other manufacturers followed Wright's example.[8] Blackwell's Bull Durham found itself surrounded by Rosebud Durham, Rival Durham, New Durham, Ten Cent Durham, Ram Durham, King Durham, Nickel-Plated Durham, Full Weight Durham, Royal Durham, Pride of Durham, Mighty Fine Durham, Billy Boy Durham, Seal of Durham, Sitting Bull Durham, and countless others, but none ever surpassed Blackwell's in popularity.[9]

Wesley Wright's victory over the W. T. Blackwell Company may have encouraged W. E. Dibrell and Company, of Richmond, to make and sell Durham Smoking Tobacco and to brand it with the head and neck of a bull. This act triggered another chain of legal events in the lives of Blackwell, Day, and Carr, who were prospering from the growing popularity of their product, but also spending huge sums of money on lawyers' fees and inordinate amounts of time traveling to and from court sessions. Nevertheless, they could not afford to ignore Dibrell, so they sued him. The case finally was decided in the U.S. Circuit Court for the Eastern District of Virginia on 18 January 1878. The presiding judge, R. W. Hughes, concluded that only those manufacturers living in Durham could so brand their tobacco, and that the W. T. Blackwell Company had "the sole and exclusive right to employ the word Durham to designate and distinguish the tobacco manufactured by them, and also to use and employ in conjunction with the said word Durham, the side view representation of a Durham bull as and for their trade mark."[10]

Four days later, the W. T. Blackwell Company, jubilant in victory, published in leading tobacco journals a letter lambasting Louis Armistead and William Dibrell in particular, and threatening their competitors in general:

> We are the manufacturers of the Only Genuine Durham Smoking Tobacco to be found in the world. Ours is the Original Durham, and but for the efforts of our predecessors and ourselves the now celebrated Durham Smoking Tobacco of world wide reputation would never have been an article of commerce.
>
> The reputation of our goods has induced other manufacturers to pirate our trade-mark and throw upon the market various brands of spurious Durham smoking tobacco. Not satis-

fied with filching a portion of our trade-mark, some of the manufacturers of this counterfeit Durham are so utterly lost to all regard for truth as to advertise their *base imitation* as the "Genuine" and the "Oldest Durham Brand" and other miserable subterfuges which they know are unqualifiedly false. . . .

Armistead of Lynchburg, when we sued him, and Dibrell and Company of Richmond, when we sued them, issued flaming circulars to the trade guaranteeing to protect them in the handling of their goods, but where are those guarantees now, and what do they amount to? We say, "Gone where the woodbine twineth."

In conclusion, buy only Blackwell's Durham, and take no other, and put no confidence in "guarantees" and trashy circulars, or you may learn too late that "he who soweth to the wind shall reap the whirlwind."[11]

This "Card to the Public," as it was titled, no doubt was created by Blackwell's advertising manager, and the reply it prompted from W. Duke Sons and Company "more than likely . . . was the work of James B. Duke," the youngest and most aggressive of Washington Duke's three sons. The Duke firm sent a letter to the *United States Tobacco Journal* early in February 1878, saying it had no desire "to use anybody's bull," but that it had a perfect right to use the word *Durham*, as did "a half dozen other manufacturers in the town of Durham"; that it intended to continue making Genuine Duke of Durham and Pro Bono Publico Durham smoking tobacco; that its customers could, most assuredly, put every confidence in their guarantee to protect them against "any loss, or trouble, from any claim for infringement of another's rights"; and that it was "able, ready, and willing to make good our guarantee."[12]

So neither Judge Hughes's decree nor the Blackwell Company's admonition impressed W. Duke Sons and Company. John H. McElwee, of Statesville, also ignored them. McElwee began using the side view of a bull on his Genuine Antebellum Smoking Tobacco in 1877, and he continued to do so despite the warnings inherent in the outcome of *Blackwell* v. *Dibrell*. Claiming that he had been a partner of Blackwell's predecessor, John Ruffin Green, McElwee further insulted the W. T. Blackwell Company by filing suit against it for infringing on his own trademark, and although the case resulted in a non-suit, McElwee was not intimidated. His Genuine Antebellum

Smoking Tobacco and Blackwell's Genuine Durham Smoking Tobacco, both stamped with side-view representations of short-horn bulls, continued to appear together on the shelves of tobacco shops and general stores, while suits and countersuits were being tried in the North Carolina courts. Even after the Supreme Court upheld the decision that had given Blackwell exclusive rights to the bull, McElwee persisted in keeping a bull on his Genuine Antebellum labels, thereby forcing Blackwell to secure yet another injunction against him and throwing Blackwell's partner, Julian Carr, into a rage. Carr advised Blackwell to threaten McElwee's customers with prosecution, and on one occasion, when Blackwell was in Baltimore on company business, Carr wrote urging him to "go to Norfolk and see who is handling McElwee's 'Antebellum.' . . . Go to see them and get them to stop it, and tell them you give them this one chance to stop it, and if they don't, you are going to put the law to them, to the very fullest extent. . . . Everything is fair in love and war, and *we must stop it.*"[13]

Stopping that kind of piracy was extremely difficult, however. Even the prestigious firms of Pierre Lorillard, of New Jersey, and Marburg Brothers, of Baltimore, apparently did not frown on it, for Julian Carr stated that "in one of our suits in the United States Court at Norfolk, we found Lorillard's lawyer managing the complainant's case."[14] Expressing his opinion of Marburg Brothers and Lorillard, Carr insisted that Blackwell visit them personally and say to them:

> that we have borne this thing long enough. That Houses that holds such positions in the trade ought not to lend their names to such dirty work. That because other Houses makes spurious Durham is a mighty poor argument from a moral standpoint for a House of Integrity to rely upon. Two wrongs never made a right . . . and the truth is, that for the force of example set by Marburg Bros. and Lorillard 9 out of every 10 spurious Durham manufacturers is encouraged in his meanness. The Houses ought to quit and in a card to the "Tobacco Leaf" ought to say as much, stating that they are satisfied that W. T. Blackwell & Co. are the rightful owners of the brand. "Durham Leaf" on tobacco labels is a miserable subterfuge used by rascals with not enough courage to shoulder their villainy.[15]

Rascal or not, John H. McElwee had the courage to fight the makers of Bull Durham for eight years, and he gave up only after the North Carolina Supreme Court denied his 1887 appeal of a verdict granting "the exclusive right of the successors of John R. Green to the use of the Bull trade mark."[16] By that time the famous trademark was a familiar sight not only throughout the United States but also in Canada, Mexico, Europe, and the Far East. Credit for that fact was due to Julian Carr, who had persuaded his partners that investments in advertising were both safe and highly lucrative.

Carr had learned the value of publicity early in life, first from his father, who "talked up" luxuries while he weighed, measured, cut, and wrapped necessities for his customers; and later from David Lowry Swain, who never missed an opportunity to promote the University of North Carolina while he was its president. Swain publicized the university not only in newspapers and periodicals, but also through personal appearances in cities up and down the eastern seaboard. Audiences heard him praise the faculty, the curriculum, North Carolina's wonderful climate, and Chapel Hill's ever-changing seasonal beauty. His eloquence convinced many young men and their parents of his university's superiority, and during his tenure enrollment increased from 89 students, in 1835, to 456 in 1859. This made it the second-largest college (next only to Yale) in the United States.[17]

Growing up in Chapel Hill, where high government officials and prominent men of affairs were frequent visitors at university commencements, Carr learned, by monitoring his own reactions and observing those of his fellow villagers, that so-called average people were impressed by celebrities and eager to identify with them. That particular lesson in human nature led him to enlist the aid of certain notable figures in promoting his company's product. For a fee— which probably included generous portions of flattery and Bull Durham tobacco, as well as money—he persuaded the erstwhile vice-president of the Confederacy, the poet laureate of England, a noted Scottish historian, a popular American author, the chaplain of the United States Senate, and five southern senators to endorse the Blackwell brand in leading newspapers and tobacco journals.[18] Alexander H. Stephens, Alfred Lord Tennyson, Thomas Carlyle, James Russell Lowell, the Reverend W. J. Milburn, and senators Coke (Texas), Blackburn (Kentucky), Butler (South Carolina), Cockrell (Mississippi), and Harris (Tennessee) publicly praised the taste and aroma of Bull Durham tobacco. Their testimony not only increased the company's sales, but also boosted America's economy by pouring vast sums of tobacco tax money into the U.S. Treasury.

Elated over these results, Carr boasted to Blackwell:

About advertising the "Durham" brand—it is beyond doubt one of the best if not the best advertised brand of tobacco before the Public, and this in a very great measure is its success. . . . It would astonish the "Natives" I reckon to know how much we advertise, yet it is a serious fact that if I ran the establishment precisely as I saw fit I would spend $2, where we now spend $1. It ain't no use to tell me that advertising don't pay, and people don't read newspaper advertisements. I have studied advertising hard, and am satisfied about it.[19]

Carr's study convinced him that newspapers were the best vehicles for advertising, but he also put great stock in signs, and as soon as he was running the establishment precisely as he saw fit, which occurred in 1883, a great deal of the publicity budget went for huge billboards. By then he had discovered that one side of a barn, one wall of a building, or a section of board fence could be rented for a relatively small sum, and many such surfaces already displayed the arresting bull he had substituted for John Ruffin Green's original animal as soon as he had the legal right to do so.

Green's bull had always faced the right side of the background on which it was painted. Carr, interpreting that side to be the East, reversed the position so that Blackwell's bull gazed toward the West, a "newer, more radical region of unlimited resources." One of the first bulls to turn away from "the more conservative, more limited East" wore the American flag and the Liberty Bell around its neck; in Carr's eyes, this jaunty beast, with its patriotic collar, was a distinct improvement over its stolid, unadorned predecessor.[20] Over the years Carr continued to display the Durham Bull in many different attitudes: "serious, boisterous, jovial, determined, frisky and otherwise"; on occasion, he even showed the animal dressed in the swallow-tail coats and bat-wing collars that were an integral part of his own wardrobe.[21]

Carr rarely missed an opportunity to deviate from run-of-the-mill advertising. When the Royal Arch Masons met in Durham in 1879, he capitalized on their convention by staging an outing for the delegates that was long remembered, not only by citizens of Durham and Chapel Hill, but also by visitors to the university's commencement exercises. Guests came prepared to witness nothing more startling than an academic procession and were surprised by a parade that would have done justice to P. T. Barnum. Carr began preparations for entertaining his fellow Masons many weeks before the convention. From Philadelphia he ordered "costly trappings" for the fifty-two horses that would pull thirteen wagonloads of celebrating delegates to Chapel Hill, where they would watch the seniors graduate and then "partake of a barbecue, prepared by Blackwell & Co. on the grounds of the campus." Carr commissioned James R. Lawrence, an employee who was both an inventor and "an artist of no mean pretensions," to design and paint twenty-six large banners, two for each wagon, that would display the Bull and enjoin the public to "Smoke Blackwell's Durham Smoking Tobacco."

At six o'clock on the final morning of commencement, the convention delegates gathered in front of Durham's Claiborn Hotel, which had been built by Julian Carr and named for his father-in-law, Doctor Claiborn Parrish. Carr greeted the delegates, presented them with long-stemmed pipes and sacks of Bull Durham tobacco, and told them to light up as soon as they reached Chapel Hill. The wagons were hung with Lawrence's red, white, and black banners, and the horses were "richly caparisoned," each with an elaborate, made-to-order cover on its back and a flag stamped with the Blackwell trademark on its head. Dozens of early risers were on hand to see the procession off, and when it reached the outskirts of Chapel Hill several hours later, the Salem Cornet Band was waiting. The horses were sweating under their colorful regalia and the Masons were aching from the long, rough ride; but despite heat and dust and weariness, they made a grand entrance into the village. Following instructions, they puffed steadily on their pipes and filled the warm June air with the scent of Bull Durham tobacco, while the brass band played and onlookers, alerted in advance by the W. T. Blackwell Company, cheered and waved from both sides of Franklin Street.

Jule Carr was in his element as the instigator of this spectacle, and he invited all visiting alumni to share the barbecue that took place in the shade of trees he had played beneath as a boy. There he and his partners presided over a feast that lasted until four o'clock in the afternoon. When "the returning procession reached Durham at 8:45 p.m. without a mishap," it may have been due partly to luck, but it was also a tribute to Carr's organizational skills.[22]

Using a variety of premiums such as clocks, razors, calendars, floating soap, and photographs of famous people, Carr gently bribed dealers to stock the Blackwell brand. Once he was given free rein, he offered smokers cash prizes for empty Bull Durham tobacco bags, a scheme that cost him almost $12,000 in 1884.[23] A less spectacular but quite effective means of advertising was the show card, which could be placed in shop windows or nailed to any flat surface. Carr preferred cards made of tin because "as a rule Paper Show Cards are the dearest Show Card, that you can put up. They get dingy and fly-specked, and are then thrown away, when a card that you can wipe off with a damp rag beats it to death."[24]

Many show cards depicted, in vivid colors, the intense rivalry between the W. T. Blackwell Company and other manufacturers of tobacco, especially Washington Duke. Duke's Pro Bono Publico brand became popular after he moved to Durham in 1874 and built a factory at the extreme western end of Main Street—out of sight but by no means out of mind, as far as Blackwell, Day, and Carr were concerned. Duke, who was known around the Blackwell factory as "Old Bono," had become a formidable competitor by 1877. In November of that year Carr told Blackwell: "I want to jump 'Old Bono.' I wish that you could see his Show Card. He has the Bull down dead, killed by his Indian, and his Indian rejoicing."

At that time Blackwell was in Baltimore conferring with Gerrard S. Watts, a prominent commission merchant and jobber who was an agent for Blackwell's products. Carr spent the better part of a week begging his senior partner to go with Watts to Cleveland, Indianapolis, St. Louis, Detroit, and Chicago, where Washington Duke was "piling it off. Just lots and scores of it, and his trade is growing fast, fast in the section where our trade is falling off rapidly. Something must be done. Go West by all means this trip and carry Watts with you through his territory."[25]

Carr wrote that he had been informed that orders were pouring in at the Duke factory, and that only the day before he himself had seen "Bono making a big shipment into this very Western territory," which included Indianapolis, Detroit, Cleveland, Muscatun, and Sandusky. "All these were at one time good markets for 'Blackwell's Durham.' Don't les' give them up to Duke," he pleaded. "Go West, and make such arrangements as will get back what we have lost, if we do no more."[26]

Apparently goaded by dark thoughts of what Washington Duke was accomplishing, Carr continued to bombard Blackwell with letters and telegrams, sometimes as many as three a day, entreating him to "look after the trade, for I tell you, my dear Brother, 'Bono' is walking into us. We must stop this, and you are the man and now is the time. Go West, carry Watts with you, tell him Duke is entering through his territory, the worst sort. Every day, my dear Sir, Duke takes a slice from us in the West."[27]

Carr had good reason to worry about Washington Duke, for although he lacked formal education the fifty-seven-year-old farmer turned manufacturer was a shrewd businessman, a tireless worker, and the father of three sons who were every bit as dedicated to getting ahead as was "Old Bono" himself. But the Dukes were not the only disturbers of Carr's peace of mind. At least a dozen tobacco factories had sprung up in Durham since his arrival there in 1870, and their owners also were eager to take slices out of the pie that once had been the exclusive property of the W. T. Blackwell Company. Carr's spirits rose or fell with the number of orders he received for tobacco, and whenever one of Blackwell's selling trips sent those welcome orders pouring into the Durham office, he was as quick with his praise as he had been with his badgering. During one highly successful trip he wrote to his partner:

> You have done so admirably well on this trip that henceforth I give you the papers, and you can do the going. Don't never say that you can't no more. Your abundant success this trip leaves no room but for us to say "Well done thou good and faithful servant." You can beat me buying and trading at home and abroad, so you are in for it henceforth.
>
> Everything and Everybody is well—first rate. Orders have been good and one entire force [of] stamp hands have been kept busy ever since you left, and our orders have taken out the goods about as fast as we got them ready. . . . The weather is open and the town just stays packed with wagons.[28]

The covered Nissen wagons used by many farmers to haul tobacco to markets were a welcome sight to Carr. Whenever there was "a cloud of white canvas" in Durham, it meant more money for the company, and excitement ran like fever in his blood.[29] Conversely, when foul weather or a poor crop kept tobacco farmers away and orders from agents and commission merchants were either slow in coming or nonexistent, his outlook turned gloomy. He once mourned, by mail, to his absent senior partner, "Everything is quiet this morning in Durham. Not even a load of tobacco in town. Not an order in the House since you left, and the Warehousemen hungry and the Bank growling. We are overdrawn this morning the rise of

Eleven thousand dollars. If I don't get an order this morning I am going to ship Watts and Co., then McDowell and Co., as I am bound to raise some money."[30]

The following day Carr reported to Blackwell that the town was still quiet and the weather cloudy and threatening. Twenty-four hours later, he was "considerably under the weather with my lungs. My right lung pains me all the time & sometimes both of them," he complained. "I can just barely get up of a morning at all. . . . I am fully satisfied now, with my lungs hurting me so much, that I have confined myself too closely to this warm room this Winter."[31]

It had been a bad winter in many ways, what with the Dibrell case pending, John McElwee and Wesley Wright usurping Blackwell's trademark, and manufacturers of "spurious Durham" cropping up with maddening frequency, not only in Virginia and the Carolinas, but even as far away as Savannah, Georgia. The legal battles dragged on, and in the spring of 1877, Carr wrote to Blackwell, "I am like you. I am tired of Wright. . . . In fact I do sincerely believe I can say from the bottom of my heart that I am tired of 'Durham Tobacco.' I have not had the chance of a Factory hand for more than a year, and it is not only hard work, but the most unpleasant kind of work. I am tired of it, and have felt now for some time that I would prefer to do something else that is not so hard and unpleasant." Before closing, however, Carr added that "it is important to break McElwee's back," and he urged Blackwell to hire the best lawyer in Norfolk to work in conjunction with Augustus Merrimon, Thomas C. Fuller, and Samuel A. Ashe, a prestigious legal threesome they had been retaining, at considerable expense, for several years.[32]

Julian Carr may have been tired of Wright and McElwee and lawsuits and hard, unpleasant work, but he had no real notion of leaving the business that was making him a power in the rapidly growing town of Durham. The population had jumped from 258 in 1870 to 2,000 in 1875. Durham's property value had increased from $15,000 in 1866 to $550,000 in 1876; the town's active capital, which had amounted to only $1,000 when the Civil War ended, had advanced to $500,000. Where there had been two small stores, one blacksmith shop, and one barroom in 1860, there were now fifteen dry goods and grocery stores, three drug stores, four confectioneries, six boarding houses, one hotel, seven restaurants and barrooms, one tin shop, five planing and lumber mills, and one combination newspaper and job printing office.[33]

This was progress in a high degree, all of it related to the manufacture and sale of tobacco, and much of it due to the leadership of the W. T. Blackwell Company, whose three partners "conducted their business with great vigor—greater, perhaps, than many Richmond manufacturers."[34] Nevertheless, vigor could not do what machinery could, and some of those Richmond manufacturers had a machine that shredded and sifted tobacco, a machine so valuable it was hidden away behind locked doors. Patented in 1866 by Hiram W. Smith, a manufacturer of farm machinery, the unique steam-powered device was something the Blackwell Company desperately needed in order to increase production and stay ahead of competition. Julian Carr acquired it, "by a process of sleuthing," and also by charming his way into certain Richmond strongholds.[35]

Perhaps Carr furthered his purpose through friends who lived in the "City on the James," men whom he had known at the University of North Carolina or in the Confederate Army. He was not one to let old cronies fade out of sight, nor was he modest about asking favors in the name of friendship. Possibly he was invited to the Commercial Club, where visiting merchants and businessmen were entertained, and in that convivial atmosphere he may have learned the whereabouts of Hiram Smith. However it happened, he did locate the inventor and persuaded that gentleman to sell the W. T. Blackwell Company a Smith machine. He returned to Durham with no intention of keeping it under lock and key, for unlike his Virginia competitors, Julian Carr was not inclined to secrecy where his latest business accomplishment was concerned. Publicity was more to his liking, and by the time the Smith machine arrived in Durham, the whole town had been informed about its wonderful capacities and promised a demonstration as soon as workers could be trained to operate it. That first demonstration of tobacco machinery sparked a flood of admiration for Jule Carr, the "go-getter"; the sweet taste of local acclaim lost some of its savor, though, when it became apparent that Hiram Smith's machine, which operated on the principle of a wheat thresher, was spewing out granulated leaf so rapidly that neither the Durham women who sewed tobacco bags nor the factory hands who packed and labeled them could keep up the pace.[36]

Carr and his partners could not foresee that twenty-five years would elapse before most of the problems associated with tobacco machinery would be solved. Their conviction that more automation was essential made them receptive to the ideas of James R. Lawrence, who believed he could make a successful packing machine, provided he had the materials and a place to work. They gave him a salary and a room in their factory, and in 1875 he became the first of several inventors, financed and encouraged by the W. T. Blackwell Company, who were to revolutionize the tobacco manufacturing process. Although he spent five years designing and building his machine, it was worth every minute of his time and every dollar of the company's money, for the Lawrence Smoking Tobacco Packer definitely influenced the southward shift of the tobacco industry and helped to rid North Carolina of its image as the "Rip Van Winkle State."[37]

During the five years Lawrence worked to perfect his invention, it became apparent that the existing factory would have to be enlarged in order to supply the ever-increasing demand for Bull Durham tobacco—a demand that was essentially the result of Carr's creative advertising and Blackwell's hard-driving sales technique. Day had made no major contributions, unfortunately, and his decline as a force in the business may have been due in part to Carr's aggressiveness. Day's easy-going temperament, his taste for spirits, and his dislike for hard work infuriated Carr, an abstemious Methodist to whom work was all important. Blackwell sometimes found himself caught in the middle of this clash of personalities, even when he was out of town. Wherever Blackwell went on business, Carr reported to him about what was going on at home, and in the spring of 1877 he wrote, "J.R.D. has hardly as much as shown himself since you left."[38] Another 1877 letter in which he alluded to Day concerned one of the company foremen, whose fondness for drink was getting entirely out of hand:

> He goes every day during work hours 2 or 3 times into Bar Rooms, and we ought not to allow it, it demoralizes the hands and has long been a great source of trouble to us. A man occupying the position toward us that he does and in Broad daylight, in work hours 3 and 4 times a day goes into Bar Rooms and the other hands see it and know it, ought to be discharged without Judge or Jury and no promises taken from him. It has mortified me 20 times to see him during work hours while you are at the Sales, standing in a crowd of a dozen drinking whiskey. We ought not to submit to it. You have not seen what I have seen or you would not I know. We condemn it in Mr. Day and we ought not to allow a hand to do what we condemn in a

Partner. Clean up this morning and les' turn over a New Leaf. Remember what is bad in a Partner is worse in a hand.

From the tone of this letter, Carr apparently had advanced from third place on the executive totem pole to second in command. But equal footing with Blackwell was what he really wanted, and shortly before it was time to renew their contract, in 1876, he demanded just that.

Although he had signed the initial agreement with understandable eagerness in 1870 and had signed a second contract in 1873, by 1876 he felt that he was being kept in a subordinate position he had long since outgrown. He decided, "after several months of careful thought and reflection," to deliver an ultimatum to Blackwell. In a four-page letter Carr implied that he no longer regarded Jim Day as important to the business; he spoke as if the company had been run, since 1870, by Blackwell and himself, and that many times it had not been run to his liking. In the two-page preface to his letter, Carr wrote:

> I know your aversion to long documents, but once in 6 years it is excusable, especially on Copartnership business. If there is anything that a man can learn, he certainly ought to learn it in 6 years of hard Study. For 6 years I have studied *hard* the manipulating of Finances and I want you to know my views on this point before we begin business as partners again. I must insist that these arrangements of our Finances be gone into if we renew our Copartnership, and that like the laws of the Medes and Persians change not.
>
> I remember that on several occasions we have agreed in conversations upon these very points, yet before anytime had passed the conversation seemed forgotten, and the agreement was time and again—*time and again*, violated. I want it this time understood that Come life or Come death, Come weal or Come woe, we are through thick & thin, going to live up to this part of our Agreement. That one as much as the other will be oposed to its being violated, under any circumstances; for I tell you now that our credit is of the very first importance, above Stock— reputation of leaf markets or anything else—and I tell you upon the honor of a man, that our credit and financial reputation and standing is not what it was 12 mos. ago. This is mighty unpleasant to admit, but it is true as the Gospel.

With the best feeling, hoping that you will read this and my 4 page letter entirely through, Carefully, I am

Your friend J.S. Carr[39]

This strongly phrased preamble indicates that Carr had ceased to think of Blackwell as his mentor; he was determined to make Blackwell view him not merely as an equal, but even as having the final word in money matters. In the letter itself he acknowledged, without mentioning Day, that he and Blackwell had worked hard for six years to make the business a success and that they could be proud of achieving that goal. If Carr was to remain in the firm, it would have to "pay due regard and protect properly and sacredly its credit." Furthermore, "the member who purchases leaf tobacco . . . [must] put into leaf tobacco what funds that they may have to spare, but stop there and then when notofied by the member of the firm whose business it is to look after the finances of the firm that the funds are out."

Carr then complained of not having as many conferences with Blackwell as he felt he was entitled to as a partner. "By degrees they have grown fewer and shorter," he said, "and I have seen my influence with you grow less and my ideas of business discarded more and more each month." After insisting that he had tried every way he knew to remedy the situation and had gotten nowhere, he stated flatly, "I can't be clerk in business and I won't be. When I can't be full partner then my interest in that business is for sale, and if I can't get one price I am going to take another, for I am coming out full partner or nothing."

Despite their differences, Carr had a sincere regard for Blackwell; indeed, the letter was not entirely accusatory. He thought they "operated together and pulled together well," and he readily admitted that Blackwell had "some of the elements of success that I have not got, and again I have some elements that you have not. And for 6 years we have been so situated that we have cultivated these elements. We know each other, we have tried each other, and the business that we both are engaged in suits us, and we might if we chose now arrange our matters so that everything might work well together. If this is agreed upon I am willing to stay in the firm."

Saying he had written because he felt it was his duty "as your partner and Brother Mason to do so," and that the letter was composed "in the very best of humor and kind feeling toward you," Carr proposed that, if Blackwell thought they could not reconcile matters, the firm should go into liquidation on 1 October 1876 "and pay off and collect up everything and dispose of everything." Adding that "I only throw out this last in case the worst must come to the worst, which I sincerely trust may not be the case," Carr then concluded, "I can by no means consent to stand what I have suffered in the past 12 mos. I will work in the field first."[40]

How Blackwell responded to Carr's feisty dictum is not known, but Buck Blackwell was a philosophical man, as well as a patient one. Because he and Jule Carr remained partners until 1883, it can be assumed that they reached a satisfactory agreement. Whether its terms had anything to do with Jim Day's subsequent resignation also remains a mystery, but Day did leave the company "around 1880" and went into manufacturing with his brother.[41] Carr continued to grumble to Blackwell about bibulous employees, and his concern for the firm's bank account remained like that of an over-anxious parent for an ailing child. Toward the end of December 1877 he wrote to Blackwell from New York, "Now if getting home I can just find our Bank Account healthy, that's all the Christmas I want. Our Bank Account has been in my mind ever since I left, more or less."[42]

In spite of Carr's chronic concern about finances, a new wing was added to the "Bull Factory." In 1880 it became the largest smoking tobacco factory in the world and "one of the marvels of North Carolina." Visitors came from far and near to see it, and many stood open-mouthed as they gazed at the sign that towered above the central entrance, a huge panel "on which was emblazoned in colossal proportions . . . the great Durham Bull, rampant and triumphant." There can be no doubt that Carr was responsible for the sign, although Blackwell was credited in print for "the whole work of enlargement." According to one writer, Blackwell "designed all the interior arrangements, rigidly inspected every piece of timber that went into the structure, and scrutinized almost every brick that was laid; and this intelligent, watchful supervision pervades every operation of the firm." It is highly improbable, however, that Julian Carr stood by silently and let his partner take complete charge of the new west wing.[43]

When that wing was completed, the four-story factory, located in the approximate center of Durham on fifteen acres of fenced-in land, was an impressive sight. Of red brick and cream-colored granite, it loomed over a number of satellite structures that housed stored tobacco, fire-fighting apparatus, machine shops, stables, a printery, and two box factories. Local citizens as well as visitors often lingered outside the surrounding fence to watch, and comment on, the activities that were visible from where they stood. The loading of boxcars was a constant attraction, as about 25,000 pounds of tobacco were shipped out each day; two large engines that generated steam for the factory machines also generated interest among the observers, to whom any kind of automation was a novelty. Supplied by four 216-horsepower boilers that gulped enormous amounts of wood, these engines kept over fifty machines running in the ten different departments that operated under the factory's vast roof.[44]

In addition to the 250 Durham women who sewed tobacco bags for the company in their own homes, 485 men, women, and children, white and black, were employed at the Bull Factory. Some worked in conjunction with machines that cut, flavored, mixed, and packed tobacco; others were box makers, printers, stampers, and labelers. Still others maintained the machines, the fire equipment, the buildings, the stables, and the horses. Small boys ran errands, attached revenue stamps to bags and boxes, and "crawled on their hands and knees searching among the floor sweepings for chance nails or stones" that might harm valuable machinery when the refuse tobacco was run through it a second time "for the preparation of an inferior product."[45]

In the drying room on the fourth floor, tobacco was thoroughly dehydrated by natural processes combined with heat coils. Then it went, via chutes, to the ground floor cutting room, where it was reduced to fragments that were subsequently transported, in elevators, to the third floor. After the stems were sifted out, the tobacco was bolted, like flour, and flavored with a mixture containing rum, tonka beans, and deer tongue, a plant that tasted not unlike vanilla. The finished product then was placed in hand-sewn bags by eleven of James Lawrence's Smoking Tobacco Packers. The Blackwell Company had been using these for almost a year prior to Lawrence's announcement, in 1880, that his invention had finally been perfected and was designed simply enough to be run by any unskilled laborer and kept in working order by any mechanic.[46]

Although Lawrence's machine measured and packed "any size package of tobacco at the rate of 15 per minute," it still fell short of perfection. Four workers were required to operate it, which increased company expense. Moreover, the packed bags were not uniform in weight, because the plunger, as it was withdrawn from a bag, often pulled out particles of tobacco and deposited them, along with a new charge, into the next bag. Whether heavy or light, each bag had to be stamped, strung, tied, and labeled by hand, a multiple task that demanded the efforts of 150 of the company's 485 factory workers.[47]

As far as Julian Carr was concerned, bags were a nuisance. The women who cut and stitched them for "pin money" could not keep up with the new machinery; even though a nimble-fingered seamstress might produce as many as six hundred bags a day, not every woman achieved that goal every day. Nor were any two bags exactly alike: that fact, in itself, made uniformity of weight impossible. To Carr, a perfectionist, the situation was a source of constant irritation.[48] Five years were to elapse, however, before he found an inventor able to alleviate it. During those years a number of significant changes took place in the management of the W. T. Blackwell Company and in the town of Durham.

5. Building a Business, a Town, and a Reputation

ON 1 December 1880, a fire that began in one of the barrooms in Durham's business district raged unchecked through almost an entire block of buildings when the "fearful condition of the streets, caused by incessant rains and freezes," prevented the volunteer fire company from moving its engine. Exactly a month later, a furniture store and the four-story building next to it burned to the ground. Two weeks after the second fire, a third occurred: a blaze that originated on the south side of Main Street was spread by a stiff wind to the north side, and within two hours property valued at $50,000 was reduced to charred rubble. Fortunately, most victims of all three fires were insured, and those who rebuilt used brick, instead of wood. So Durham, like the phoenix, "rose proudly from her ashes" and began paving streets, bordering them with trees, and passing laws regarding sanitation.[1]

It was an appropriate time to refurbish the town, for in April 1881 it became the seat of a new county carved, with much legislative pain, out of parts of Orange and Wake. The movement to create Durham County was instigated by W. T. Blackwell and his brother, J. R. Blackwell; Julian S. Carr and his brother-in-law, E. J. Parrish; and businessmen Samuel T. Morgan and J. C. Angier. Fortunately, they had the support of W. K. Parrish and Caleb Green, two state legislators from Orange County who lived in Durham. All of these men had watched their town grow and prosper to such an extent that by 1880 its governing body, consisting of a mayor and five aldermen, was inundated with business having to do with deeds, mortgages, and the various kinds of litigation that inevitably accompany economic and physical growth.[2] Most of that growth could be traced to the success of the W. T. Blackwell Company, which was largely responsible for the fact that North Carolina's production of smoking tobacco reached 4,379,566 pounds in 1880. The state of Virginia, with only 1,275,570 pounds to its credit that year, had to renounce its long-standing leadership to the land of tar, pitch, and pork, and Durham, which had been "a houseless old field" in 1865, was on its way to becoming the tobacco capital of the world.[3]

As long as Durham remained part of Orange County, the bulk of its legal business had to be transacted in Hillsborough, which was fifteen bone-bruising miles away, difficult to reach even in the best of weather and often inaccessible in the worst. Valuable time was lost and progress was impeded by ever more frequent trips to the county seat. Because it was obvious that something had to be done, Carr, Parrish, Morgan, Angier, and the Blackwell brothers employed the Raleigh-based law firm of Merrimon and Fuller to draw up a bill for the creation of Durham County and to help them secure its passage in the General Assembly.[4]

When it became known that Durham proposed to make itself the seat of a new county by snatching parts of Orange, Wake, Chatham, and Granville, influential citizens in Hillsborough, Raleigh, Pittsboro, and Oxford began to howl their protests. Why, they demanded, should upstart Durham be allowed to confiscate not only Lebanon, Mangum, and Patterson townships, among the richest in Orange, but also certain portions of Oak Grove and Cedar Forks townships in Wake? And why should Durham steal Williams Township from Chatham, and Dutchville Township from Granville? Granville would be especially hard hit because it already was threatened by another movement to establish a new county (Vance) just east of Oxford.

To these questions, as well as to other expressions of outrage, the six Durham men responded by exerting their own influence. Their attorneys, Augustus A. Merrimon and Thomas C. Fuller, one a former United States senator and the other a future federal judge, were among the best legal minds in the South. The twenty-three-year-old Williamson Whitehead Fuller, newly admitted to the bar and to his father's firm, had earned a reputation for brilliance at both the University of Virginia and the Dick and Dillard law school in Greensboro. This young man, guided by his senior partners, wrote the bill for the creation of Durham County and was responsible for its passage in the 1881 session of the General Assembly.

Introduced by Caleb Green, a representative from Orange, resident of Durham, and friend of the unofficial committee of six, the original bill met with furious opposition from such powerful lobbyists as Paul Cameron and his son, Bennehan, of Orange; Walter Clark and Fabius Busbee of Wake; and Henry A. London of Chatham. As a concession, and on the advice of Will Fuller, proponents eliminated the inclusion of Williams Township, in Chatham, and Dutchville Township, in Granville. After much heated debate, this second version of the bill passed its third reading in the House on 10 February 1881. But the battle was not over, and the measure ran into a great deal of difficulty in the Senate after it passed its first reading. It was vehemently opposed by William T. Dortch of Goldsboro (who, incidentally, had a number of relatives in Hillsborough).

Dortch, who was president pro tempore of the Senate, contended that the creation of any more counties would prove too costly for the state to administer, and he tried to kill the bill by moving that a decision be postponed indefinitely. His motion carried, 25-13, but immediately Senator J. N. Staples (who, incidentally, was Will Fuller's father-in-law) moved to reconsider the vote. Throughout the next week a vote on Staples's motion was postponed repeatedly in an effort to gain support for the new county of Durham, but on its second reading the bill fell six votes short of passage in the Senate. Dortch then moved to put what traditionally was known as a "clincher" on the defeat of the measure by moving for reconsideration of the bill and then tabling the motion without a vote.

Ordinarily such a move would have halted any further action, but only a few hours later, when Dortch gave his outspoken support to the establishment of Vance County, his inconsistency aroused a wave of support for Durham County, and its proponents seized the opportunity to reenter the fray. Acting again on Will Fuller's advice, they argued that simple justice required the legislature to correct its own mistakes when new information (Dortch's inconsistency) came to its attention, and that it was entirely legal for the Senate to "reconsider the vote by which it had voted to reconsider and lay that motion on the table."

Although the point was raised that no bill could be reconsidered more than once, the lieutenant governor, as president of the Senate, agreed with Fuller's "sound proposition" that no power existed that limited a legislative body where its own actions were concerned, and that a majority must rule. So by passing, reconsidering, tabling, and reinterpreting motions, Durham County was created on 28 February 1881, "after a contest notable for its consideration of legislative custom."

While that contest was also notable for its bitterness and its innuendos concerning "undue influence," those who accused certain "honorables" in the legislature of allowing the powerful bellow of Black-well's bull and the persuasive logic of Will Fuller's arguments to drown out the dictates of their own consciences were in the minority. The final vote on the boundaries of Durham County revealed that in Orange there were 1,464 in favor and 250 against; and in Wake the count was 275 in favor and only 47 against. The people had spoken. On 16 April 1881, Governor Thomas J. Jarvis issued a proclamation establishing the new county of Durham and granting it "all the rights, powers, privileges, advantages, and immunities that belong and appertain to other counties in the state."

Two months later, Williamson Whitehead Fuller moved from Raleigh to Durham with his wife, the former Annie Staples, of Greensboro, and their infant son. The Blackwell Company immediately retained Fuller to help fight its legal battle against John H. McElwee. The case had been going on for two years and would continue for another six; during those years the fledgling lawyer polished his skills, acquired one of the most lucrative practices in North Carolina, and built an imposing mansion diagonally across the street from his friend, Jule Carr. Will Fuller began to develop a courtroom style that was to make him famous; once that style caught the shrewd eye of James Buchanan Duke, it made Fuller enormously wealthy as well.

But before Will Fuller became associated exclusively with the Dukes and the giant American Tobacco Company, he performed many legal services for Buck Blackwell and Jule Carr. One of the most significant of these occurred in 1883. Blackwell, perhaps tired of constant travel, seemingly endless lawsuits, and the fierce competition that was an integral part of the tobacco business, decided he wanted a less strenuous life. His company had eight competitors in Durham, an additional 296 in other parts of the state, and 220 in Virginia; and all of them "shared the determination of James B. Duke to stop the Bull."[5] Because such intense rivalry precluded the dignified, peaceful existence that Blackwell wanted, and now could afford, he sold half of his interest in the company to M. E. McDowell and Company of Philadelphia, a nationally known jobbing house with which he had been doing business for many years, and the other half to Julian Carr. Carr said of the transaction: "Thirteen years after my father had purchased an interest in the Durham Tobacco business, I purchased of Mr. W. T. Blackwell an interest in his Trade Mark, for which I paid him Sixty Two Thousand, Five Hundred Dollars . . . and if I had not mastered as I did the details of the business and gotten control of the financial management of the business, I never would have been able to have gotten an interest in the trade mark."[6]

Apparently Carr paid Blackwell $12,500 in cash; then, with Will Fuller as a witness, he signed a promissory note for the balance: "On the first day of July, 1885, with interest from date at the rate of six per cent per annum, I promise to pay to William T. Blackwell on order Fifty Thousand Dollars, value received in purchase of Factory and Trade Mark. Witness my hand and seal the day and year above written." The note, in Fuller's handwriting, was dated 20 January 1883.[7]

Carr then joined forces with McDowell and Company, a firm that realized the value of Blackwell's name and arranged to retain it, in slightly altered form. On 24 January 1883, Blackwell's Durham Tobacco Company, with a paid up capital of $500,000, was chartered by the North Carolina legislature. Carr became president and chief stockholder of the new company, which listed Marcellus E. McDowell as vice-president, J. A. McDowell as secretary, and Samuel H. Austin, who had been the western agent for Bull Durham tobacco for six years, as treasurer.[8]

These three men, the possessors of "generous capital and branch houses in New York, Chicago and elsewhere," saw eye to eye with Julian Carr on the importance of advertising. Carr, free at last to spend as much as he liked on pushing the Durham Bull, was soon boasting "that he would have that animal painted on the pyramids of Egypt, and that in America he would grow so big his head would be in the Great Lakes and his tail in the Gulf of Mexico and he would bellow so loud that it would be heard from ocean to ocean."[9]

In making good that boast, the new president of Blackwell's Durham Tobacco Company bought the services of Jule Gilmer Korner, a talented and eccentric decorator, designer, portrait painter, photographer, and sign writer whose home near Winston-Salem had been attracting state-wide attention since 1880. Five years of study in Philadelphia had sharpened the artist's talents, and successful real estate ventures had made him rich enough to indulge his eccentricities. He constructed, under one vast roof, a studio, office, stable, carriage house, reception hall, ballroom, and living quarters for himself, his wife, and his two children. Known as "Korner's Folly" and said to have cost $200,000, this remarkable edifice no doubt convinced Julian Carr that its creator could deliver something spectacular in the way of advertising, and Korner did not disappoint him.[10]

Working under the professional name of Reuben Rink, Korner produced 66,000 feet of Bull Durham signs in 1883. His fiery, spirited bulls, no two exactly alike, provoked much critical comment from newspaper editors and thus gave Blackwell's Durham Tobacco Company additional free advertising. Highly pleased, Carr arranged to have Korner's originals duplicated and enlarged by four gangs of sign painters, some under contract and others hired by the day, to confront the public with enormous likenesses of the Durham Bull on billboards that frequently measured 80 by 150 feet. When he was approached by a reporter from the *United States Tobacco Journal* and asked about the huge new signs, Carr asserted that he had to have something striking, no matter what it cost, because ordinary signs were "played out," and that "every sign that Reuben Rink paints creates a sensation." Warming to one of his favorite subjects, Carr explained how the four gangs of painters were covering the country. "One gang is following the railroads through the South to New Orleans and Texas, and later on to Mexico," he said. The three remaining gangs were working from New England down through New York and Washington; between New York and Philadelphia along the tracks of the Pennsylvania and Bound Brook railroads; and from Chicago "all through the West and over the Northern Pacific Railroad clear to Seattle, Washington Territory."

Carr did not tell his interviewer exactly what the signs "in every State in the Union, Manitoba and parts of Canada" would cost, but he readily admitted that his company would spend, in only one year, $150,000 for newspaper ads and $60,000 on mantel clocks, by far the most elegant of all the premiums he was offering to dealers.[11] In a letter to distributors of Bull Durham tobacco that Carr also used as a newspaper ad, he explained the reasoning behind these timepieces, which were a foot high, eight inches wide, and made to look like bales of tobacco:

> It has been our aim for some time to supply you with an article that would not only advertise our brand . . . but also be useful to you and an ornament to your place of business . . . and we regretted to spend such an enormous sum on anything that would not last and be of some value. The novel idea finally

struck us of producing a bale of Bull Durham Smoking Tobacco, containing "Works" instead of the original well-known article, guaranteed to furnish you with Correct Time and to be a pleasant reminder when your orders should be sent in for the "Bull."[12]

Any dealer who ordered fifty pounds of Blackwell's tobacco from his jobber got this unusual clock "free." Less expensive premiums (razors, calendars, etc.) were available, too, and in the summer of 1884 Carr offered just under $10,000 in prizes for empty Bull Durham tobacco bags. His aggressive advertising was creating an ever-growing demand for the contents of those bags, even as the bags themselves were impeding the manufacturing process and slowing down production. Bags were a problem that Carr pursued continually, like a terrier after an elusive rat, until he found a possible solution in the person of William Hall Kerr, a textile manufacturer from Concord, North Carolina.

Kerr approached the president of Blackwell's Durham Tobacco Company in 1885 with a plan for a machine to manufacture bags. Carr, immediately enthusiastic, agreed to finance the experiment, which Kerr wanted to conduct in Ilion, New York, in order to have access to other machine builders. Carr's faith in the would-be inventor was justified: William Kerr proved to be a mechanical genius who created, within twelve months, a complicated device that could be operated by a single worker and was capable of producing from 10,000 to 15,000 bags a day. Minor adjustments increased that output to 25,000 bags, but Kerr continued to perfect his invention, which was patented on 5 November 1886. At a demonstration staged for the people of Durham three weeks after it was installed in the Bull Factory, the machine outdid itself by cutting and stitching 90,000 bags in one day. Local citizens gaped in astonishment, and Julian Carr, who loved the limelight and rarely missed an opportunity to bask in its glow, pointed out the almost human qualities of his latest acquisition, seeming as pleased and proud as if he had invented it himself.[13]

Realizing that there was a wide market for bags, Carr lost no time in establishing a company to produce them wholesale, not only for the tobacco industry, but also for manufacturers of coins, sugar, table salt, flour, meal, and feedstuff. The new business, which he called "The Golden Belt Manufacturing Company," attracted workers to

Durham and enhanced his growing reputation as an entrepreneur; but it did not distract his attention from existing problems at Blackwell's Durham Tobacco Company, where each improvement in the manufacturing process made him more conscious of stubborn defects.

One of the most irritating of these was the Lawrence Tobacco Packer's inability to stuff identical amounts of tobacco into the identical sacks that now flowed, with such satisfying speed, from the Kerr machine. Carr also continued to fret about the fact that every bag, whether light or heavy, still had to be stamped, strung, and tied by hand. These "bugs" eventually were eliminated when a factory employee, Charles Vinson Strickland, improved Lawrence's plunger by adding a piece of rubber, and Rufus Lenoir Patterson of Salem, North Carolina, collaborated with William Kerr on a machine to stamp and label bags.[14]

Rufus Patterson was fourteen years old when William Kerr's bag machine was patented. He may not have been much older when he decided "to devote his life to the problem of tobacco machinery," for he was only twenty-two when he and Kerr joined forces, in 1894, with the intention of building an automatic packing and labeling machine. At that time, the thirty-seven-year-old William Kerr was president and treasurer of the Thistle Mills Company, a Baltimore concern that manufactured gingham, denim, sheeting, and worsteds; he continued to experiment with machinery, and in Baltimore he had access to the Murrell and Kerzer Company, which manufactured models, presses, patterns, and dies and proved indispensable to his efforts as an inventor. Apparently he and Patterson approached Julian Carr about financial backing for their proposed machine but failed to obtain an immediate affirmative answer, for in December 1894 Kerr wrote to Patterson from Baltimore: "I do not think, Rufus, that we should think of stopping this in case Mr. Carr does not see fit to join us."[15]

But Carr did see fit to join the two inventors before the month was out, and by the middle of January 1895 he had drawn up a contract stating that he and Patterson would provide William Kerr with $5,000 to be used in connection with the invention, development, and construction of the machine; that they would invest $1,000 in the procurement of patents; that they would bear the expense of manufacturing additional models once the original had been perfected; and that they would pay Kerr one-twentieth of one cent on each pound of tobacco handled by his machines. If his royalties fell below $1,200 a year, Carr and Patterson would make up the amount lacking; and if royalties exceeded $1,200, then "a royalty shall be paid by the parties of the first part to the party of the second part at a rate hereafter agreed upon between said parties."

Kerr complained to Patterson, "I feel that I am not to be paid as I should for a big job," but in spite of his misgivings, he proceeded with the work. On 14 April 1895 he was able to tell Patterson, "We are making very good progress now on the machine and I hope it will come out in good shape." Two weeks later he wrote again, saying, "I have the weighing apperatus of our machine in good shape, and if you come [to Baltimore] about the 20th of May I can show you that, and the packing part well under way. I think you will like the work done, Rufus. . . ."[16]

Exactly how much physical and mental effort Rufus Patterson contributed toward the invention of the Automatic Packing and Labeling Machine prior to the summer of 1895 is not known, but Kerr's remarks seem to indicate that it was he who did most of the actual work—at least until June of that year, when his life was tragically cut short by accidental drowning. Patterson was left to complete the invention alone, which he managed to do before the year's end. The result, an apparatus that weighed, packed, stamped, and labeled bags of uniform size at the rate of twenty-five per minute, "enabled one operative to equal the output of 42 handworkers." That meant a savings of more than 80 percent in labor for Blackwell's Durham Tobacco Company.[17]

Inspired by the success of this phenomenal device, Julian Carr, Rufus Patterson, and Thomas B. Fuller, an accountant for the Blackwell firm, organized the Automatic Packing and Labeling Company of Durham in February 1896 and began to lease the machines, on a royalty basis, to manufacturers whose products required bags as containers. Their list of customers grew as word of Kerr and Patterson's extraordinary invention spread, but James B. Duke, president of the American Tobacco Company, did not avail himself of it until the end of 1897, when he made a special trip to Durham to watch it perform. Duke called it the most ingenious piece of tobacco machinery he had ever seen and began to look with barely concealed interest at the young man who had helped to invent it. Rufus Patterson, glowing from Duke's high praise, reported the compliment to his mother and described Duke as "the greatest Tob[acco] man in the Country."[18]

Patterson's exalted opinion of Washington Duke's youngest son was not shared by Julian Carr, who had known ever since the American Tobacco Company was formed, in 1890, that Buck Duke was out to get Blackwell's Durham Tobacco Company. By consolidating W. Duke Sons and Company with Allen and Ginter Company, of Richmond; F. S. Kinney Company, of New York and Richmond; W. S. Kimball and Company, of Rochester, New York, and Oxford, North Carolina; and Goodwin and Company, of New York City, Buck Duke had created a powerful combine that had systematically begun to acquire control not only of the cigarette industry, in which he was chiefly engaged, but also of the smoking and chewing tobacco interests. His earlier intent of "stopping the Bull" had not lessened. Duke's "tobacco trust" was anathema to Carr, who spoke out against it at every opportunity.[19] In an address to a combined meeting of the North Carolina United Daughters of the Confederacy and the Piedmont Poultry Association, he said, with considerable heat:

A great evil which is growing and is daily assuming large proportions is the formation of the great combines. Like a gigantic octopus the immense aggregation of capital is spreading out its long monied tentacles to gather in and feed upon all sections of our land in defiance of the people, the law, and the Constitution. . . . I am for the underdog in the fight, therefore I am against the abominable, unholy, unrighteous trust. . . .

Any system which is making multimillionaires on the one hand and millions of paupers on the other is wrong [and] I swear here in this presence eternal war against the trusts. . . . My countrymen, the times are sadly out of joint when one man lies awake at night studying how he shall spend his 500 millions of dollars, the accumulation of a short 20 years, when I see as I go up and down throughout North Carolina so many evidences of my fellow citizens having a hard fight for Bread.[20]

Carr was by no means alone in his anger against the giant corporation that had its beginnings in "the dusty little factory" that Washington Duke and his sons had built in Durham in 1874. Other manufacturers cursed it because they could not compete successfully against it; organized labor cursed it for its open-shop policy; leaf dealers and speculators cursed it for buying directly from farmers; and farmers cursed it for dictating prices.[21] As the American Tobacco Company continued to buy up its biggest competitors and force smaller ones into bankruptcy, it "aroused a hatred which permeated local tobacco circles and even political, educational and religious life of the Old Bright Belt." Despite the comfort Julian Carr may have derived from such widespread animosity to the trust, however, he must have realized that, sooner or later, it would swallow up every independent tobacco manufacturer in the country, himself included.[22] Long before that could happen, he began the diversification of his business interests that was to continue until the end of the century.

Like many southerners who had "struck it rich" after the war, Carr started with a cotton mill. Southern cotton manufacturing, a prosperous antebellum industry, experienced a revival soon after Reconstruction ended and leading citizens (those who had the most money) realized that something had to be done about the poor white farmers who had never recovered from the war and were having to compete with freed Negroes. A sense of noblesse oblige, born into some and acquired by others, impelled the "aristocracy" to provide these unfortunates with a means of subsistence. All things considered, cotton manufacturing seemed to be the logical answer to a knotty economic problem.[23]

In Durham, as in other southern towns, the pulpit and the press began to urge community leaders to start a cotton factory "for the town's sake, for the poor people's sake, for the South's sake, literally for God's sake." Julian Carr, who liked nothing better than being first, answered the call. In 1884, the year after he became president of Blackwell's Durham Tobacco Company, he decided he had enough income to support his wife and five children in elegant style, to give generously to religious and educational institutions, and to start a textile enterprise. But in spite of his zeal for new ventures, and his pleasure in being viewed by so many of his fellow citizens as Durham's leading light, Carr's feeling of moral responsibility did not overshadow his hard-nosed approach to business. He conducted a thorough investigation of the fiscal possibilities before he made a decision.

Raw cotton was available in Durham County, as well as in eastern North Carolina, and it was cheap. Furthermore, freight rates were low, and labor was cheap and plentiful; many families who could barely scratch out a living on their rundown farms were eager to live in a town and work in a factory or a mill. Any wage, however low, was better than no wage at all. While Julian Carr prided himself on being an ideal "boss man"—benevolent, protective, and always accessible—

he saw nothing amiss in making large profits from cheap labor, nor was he alone in his viewpoint.

Throughout the South, factories and mills were being run the way plantations had been run before the Civil War, when the master delegated a certain amount of authority to a trusted overseer, who gave orders to the slaves who did the work. Now, with industry replacing the plantation, the president of a company delegated authority to a manager, who gave orders to a foreman, who passed them on to the employees who did the work. Nothing had changed very much, except names. In antebellum days, the master of two or three plantations had enjoyed a higher social position than the master of only one; so it was also in the latter part of the nineteenth century. The head of several corporations had a great deal more status than the president of a single company, no matter how successful that company, and Julian Carr was not indifferent to status.

Once his decision was made, Carr began to look for partners and additional capital for his proposed new business. When he found none among his friends and business associates in Durham, most of whom strongly advised him against his new venture, he shrugged off their warnings and went to other sources. James A. Odell, John M. Odell, and William H. Branson, all of Greensboro, and William R. Odell of Concord were men with wide experience and important connections in the textile industry, being associated with mills in Salisbury, Bessemer City, and Concord. Happily for Carr, they shared his enthusiasm for the venture and agreed to join him. With Carr as vice-president and chief stockholder and James Odell as president, the Durham Cotton Manufacturing Company was capitalized at $130,000. William Branson, who was named secretary and treasurer, agreed to move to Durham to manage the new firm.[24]

Carr decided to locate the mill on a large tract of land he owned in the eastern section of Durham. He would build houses for the workers around it, as he and Buck Blackwell had done for their factory hands, only this would be different—not just row after row of identical houses, but something better. He envisioned a community with orderly streets and neat homes, with trees and flowers, a church, and perhaps a school for children who were too young to work with their parents in the mill. The houses, some with three rooms and others with five, would be well constructed; they also would be painted, and each would have a porch in front and a privy out back. He would have to charge rent, but it would be not more than a dollar a week;

for a real home, not just a shanty, any mill family ought to be glad to pay that. After all, he reasoned, weavers made from $3.85 to $5.60 a week, spinners from $2.20 to $3.30 a week, and even bobbin boys took home $.20 a day.[25]

Fired with characteristic zeal and eager to publicize his new project, Carr arranged a cornerstone-laying that took place on a sizzling day in July 1884. Ministers from Concord and Durham prayed and preached, the choir from Trinity Methodist Church sang "an appropriate hymn," and the editor of the local *Tobacco Plant*, who had been campaigning for a cotton mill for two years, called it a "joyous day for Durham citizens."[26]

Manufacturing began the following spring in a four-story brick building that measured seventy-five by one hundred feet and boasted a belfry that rose an additional three stories. At first the looms wove only muslin cloth for Bull Durham tobacco bags, but within a short time they were turning out ginghams, chambrays, and colored goods. By 1889, when the Durham Cotton Manufacturing Company was able to increase its capitalization to $150,000, local men who had declined Julian Carr's invitation to invest in the mill began to regret their lack of vision, and the Duke family began to think seriously about entering the textile business.[27]

Jule Carr was too busy promoting other ventures to concern himself about competition from "Old Bono's" two oldest sons, Ben and Brodie Duke. Within the short span of four years, while the Durham Cotton Manufacturing Company was becoming a success and the village of East Durham was growing up around it, Carr established a bank and an electric lighting company, bought a weekly newspaper and turned it into a daily, built an elaborate hotel, and invested heavily in four railroads. He also hired a New York architect to design and build a costly Victorian mansion to replace Waverly Honor. Furthermore, on 14 August 1885, he bought his father's interest in Blackwell's Durham Tobacco Company.

The latter transaction took place a few months after the cotton mill began operations. It was witnessed by W. T. Blackwell, the erstwhile partner of John Wesley Carr and his son Jule. The buyout drew strong criticism from some members of the Carr clan, who did not like the idea of all future profits from Bull Durham tobacco going to Jule and his Philadelphia partners and none to the family's patriarch, who very likely would have far less to leave his heirs. They were not reticent about verbalizing their opposition, either among themselves or to outsiders, and Jule reacted to their disapproval with deeply wounded feelings, which he nursed until after his father's death in 1889. Then, after making a written statement about what he considered to be the facts of the unhappy matter, he secured corroboration from Buck Blackwell. Both statements were made, he said, in order that "those who have persistently mis-stated the circumstances may know how far they have wandered from the truth." He emphasized that what he had written was written "WITH CHARITY TOWARDS ALL AND WITH MALICE TOWARD NONE."[28]

The gist of Carr's three-page document was that the sale was fair in all respects, and that John Carr was not only satisfied with it, but actually pleased. Blackwell's declaration, duly witnessed and notarized, was in total agreement with that premise. Carr's statement said, in part, "I married in 1873 [and] I felt as my family began to gather around me that it was due to them and to me that the co-partnership arrangement with my father should terminate, and that my efforts should be expended in building up a business of my own, one in which my own family only should share and to which my boys should succeed."[29]

How much return John Carr realized on his initial investment was not spelled out; however, Julian asserted, "I returned him considerably more than the $4,000. . . . and besides this, at the end of 15 years, say 1885, I paid my father a satisfactory price for his interest in the business, he being entirely pleased with the result, and was told by our mutual friend, Mr. W. T. Blackwell, whom he advised with and trusted implicitly, that the trade was fair and equitable to both." Carr further stated that "Col. Blackwell was present pending these negotiations betwixt my father and myself and advised with us both, and was impressed with the equitableness and fairness of the settlement as his statement shows."

Blackwell, who was then a banker, said he was "called into the transaction being a friend of both the parties in interest," and that he saw

> the payment of several thousand dollars, made by the said Julian S. Carr, to his father, John W. Carr, and the said John W. Carr executed to his son, Julian S. Carr, a release in full of all claims against him, of whatever nature and in my presence signed and gave to his son, Julian S. Carr, a receipt in full for any and all claims against him, and for all and every interest

which he claimed to have in any business in which his son, Julian S. Carr, was interested.[30]

Asserting that the settlement was "with my full knowledge and was full, complete and absolutely fair, and both parties to the transaction expressed the highest satisfaction over the terms of the settlement," Blackwell went on to say "that Mr. John Carr was in full health and of sound mind, driving over to Durham from Chapel Hill, in his buggy, on that day, for the express purpose of making this settlement."

Then, after declaring once more that "the settlement was honorable and fair, on the part of both, and was full, complete and final, and the money paid, and the receipts given," Buck Blackwell went an extra mile with his former partners by adding, "Having entertained for Mr. Jno. Carr the highest regard and esteem, and for his son, Julian S. Carr, likewise, and knowing the facts in the matter as I do, I take pleasure in making this statement, as an act of justice to both the gentlemen concerned."

Presumably Carr distributed both documents among "the several members of my father's family who have said unkind things about me," but he did not specify who those members were. Because most of his Carr relatives reaped many benefits from his wealth, his attempt to vindicate himself must have met with success. In addition to sending a number of nieces, nephews, and cousins to college, he insured the lives of his three sisters and their children, paid his brother Robert's medical bills (which at times were considerable), and continually saw to the needs of his aging parents, especially when "the dark shadows rested upon their home, by reason of my father's ill health."[31]

John Carr was frail and prone to nervous disorders in his latter years. Whenever he was too ill to manage his store, Julian's sense of filial duty sent him to his old home on Franklin Street, where he took stock of his parents' situation and then proceeded to set things straight. Writing of those times, he said:

> There was then no railroad to Chapel Hill, but once a week, and sometimes oftener, I drove over to Chapel Hill, through rain, snow and mud, to superintend and direct my father's affairs, and to look after the family . . . each time my father was compelled to leave home, I restocked the store, gathered the trade back in large measure, paid off all pressing debts, and each time my father returned home, his health improved to such a degree

that he could undertake the management of the business, it was turned over to him in a very much improved condition . . . although it cost me considerable, to say nothing of the wear and tear on me mentally and physically.[32]

Despite periodic concern about his family in Chapel Hill, and despite complaints about the effect of that concern on his own well being, Carr's physical and mental health was extremely good. His success as a business and civic leader no doubt contributed substantially to that fact. In 1870 he had likened Durham to "the scrub end of an old field," and being partially responsible for its almost unbelievable metamorphosis had imbued him with possessive pride. Having "put it on the map" by his aggressive advertising of Bull Durham tobacco, he intended to continue as a force—the prime one, if possible—in the community's development.

6. Entrepreneur

IN 1870, when Julian Carr came to live and work in Durham, only four of the North Carolina Railroad's trains arrived and departed each day, two eastbound and two headed west; of the four only two carried freight as well as passengers. For the W. T. Blackwell Company, the situation was less than satisfactory. In 1871, when the North Carolina Railroad was leased to the Richmond and Danville railway system, there seemed no possibility of improving matters. Blackwell, Day, and Carr found themselves at the mercy of a single railroad just when the demand for Bull Durham tobacco was increasing their need for transportation.[1] They could ship to northern outlets over the Richmond and Danville road from Greensboro to Danville, and also over the Raleigh and Gaston road that made connections with Virginia at Weldon, North Carolina; and by 1873, it was possible to ship southward to Atlanta and Columbia via Greensboro and Charlotte. But the service was poor and the freight rates, being exempt from either state or federal regulation, were extremely high.[2] North Carolina's pioneer tobacco market was dominated by a Virginia railroad company that wanted no competition, and no attempts were made to create any until 1880. By that time Julian Carr's best friend, Eugene Morehead, had moved to Durham and established the town's first bank. Being eager to upgrade his surroundings, Morehead collaborated with Carr, Ed Parrish, and Buck Blackwell in promoting the Durham and Roxboro Railroad. It was his first business venture with his friend Jule, but it was not to be his last.[3]

The strong bond between Gene Morehead and Jule Carr, which began when they were freshmen at the University of North Carolina, suffered a temporary lapse during the Civil War and resumed after Morehead returned from service in the Confederate Army to finish college. An inveterate journal-keeper, Morehead described his arrival in the village: "Every branch, house, tree, corner of the fence suggested something, all of which was sadly pleasing. I found all my friends in Chapel Hill well, but few of my old Chapel Hill friends were there, nearly all gone. It is not inappropriately termed the deserted village of the South." But in spite of drastic changes in both

Eugene Morehead (courtesy of Laura Noell Carr Chapman)

the university and the village, Gene found Jule's parents, his two unmarried sisters, Emma and Lizzie, and his brother, Robert, nicknamed "Tankie," very much the same: "I don't think I ever did anything with better spirit than I returned to College after the war. . . . I found Mr. and Mrs. Carr the same good warmhearted friends I left. Mrs. C. is improved some—looking very well—just as jolly as ever. Miss Emma is looking about the same. She is a darling girl—so clever to me. Lizz is a chuffy & warmhearted as ever. She has grown much fatter, nearly as broad as long . . . & Tankie is still the same little boy—modest and neat."[4]

Unfortunately, Jule Carr was in Little Rock at the time. How much the two young men were able to see each other during Morehead's second stint at the university is not known, but the house on Franklin Street was like a second home to him until his graduation, with first honors, in 1868. After a vacation in the North Carolina mountains, where he reached the conclusion that "for nice and pretty women I have never yet seen Morganton, N.C. approximated," Morehead returned to Greensboro, went to work in his Uncle Jesse Lindsay's bank, and also engaged in the leaf tobacco business. All work and no play, however, was against his principles, and as a popular young bachelor whose inherited wealth had survived the collapse of the Confederacy, he liked to "stand treat," as he called it. He often took friends on excursions to various towns around the state. Wherever they chose to stay, they visited the local belles, went on picnics, played croquet, danced, flirted, and fell in and out of love.

A confessed dandy, Morehead said of himself: "I liked to wear the longest coats, the biggest legged pants, the slenderest canes"; a list of what he planned to put in his traveling bag for a pleasure trip included pomade, facial soap, kid gloves, a music box, and various brushes for his hair, his hats, his clothes, his teeth, and his fingernails. "Quite a medley," he called the contents of that very necessary bag, which he was no doubt carrying when he boarded a train in Charlotte early in May 1869 and "met Jule Carr going to Ark[ansas] from which place I expect him in about a week or so. He has been most of the time in Little Rock, has visited the Choctaw nation, etc."[5] Before leaving the train at Greensboro, Gene invited Jule to visit him at Blandwood, the Morehead estate. Carr, arriving there a few weeks later for a ten-day stay, enjoyed the ministrations of Tinnen, Gene's valet, and the excellent meals provided by "Aunt Hannah," whose domain was the kitchen and whose cooking was fabled.[6]

Carr also enjoyed the company of young ladies at a number of social affairs, including one Presbyterian Sunday School picnic where "there must have been 250 persons present." Gene, Jule, and Ike Strayhorn, a mutual friend from Hillsborough, escorted Alice Alderman, Mary Campbell, and Berta Sloan to this function, and Morehead later recorded that they had "a perfectly delightful day" playing croquet and cutting their names on "a huge tree up near the fence . . . at the Buffalo picnic ground."

Morehead also noted one special conversation with Carr during that visit to Blandwood in 1869: "Jule was pretty well pleased with the country [Arkansas] and having good offers. But he much preferred the Old North State & wishes to enter business in Greensboro, & I sincerely hope he will as he & I have been friends since 1863 and I like him muchly. He is strictly moral, good sense, merry, & as good a hearted man as ever frolicked."[7]

Carr and Morehead continued to frolic with other friends in Greensboro, Hillsborough, Chapel Hill, and New Bern until the end of June. Then Carr reluctantly returned to the mercantile business in Little Rock, and Morehead resumed his job in the Bank of Greensboro, where he and his Uncle Jesse and his brother-in-law, Julius Gray, were "doing most admirably . . . loaning out all the money we can get a hand on."[8]

Although Carr's impulsive wish to locate in Greensboro never bore fruit, it was largely through his efforts that Morehead moved to Durham in 1878 "to act as stamp agent for the United States Department of Revenue" and to establish the first local bank. Until that time, federal revenue stamps that had to be affixed to each sack of smoking tobacco were obtained, at great inconvenience, from the internal revenue office in Raleigh, twenty-seven miles away. Virtually all major financial transactions occurred there, too, unless money could be secured from northern brokers and wholesalers "who had faith in the selling qualities of Durham tobacco."[9] As the town grew and the need for a revenue office and a bank became more acute, Jule Carr convinced himself and others that Gene Morehead, with eight years of experience in banking and a first-hand knowledge of the leaf tobacco business, was just the man to fill that dual need.

With characteristic eagerness, Carr took a train to Greensboro. There Morehead, now married and the father of two small daughters, was master of Blandwood and still dispensing the lavish hospitality that had made his Tuscan villa famous all over the state. Cloistered in the library, the two friends discussed the business at hand. Morehead, persuaded that considerable profit could be derived from meeting the needs of Durham's fast-growing tobacco industry, and possibly challenged by the idea of establishing his own banking house in virgin territory, agreed to make the move.

Carr was elated. He hurried home to spread the good news to Durham's tobacco manufacturers and warehousemen, who were thoroughly tired of handling most of their money matters in Raleigh. They "rejoiced, in October, 1878, at the establishment in their town of a branch revenue office which proved a great convenience and saving to them," and they were even more pleased in December, when the state of North Carolina chartered the firm of "Eugene Morehead, Banker."[10]

Immediately the bank began to do a lucrative business with every factory and warehouse in town. Its owner soon became involved in "the improvement of social conditions," a goal he shared with his wife, whose father, James W. Lathrop, was founder and president of the Cotton Exchange in Savannah, Georgia. Lucy Lathrop Morehead, who was accustomed to a more refined atmosphere than that which prevailed in Durham in 1879, found an understanding friend in Jule Carr's wife, who had also grown up on a plantation, who had been waited on by slaves, and who had married a man whose ambition was barely concealed by his charm. Nannie Carr, the plump, pretty mother of two little girls and a baby boy, was the first Durham hostess to entertain the Moreheads, and Nannie and Jule were staunch supporters of any efforts to improve the social and cultural climate of their town.

Although the Moreheads built their home on the southwestern outskirts of Durham, several miles from Waverly Honor, the two couples saw each other frequently; however, it was chiefly in the business world that the friendship between Julian Carr and Eugene Morehead was strengthened. For almost nine years, unless one or the other was out of town, very few days passed that they did not meet and talk, either on the corner of Main and Corcoran Streets, the favorite gathering place for Durham's business and professional men, or indoors, at Carr's office at the factory, Morehead's office at the bank, or the Commonwealth Club, "an organization that was formed for the very purpose of concentrating the energies of the business men on enterprises of improvement."[11] No doubt it was in the smoke-filled environs of "The Club" that Carr and Morehead, along with other interested members, decided to make a concerted effort to increase railway facilities in Durham.

When it became known, in 1885, that the Richmond and Danville railway was extending its road to Oxford, North Carolina, and that the Norfolk and Western was laying a track from Lynchburg, Virginia, to Roxboro, North Carolina, a contingent made up of Buck Blackwell, Jule Carr, Gene Morehead, Ed Parrish, Caleb Green, and Peter M. Wilson determined to establish railroads in Durham to connect with these two points. Local support for the effort was immediate and enthusiastic, since over a hundred businesses stood to benefit from it. But opposition from the Richmond and Danville Railroad was strong, and had it not been for James A. Long, a legislator from Person County, the movement might have failed.

Because Assemblyman Long wanted to establish a tobacco market in his hometown of Roxboro and favored a railway connection to Durham, he used his influence to help Blackwell, Carr, Morehead, and Parrish secure a charter for the Durham and Roxboro Railroad in 1885. During that same legislative session, Carr, Green, and Wilson successfully incorporated the Durham and Clarksville Railroad, which would pass through Oxford and thus connect with the Richmond and Danville's extension. But Carr, Morehead, Blackwell, and Parrish were not yet satisfied. Two years later they chartered the Durham and Northern Railroad in order to connect Durham with the Raleigh and Gaston road; and Carr and Morehead, with their mutual friend and legal advisor, Will Fuller, acquired still another charter for the Durham and Southern, to connect with the Raleigh and Augusta Railroad.[12]

Washington Duke and his sons gave $100,000 toward Durham's struggle to free itself from exorbitant freight rates and limited railway connections. Matching a subscription made by Durham County, W. Duke Sons and Company reaped immeasurable benefits from its investment, but not until the Lynchburg, Halifax, and North Carolina line merged with the Durham and Roxboro and became the Lynchburg and Durham, which connected with Norfolk and its ports in the east and with Cincinnati in the west. Until that time, most of the Dukes' experiences with railroads were painful, to say the least.[13]

One extremely painful occurrence followed the Durham and Northern Railroad's completion in 1889. The first of its trains arrived in Durham on 26 March, steaming and whistling its way to the terminal at the foot of Dillard Street and stopping before a crowd of onlookers, one of whom was Julian Carr. Fortunately for Carr, the terminal was very near Blackwell's Tobacco Company, but it was fully a mile from Washington Duke's factory, and because the Richmond and Danville refused to share a small portion of its right of way, the Durham and Northern had no direct access to W. Duke Sons and Company. The Dukes and most of Durham found the situation deplorable, and when a group of angry citizens decided to lay a section of track from the terminal to the eastern end of W. Duke Sons and Company, they did so with the town council's blessing.[14]

Starting work at midnight on Monday, 9 April, under the supervision of a group of Durham and Northern engineers, the men managed to cover about half the distance to the Duke factory by daylight on Tuesday. Unfortunately, the route they took traversed land that had been leased to the Richmond and Danville, and by noon that company had sworn out a warrant for trespassing against every man who was involved. After a five-hour court session presided over by three Durham justices, the warrants were dismissed. Work on the track was resumed that night, and by Wednesday morning it was completed.

Elation at the Duke factory was short lived. Only a few hours later a work crew debarked from one of the Richmond and Danville's construction trains and began to tear up the new track; they had managed to demolish about one hundred feet of steel before Durham police put a stop to the vandalism. Late that afternoon a federal judge in Greensboro issued an order restraining the Richmond and Danville from interfering with repairs to the Durham and Northern tracks, and a number of Durham citizens took up arms to prevent the Virginians from further damaging what they had christened the "Moonlight Railroad."

The inevitable lawsuits that followed these demonstrations lasted for almost a year. On one occasion the court proceedings became so heated, because of local prejudice, that they were transferred to Chatham County. Not until the summer of 1890 did a favorable verdict, granted by the North Carolina Supreme Court to the Durham and Northern Railroad, give the tobacco manufacturers who had contributed so liberally to its establishment the legal right to use it.[15]

Although this was not the last battle that Durham would fight in order to link itself to the rest of the world, it laid the groundwork for future connections with four railway systems: the Norfolk and Western, the Norfolk and Southern, the Seaboard Air Line, and the

Southern. These connections encouraged the industrial expansion that was making Durham the "livest" town in the South, according to the editor of the local *Tobacco Plant*, who asked his readers: "With three new railroads entering the town and yet another most favorably agitated, what is it we are not justified in doing?"[16]

That rhetorical question reflected the attitude of Julian Carr, who had bought the newspaper in 1886 from his friend Caleb Green. Green, undoubtedly a prodigy, had started the first job printing office in Durham when he was only fourteen years old; at sixteen he was publishing the town's first newspaper, a weekly he called the *Tobacco Plant*, and selling it to subscribers for a dollar and fifty cents a year.[17] The first edition appeared in January 1872, and the following month Carr bought enough advertising space to announce that he was the agent for Averell's Chemical Paint, which was "cheaper, handsomer, more durable and elastic than the best of any other paint," would not fade or "chalk off," and required "no Oil, Thiner or Drier."[18] Carr only temporarily sold paint, as a sideline to his job of managing the office and traveling for the W. T. Blackwell Company, but his belief in the importance of advertising made him a valuable source of revenue to Caleb Green. Because they shared a love for the Democratic party and a strong faith in the future of their town, the two became close friends.

In 1886 fire destroyed Green's office and damaged his home. When he decided to sell the *Tobacco Plant* and to devote his time to a drugstore he owned, Carr bought the paper and hired W. G. Burkhead, a Trinity College graduate, to be his editor.[19] Burkhead, on orders from the publisher, enlarged the sheet, printed sermons and fiction on the front page, wrote much longer editorials, and included items of local interest in his layout; the first edition under Carr's ownership, dated 15 September 1886, exemplified these innovations.

A lengthy sermon entitled "Moral Wrecks" and a statement of the *Plant's* intention "to stand fairly and firmly by the Administration and President Cleveland" later appeared on the front page, along with a reference to the manner in which the president and the first lady conducted themselves in church: "She doesn't fidgit as he does . . . but fans herself constantly."[20] Julian Carr was an enthusiastic supporter of Cleveland and a frequent visitor to Washington, so he may have dictated that thumbnail sketch to Burkhead. There can be little doubt that, as time went on, his hand touched other parts of the paper as well. "Factory Scraps," for instance, told readers that "Durham can justly claim the largest Cotton Factory in the State, the largest Cigarette Factory in the South, and the largest Smoking Tobacco Factory in the World," and that the "big new engine Blackwell's Durham Tobacco Company are arranging to put in their factory is being built at Chester, Pa. by the Wetherill Corless Co." A column of personal items included mention of Mrs. John Wesley Carr's recovery from an unnamed illness and her subsequent visit with "her boys" in Durham. Prominent among the space-fillers was a statement that Julian S. Carr had given $200 of the $362 collected in Durham for relief of the Charleston, South Carolina, earthquake victims.

The elegantly phrased "Hints on Dinner Giving," obviously aimed at female readers, contained advice on how to issue invitations, how to accept and decline them, when to arrive, how to enter and leave the dining room, and how much food one should put on one's plate. Hostesses were told to invite "sensible, social, unaffected and clever people" and warned never to attempt a new dish at a party. "For reasonable and sensible people," the article stated, "there is no dinner more satisfactory than one consisting first of a soup, then a fish garnished with boiled potatoes, followed by a roast also garnished with one vegetable, perhaps an entree, always a salad, some cheeses, and a dessert. This, well cooked and neatly and quietly served, is a stylish and good enough dinner for anyone."

Burkhead (and Carr) believed not only in eating well but also in boosting Durham. "Her cotton factory, her wooden factory, her fertilizer factory, her merchants, her minor industries, are all alive," the paper said in its second edition. "Nothing stands still. There is very little loafing in Durham. A man who stands on the street corner and gazes at the sky is apt to be run over. Everybody works. Everybody is busy. The word 'Durham' is synonymous with 'Business.' " Editor and publisher also believed in prodding local officials to remedy unsatisfactory conditions in the town. "Bad smells coming from the jail yard and around the market house ought not to be," they asserted; and "crowds congregating at the depot about train time are getting to be a nuisance. In danger of getting hurt, and they deprive travelers of comfortable uses of the very conveniences the railroad places for its travelers."

Other nuisances were "a very muddy mudhole in the road leading to the Cotton Factory" and the sidewalk planks on Main Street, which were out of plumb. "Somebody will get hurt if they are not repaired. Have it done, Mayor," the *Tobacco Plant* demanded. Mayor J. F. Freeland evidently took immediate action, for the paper reported a week later that good sidewalks had been promised, and that the town council also had made arrangements "to grade the streets and provide for a sewer system and water mains."

That particular issue of the *Tobacco Plant*, its third under the aegis of Carr and Burkhead, included poems and stories, a farm and home column, further hints on etiquette and good manners, news from around the state, the honor roll list from the Durham Graded and High School, and a report on the successful revival being conducted by the Reverend W. S. Creasy at Trinity Methodist Church. "Monday night there were 35 to 40 penitents at the altar and several conversions," the paper alleged. "The spirit of the Holy Ghost seems to be moving very largely upon the hearts of almost the entire community, and it looks as if Durham might be won to Christ and laid as a trophy at His feet." In the same issue, the community was informed that "We don't propose to run a Cheap John paper, or try to conduct one on the credit system."[21]

Burkhead had been editor for almost two years when Carr decided to publish the *Tobacco Plant* on a daily basis and raise the subscription price to four dollars. He hired J. B. Whitaker as assistant editor and business manager. The first daily edition appeared on 2 June 1888. A startling new masthead displayed the paper's name in bright red script above an oversized pair of scissors, flanked by an inkstand, a paste pot, and two green, luxuriant tobacco plants. The lead editorial said, in part,

> Time and time again we have been solicited to convert the *Plant* to a daily. For numerous reasons we have not seen our way clear to do so. But we believe now that the time has arrived to throw our banner to the breeze, and we do so without the slightest misgiving, knowing that if we have merit, Durham will sustain us, if we have not, we will die as we ought. . . . We have started out to boom the livest, biggest, best, most pushing, most meritorious, and best all round town in the South, and if anything or anybody stands in our way, all we propose to take time to say is "Look out thar!"[22]

Emphasizing that it would not be the organ of any man, clique, or party, the *Plant* nevertheless endorsed "most heartily" the administration of Grover Cleveland, the first Democratic president since 1861, and swore to have "no master other than the best interest of the town of Durham and the success of the Democratic Party." The party's platform, which had been adopted at a recent state convention in Raleigh, was printed, along with a listing of the Democratic candidates for federal and state offices and an announcement that J. S. Carr and E. J. Parrish would be among the North Carolina delegates at the Democratic National Convention in St. Louis on 5 June 1888.

Media reaction to the *Daily Tobacco Plant* was generally favorable throughout North Carolina. The Danville *Register* dismissed it as "a newsy little sheet" with a masthead that was "something new under the sun . . . but most too flashy"; nobody, however, expected a Virginia editor to praise a newspaper published in the pushy tobacco town of Durham. It was enough that the conservative *Wilmington Star* pronounced the *Plant* "handsomely printed and well edited in all departments . . . a credit to the thriving town in which it is published," and that the Raleigh *News and Observer* called it "the handsomest daily in America, so far as we know, and for that matter in the world." Statesville's *Landmark* declared, "It is a beautiful thing and is filled with the choicest reading matter." The Goldsboro *Argus* echoed, "It is a thing of beauty, the handsomest paper we have ever seen . . . enhanced by the rare productions of gifted intellects, the strokes of genius and flashes of wit that await you there."[23]

This auspicious beginning did not portend smooth sailing for Durham's first daily. Before the month was out, Burkhead left to become editor of a new sheet called the *Daily Progress*, reputedly an organ of the Prohibition party. J. B. Whitaker assumed Burkhead's duties until the summer of 1889, when Julian Carr sold the paper to Edward Oldham of Wilmington. Described as "a prominent journalist of the new generation," Oldham also was a restless young man who took a jaundiced view of "the policies and aims of existing newspapers." After changing the *Plant*'s name to the *Globe*, he published it for a scant three months and then left town. Apparently Oldham had been owner in name only, for the paper reverted to Carr, who sold it again in 1890 to Al Fairbrother, formerly of the *Omaha Bee*. An editor with iconoclastic leanings, Fairbrother criticized Durham's moral and social conditions, shocking the entire town and enraging most of its leading citizens.[24]

On one occasion Fairbrother's target was the management of "the cotton mill in East Durham, which has worked hands until 8 o'clock at night and startled the hands from sleep at 4:30 in the morning and given men like Odell a chance to get very rich and fellows like the creature Branson to get fat off of human toil . . . well the concern, we learn, has sold its 'company store' and will hereafter pay by the week and let the poor devils spend the little they get wherever and however they may please." Nor were executives of the Durham Cotton Manufacturing Company (of which Julian Carr was president) the only men to be lambasted by the *Globe*. An editorial aimed squarely at Washington Duke did nothing to endear Fairbrother to that gentleman. Speaking of a mausoleum made of "granite, with a marble lining and tiled floor and stained glass windows and bronze gates" that Duke was planning to build in Maplewood Cemetery at a cost of $29,750, Fairbrother said, "Uncle Wash is shrewd enough to know unless he builds this monument to himself that posterity will never do it for him. But even the marble lining and tile floor will not stifle the cries of the poor North Carolina farmers and their breadless children, which must haunt the sleep of those who will rest in this twenty-nine thousand dollar tomb."[25]

Julian Carr's private opinion of the Nebraskan who bought his newspaper is not a matter of record, probably because Carr knew the value of favorable publicity. As a rule he stayed on friendly terms with the press, and he gave financial assistance to several struggling journalists during his lifetime. One of the first to benefit from Carr's generosity was Captain Randolph Shotwell, a Civil War veteran who later became a legislator from Mecklenburg County and, ultimately, a resident of Raleigh. Shotwell, like Carr, was "a Confederate to the end of his life . . . the soul of chivalry toward women . . . and severe only toward those who did not militantly fight the Reconstructionists." His friendship with Carr had its roots in shared experiences in both the army and the Confederate Veterans of America.[26] When Carr learned that Shotwell had started a newspaper called the *Farmer and Mechanic* and was not having an easy time of it, he went to Raleigh and offered to help. No papers were signed, but Shotwell kept a careful record of the checks Carr sent to him periodically for several years. In 1885, when he merged his *Farmer and Mechanic* with Walter Hines Page's two-year-old *State Chronicle*, "he placed the majority of the stock of the combined companies in the name of General Carr."

Shotwell died a few months after the merger, and Josephus Daniels, a young man who was pursuing a newspaper career in Wilson, North Carolina, inquired about buying the *Chronicle*. Told by Shotwell's lawyer that Julian S. Carr was the chief stockholder, Daniels "took the first train to Durham and asked General Carr what he proposed to do with his paper." Describing his encounter with the president of Blackwell's Durham Tobacco Company, Daniels said Carr had no idea that he owned the paper; he had kept no account of the money he had sent to Shotwell and was surprised to learn that it amounted to several thousand dollars. When Carr asked if Daniels thought he could make the *Chronicle* pay, Daniels answered that he wouldn't be trying to buy it unless he thought he could. "That's the stuff that wins," Carr said, and then he made Daniels a gift of the stock. "I'll have it transferred to you," he told the surprised young man, "and if you succeed, you can pay me what you think it is worth."[27]

Eventually Josephus Daniels paid Julian Carr a thousand dollars, which Carr said was a thousand more than he had ever expected to receive. But the public support that Daniels gave him for the rest of his life was something Carr probably did expect, especially in view of the fact that he financed the Raleigh editor again in 1894 when the *News and Observer*, fallen on hard times, came up for auction. Knowing that Daniels was eager to buy it, Carr offered to back him "up to the limit with needed finances." Although ten years passed before Daniels was able to liquidate the $10,000 loan, Carr never called for payment of either interest or principal. The one thing he did ask of Daniels was permission to design a new masthead for the *Observer*. When that permission was readily granted, he drew one "with his own hands . . . which was ornate and had true Tar Heel flavor."[28]

Julian Carr added his own flavor to Tar Heel news during the 1880s, when his involvement in almost every phase of Durham's rapid development kept his name continually before the public. Success in tobacco and textiles whetted his appetite for more business, and once the Durham Cotton Manufacturing Company was functioning, he turned his attention to supplying the town with electric lights. His travels in connection with Blackwell's Durham Tobacco Company had given him a knowledge of big cities that made him eager to transport some of their conveniences to Durham, and although electricity was still rare in North Carolina, he knew it would one day be as commonplace as the gaslights that had all but replaced kerosene lamps and candles.

Other Durham citizens shared Carr's views, but only Eugene Morehead and George Washington Watts were willing to invest in a scheme to promote electric lights. Watts was a close friend and business partner of Washington Duke, but that alliance did not prevent him and Carr from getting along if there were profits to be made from a mutual effort. Morehead and Watts, whose wealthy backgrounds had given them an appreciation of the finer things of life, were in favor of improving their rustic surroundings; but they, like Carr, were chiefly motivated by profit, and they were shrewd enough to know that bringing electric power to Durham was bound to be profitable.

Carr, Morehead, and Watts set about incorporating the Durham Electric Lighting Company. After securing from the board of aldermen the exclusive right to supply the town with electricity for fifteen years, without taxation, they arranged to have a power house constructed not far from the center of the business district, and to have the poles for transmission lines erected along the streets and alleys. These preliminaries were conducted in 1885, and in 1886 the people of Durham saw their little city illuminated by arc lights.

Initially everyone was delighted by these glowing signs of progress, but by 1887 complaints about poor service and the high rental rate (ten dollars a month per light) started a series of squabbles between municipal authorities and the Durham Electric Lighting Company. These altercations continued for years, and although Carr and his partners frequently offered to sell their facilities to the town, the offers were always refused. Occasional concessions were made on both sides, but the bickering continued as long as the exclusive fifteen-year franchise.[29]

In the meantime, Carr's enthusiasm for electricity led him into another controversial situation. In 1885, with his former partner, Buck Blackwell, and a local druggist, Richard Blacknall, he organized a street railway company. In addition to offering passenger service, the three men planned to run freight cars between various factories and the railway depot; they hoped soon to operate the whole system electrically, instead of with horses. Almost two years passed, however, before the Durham Street Railway, capitalized at $10,000, became a reality, with Blackwell serving as president, Carr as vice-president, and Blacknall as secretary and treasurer. The *Tobacco Plant* stood solidly behind the venture, opining that the men responsible for it "always mean business when they take hold of anything" because all three had "the pluck and the cash necessary." When work on the tracks began two months later, the newspaper put out an extra edition with 72-point headlines that shouted: "DURHAM STREET RAILWAY INAUGURATED!"[30]

The special edition described the ceremony staged on 10 March 1885 at the foot of Redmond's Hill, where eight young ladies and their escorts arrived on a bunting-draped bandwagon drawn by four horses. A large part of Durham's population was on hand to hear a local minister offer up a prayer before the young people began to break ground for the railway, using picks and shovels decorated with red, white, and blue ribbons. After a sufficient amount of earth had been turned, there were speeches. Lawyer Will Fuller praised the instigators of the new transportation system at some length before he announced that fares would be reduced during certain hours so that all working people, "however slender their means," could ride on the cars, and that special rates for schoolchildren already had been established.[31]

But the saga of the Durham Street Railway was riddled with dissension almost from its beginnings. Laying of the tracks had left Main Street so full of rocks and mounds of earth that people found it almost impossible to cross; the tracks themselves, fully six to eight inches higher than ground level, were an added hazard to both pedestrians and vehicles. Constant complaints from disgruntled citizens and irate town authorities made life less than pleasant for Blackwell, Carr, and Blacknall, and because their ambition to substitute electricity for the mules and horses that powered the cars was frustrated, it was with considerable relief that they sold out in 1891, just four years after the colorful inauguration ceremony. The street railway was absorbed by the Durham Consolidated Land and Improvement Company, and the electric lighting firm was sold, in 1901, to the Durham Traction Company. Not until 1920, however, did Julian Carr see public transportion and the production of electric light and power combined into one public utility, something he had hoped to accomplish himself.[32]

Although his experiences with municipal franchises were neither pleasant nor profitable, they failed to blunt Carr's appetite for new business. During the summer of 1887, while the electric lighting company was feuding with the town commissioners and the street railway was tearing up Durham's main thoroughfare, Carr was making plans to become a banker. Both Eugene Morehead and W. T. Blackwell had preceded him in that field, Morehead in 1878 and Blackwell in 1886; but the Morehead Banking Company and Blackwell's Bank of Durham were state banks, and Carr was of the opinion that "the Durham of approximately five thousand people, with several important industries," needed a national concern, with more extensive powers and resources.[33]

His decision could have been influenced by the fact that Morehead, in failing health, was spending more and more time out of town, seeking a cure that no medical specialist had yet been able to provide. Carr may have reasoned that, if no cure was found, Gene Morehead's bank might pass into the hands of Gerrard Watts, a partner in absentia from Baltimore. Although Carr probably would not have set out deliberately to compete with his closest friend, he had no misgivings about competing with the father of George Watts, who was, like George, an ally of the Dukes. Nor was he hesitant about competing with his erstwhile partner, Buck Blackwell, for they had shared the buffalo-goring tactics of the tobacco industry. Both of them knew that if a man wasn't your partner, he was liable to be your competitor—and sometimes he turned out to be both.

Because "conditions were ripe and capital was all that was lacking" in order to establish a third bank in Durham, Carr approached James Augustus Bryan, a friend and fellow Confederate from eastern North Carolina. Bryan's wealth made him a likely source of capital, and his position as president of the National Bank of New Bern qualified him as an expert source of advice and information. The fact that Bryan wanted to launch his son, Charles, on a banking career possibly influenced his response to Carr's overtures. Young Charles, having just graduated from Princeton, apparently was not averse to exchanging the staid confines of his father's establishment for the excitement of working with the ebullient Mr. Carr in the frontier town of Durham. The elder Bryan was a cautious man, however, and Carr had to make several trips to New Bern that summer before his friend was persuaded to supply over half of the $100,000 needed to establish a national bank in Durham. Carr himself invested $11,100, and he was able to round up the balance among twenty-four subscribers, most of them Durham residents.

On 9 November 1887, the United States Treasury Department granted a charter to the First National Bank of Durham, authorizing it to conduct general banking business and also to issue notes. On 1 December the new institution invested $25,000 in 4 percent bonds, paying a premium of approximately $26 on each $100. At the same time, the bank placed over $9,000 in the National Bank of Raleigh and sent deposits of $5,000 each to the Manufacturers National Bank of Philadelphia and the National Bank of the Republic of New York City "in order to establish banking relations elsewhere."[34] These arrangements undoubtedly facilitated the financial operations connected with Julian Carr's various business enterprises, the most lucrative being Blackwell's Durham Tobacco Company.

The First National Bank of Durham, located in "a large store building, almost large enough for the bank to get lost in," opened its doors on 6 December 1887, and the wife of the bank's president was its first customer. Mrs. Julian S. Carr deposited $622.70 in a personal checking account, and during the day "five other depositors appeared and went away with checking accounts on the books." That evening the big safe that substituted for a vault contained $5,714.95.[35]

At the end of its first month of operations, the bank had averaged about $5,000 worth of business each day and had a net profit of $851.19. Eight months later, on 3 August 1888, the number of depositors had increased to 131, "representing all classes of people." The examining committee of the board of directors reported that the institution was prosperous and healthy, its books well kept, and its officers faithful, intelligent, and diligent.[36]

Those exemplary officers, in addition to Julian Carr, were Charles Shepard Bryan, the twenty-three-year-old vice-president and bookkeeper; Leo D. Heartt, who had left the State Bank of Raleigh to become Carr's cashier; and Charles A. Jordan, teller (who eventually would leave Carr to work for W. Duke Sons and Company). Both the president and the teller received $1,000 a year; the cashier drew $2,000, and the vice-president and bookkeeper (who, incidentally, was the largest stockholder) earned $600.

The board of directors included Carr, the two Bryans, attorney Will Fuller, and six Durham men who were involved in either the manufacture or the sale of tobacco: E. J. Parrish, H. N. Snow, J. T. Mallory, T. D. Jones, J. W. Walker, and A. H. Stokes, all friends of Carr's who agreed that Durham's third bank should operate "in a conservative, but sufficiently liberal manner," and that "a continuance of the present strict adherence to business methods will benefit the community and advance the interests of the stockholders of the bank."[37]

The president of the First National Bank of Durham watched with pleasure a modest but steady advance of the stockholders' interests during the next five months. On 31 December 1888, deposits totaled $125,265.15 and the books showed a profit of $7,276.10.[38] His latest business venture was fast becoming his greatest love, and 1 January 1889 would have been a truly happy New Year's Day for him had it not been for the fact that Eugene Morehead, ill at his wife's former home in Savannah, Georgia, was not expected to recover from the malady that had plagued him for over two years.

Morehead had spent much of that time away from Durham, consulting various medical specialists. After a fruitless trip to New Orleans, he had returned home in the spring of 1887 to find a brass band and a large crowd waiting at the depot, primed to welcome him with speeches and music before they escorted him to his house on Morehead Hill. In that spectacle he must have seen the flamboyant hand of his friend, but if Carr planned the demonstration, he had widespread support for it in the community. During Morehead's eleven years in Durham, he had become one of the most popular members of "a social circle appreciated for its excellence and esteemed for its culture and virtues." When he died on 27 February 1889, just six months before his forty-fourth birthday, the gregarious young man from Greensboro, who "could not resist inviting friends as well as passing acquaintances into his home for a meal or a visit," was widely mourned in the town he had adopted for his own.[39]

Carr's grief was especially keen. He told Cornelia Phillips Spencer, "I had no better friend, and certainly none I esteemed more highly." One of his great sorrows stemmed from the fact that he and Gene were never together in Somerset Villa, the Victorian mansion he began to build in the summer of 1887 and completed the following year.[40]

7. Somerset Villa and Charlie Soon

John B. Halcott of Albany, New York, the architect who designed and built Somerset Villa for Julian Carr, also dismantled Waverly Honor, moved it across the street, and rebuilt it for Carr's younger brother, Albert, who had come to Durham to practice medicine. In a "History of Somerset Villa," possibly written at Julian Carr's request, the architect stated that "work of demolition of the old building was begun on the ninth day of July 1887 and the ground was cleared and the excavation for the present building commenced on the thirty-first of July 1887."[1]

For some time Carr had felt that Waverly Honor no longer could accommodate two adults, five children, several servants, and a great many visitors; nor was it grand enough to satisfy his growing taste for elegant surroundings. Because he liked the location, however, he directed Halcott to build his second residence on the site of the house in which he and Nannie had lived for thirteen years. Sentimental attachment to that first house kept him from destroying it, so Waverly Honor was "taken down and re-erected upon the South side of Peabody Street—near Dillard Street."[2] The constantly changing audience that gaped at the fall and rise of Waverly Honor also saw the building of Somerset Villa, in a show that ran for almost nine months.

During that time Carr was president of Blackwell's Durham Tobacco Company, the First National Bank, the Durham Electric Lighting Company, the Golden Belt Manufacturing Company, and the Atlantic Hotel Corporation. He was said to be the richest man in North Carolina, and he made it clear to John Halcott that money was no object. Only the best was good enough, and Carr's idea of the best was a three-story Queen Anne mansion with a massive reception hall, two parlors, a smoking room, a dining salon big enough for a banquet table, a kitchen big enough for a hotel-size range, oven, and broiler, five bedrooms with connecting dressing rooms and baths, quarters for two live-in servants, and a billiard room.[3]

Halcott, who espoused the so-called new school of architectural

Waverly Honor, Durham, North Carolina
(courtesy of Laura Noell Carr Chapman)

reform that had been sweeping the country since 1880, must have been delighted to learn that his wealthy client yearned for exactly the kind of house he wanted to design—one that exhibited projecting bays, rounded towers and porches, and a dramatic and complex roofline of gables, dormers, and conical turrets. Knowing that the owner was giving him carte blanche in construction of this house must have been an added source of pleasure to the architect.

In his attempt to "faithfully perform the offices entrusted to his care," Halcott used timber, brownstone, granite, marble, stucco, pressed brick, slate, terra cotta, and bronze in the construction of Somerset Villa; he adorned it with cupolas, gables, archways, dormers, recessed panels, and gingerbread fretwork. There were two upstairs porches and a catwalk, in addition to two balconies. A turret rising twelve feet above the crest along the irregular ridges of the roof supported an ornate copper weathercock, which gleamed in the sunlight and was visible for half a mile in all directions. A wide veranda, with colonnettes linked by a turned balustrade and spindle frieze, curved and jutted its way around the lower floor. The panels beneath it, designed to hide the underpinnings and basement, were made of bronzed iron grillwork. A double stairway from the main entrance of the porch to the front lawn formed an enclosure for a stone fountain and pool. On the right-hand side of the veranda, an

*Albert Gallatin Carr, physician and brother of Julian S. Carr
(courtesy of Laura Noell Carr Chapman)*

elaborate porte cochere with a clipped gable roof protected the occupants of carriages (and later of automobiles) from bad weather.[4]

Somerset Villa (named for Robert Carr, the earl of Somerset and a favorite subject of King James I) was heated by steam, illuminated by both gas and electricity, and guarded by an unusual system of burglar and fire alarms. The separate two-story kitchen with its walk-in ice room especially pleased John O'Daniel, the butler who ruled Carr's lesser servants and kept a proprietary eye on his children. Those children were pleased to have their own special bathrooms, one for the two sisters and another for their three little brothers. Each bath had marble fixtures, a shower bath, and picture-book tiles decorated with reeds, cattails, pond lilies, frogs, turtles, and storks.

Out of deference to his client's Tar Heel origins, Halcott used North Carolina products and local labor whenever possible, but since most of the materials and many of the workmen came from northern cities, apparently his standards were not easily met. The only Durham firm to profit from Carr's mansion was the Robertson-Lloyd Company, which furnished part of the hardware. Four contractors from Raleigh fared better: John Whitelaw supplied and set the cut stone; J. C. Brewster installed the piping, the heating system, and the speaking tubes; M. S. Clark laid the slate roof and ridge castings; William John Wier set the terra cotta tile ornaments in the gables. Other North Carolinians who participated in the project were J. A. Wilson of Wilson's Mills, who supplied the rough lumber and the exterior finished wood; B. H. Tyson of Wilson, who installed the lightning rods; and J. Gilmer Korner, Carr's favorite painter of Durham bulls, who used his talents to embellish some of the interior walls and ceilings and also saw to it that every surface requiring polish was buffed to a high gloss.

Halcott contracted for cabinets, interior woodwork, stairways, plumbing, wrought iron, weathervanes, and kitchen equipment in his home town of Albany, New York. To obtain for Carr the finest plate glass, stained glass, floor tiles, heat registers, window guards, sash chains, pressed brick, and electrical devices, he went to Bridgeport, Connecticut; Wilmington, Delaware; and New York, Boston, and Baltimore. All of the hearths, mantels, fireplaces, chandeliers, lighting fixtures, ceiling and wall decorations, furniture, curtains, and carpets were shipped to Durham from Philadelphia, which was Julian and Nannie Carr's favorite metropolis. As huge boxes and crates, addressed "To J. B. Halcott, c/o J. S. Carr," began to arrive at the little

John B. Halcott, architect of Somerset Villa
(courtesy of Laura Noell Carr Chapman)

Somerset Villa, Durham, North Carolina (courtesy of Albert G. Carr)

depot at the foot of Church Street in ever-increasing numbers, conjecture about the big house at the eastern end of Main Street cropped up in many conversations.

It was reported that over half of the $125,000 Carr spent on the construction of "one of the most beautiful and complete private houses in the world" was for the interior. There "a richly carved mantel, reaching to the ceiling and costing $1,800" dominated the reception hall, and the two carved newel posts at the base of the broad main staircase cost $500 each. To make sure he would have "a palace home . . . perhaps the finest of its kind in the South," Carr invested $5,000 in chandeliers, $40,000 in carpets and furniture, and $6,000 in stained glass windows. The largest of these windows, placed high above the main stairway, was inspired by the poem, "Curfew Must Not Ring Tonight," and depicted a young woman clinging to the clapper of a huge golden bell. On sunny days the massive window blazed with color, and the agony on the maiden's face was clearly visible as

> Out she swung, far out; the city seemed a speck
> of light below,

Interior of Somerset Villa (courtesy of Rufus Tucker Carr)

She 'twixt heaven and earth suspended, as the
bell swung to and fro.[5]

An architectural journal published in Richmond, Virginia, called
Somerset Villa "*the* conspicuous landmark [of Durham] upon which
the eye first falls and upon which it loves to linger." The reporter
described many of the rooms in detail, with special attention to mantels carved from white maple, sycamore, and oak; to stairway plat-
forms inlaid with rosewood and ebony; and to the bedroom designed
for Carr's two daughters, where J. Gilmer Korner, alias "Reuben
Rink," had painted the ceiling with clouds, life-size cupids, and "a
frieze representing water."[6]

In order to create a setting worthy of his spectacular new house,
Carr hired Dutch and French landscape gardeners to work with Reuben Hibberd, a local horticulturist. The trees these experts planted
ran the gamut from ordinary to exotic: magnolias, lindens, cedars,
pecans, crepe myrtles, and cork maples mingled with palm, banana,

Interior of Somerset Villa (courtesy of Rufus Tucker Carr)

and coffee trees; blue spruce, golden arborvitae, and Chinese box-wood grew alongside the hardy hydrangea and the canna lily. Almost every kind of flower that would grow in Durham soil found its way into the carefully tended beds and borders, and many varieties of carnations, chrysanthemums, and long-stemmed roses thrived all year in a spacious greenhouse behind the tall privet hedge that separated Somerset Villa from its dependencies.

Carr, who loved everything that bloomed, was proud of his gardens and grounds, and it especially pleased him to hear them equated with those at Biltmore, the Vanderbilt estate in Asheville, North Carolina. Once, in a burst of patriotism, he commissioned Reuben Hibberd to plant a forty-foot floral replica of the American flag on one side of his front walk, and a twenty-foot likeness of the American eagle on the opposite side. Sometimes, when he saw passersby stopping to peer through the fence at these phenomena, he invited them in for a closer look and a sample of the Old South charisma that was becoming his hallmark.

*Somerset Villa's cornerstone box after being opened around 1925
(photograph by Charles Cooper, Durham, N.C.)*

On 29 September 1888, at what John Halcott described as "a ceremony of dedication," twenty-seven of Carr's relatives and friends
signed the architect's "History of Somerset Villa" and watched their
host place it, "together with other suitable articles," in a copper box
that later was sealed into the cornerstone.[7] Those other articles were
three books in which he figured prominently; four newspapers containing stories about him; letterheads and envelopes currently being
used at Blackwell's Durham Tobacco Company and the Golden Belt
Manufacturing Company; a two-ounce bag of Genuine Bull Durham
Smoking Tobacco; a Bible published in 1888 "from the original
tongues"; a five-dollar bill issued by the First National Bank of Durham; eight copper and silver coins of various denominations; Confederate currency ranging from fifty cents to one hundred dollars; a
copy of the charter of the town of Durham; lists of the names of
Durham County officers, state officers, and members of the state
legislature; a group picture of the North Carolina Methodist Confer-

Julian S. Carr (courtesy of Austin Heaton Carr, Jr.)

ence of 1887; and thirty-seven photographs. Pictured were John Halcott, President and Mrs. Grover Cleveland, numerous Carr and Parrish kinsmen, a dozen close friends, and Somerset Villa's owner, his wife, Nannie, and his five children: Eliza Morehead, Lalla Ruth, Julian Shakespeare, Jr., Albert Marvin, and Claiborn McDowell, the baby in the family at the time.[8]

An extremely significant item that Carr included was a sepia print of a Chinese boy dressed in stylish American clothes. The boy, named Soong Yao-ju, was taken into the Carr family when "one of the romances of modern Christianity brought them together" in 1881.[9] Among several versions of that so-called romance, each laced with myth and riddled with conflicting evidence, one fact stands out clearly: the "slender little fellow with almond eyes" who became known as Charlie Soon was exceptionally lucky, especially with regard to his Western benefactors, all of whom were devout Methodists.

Soon's phenomenal luck is one of the few things about which historians and biographers agree. Other details—his true Chinese name, his family's occupation and financial status, his character and intelligence, the reason for his coming to America, and the means by which he reached North Carolina—have provoked considerable disagreement. A fire at Durham's Trinity Methodist Church destroyed the bulk of Julian Carr's testimony regarding the lad, who later sired one of China's most powerful families. More of the truth about Charlie Soon might also be known today if Carr had been less reticent, in his personal diary, about recording details of his 1917 visit to Shanghai.

In the early 1880s in Durham, however, it became generally known that Soong Yao-ju was born in 1866 at Hainan Island, off the south coast of China, and that he was brought to America in 1875 by his mother's brother, who owned a tea and silk business in Boston. This uncle, having no sons of his own, planned to make the boy his apprentice and heir. The arrangement contrived by his elders held no appeal for Yao-ju, who became even more disenchanted with it after he met two students from Shanghai who extolled the advantages of a first-class American education. He begged to be allowed to attend school during the day, instead of for only a few hours at night, but his uncle replied that it was his duty to learn the business. Although outwardly obedient to this ultimatum, Yao-ju was determined not to be a shopkeeper, and when he was about fourteen years old he ran away.[10]

The least colorful and probably most factual account of his adven-

Nancy (Nannie) Graham Parrish Carr
(courtesy of Laura Noell Carr Chapman)

Eliza Morehead Carr (courtesy of Laura Noell Carr Chapman)

Lalla Ruth Carr (courtesy of Laura Noell Carr Chapman)

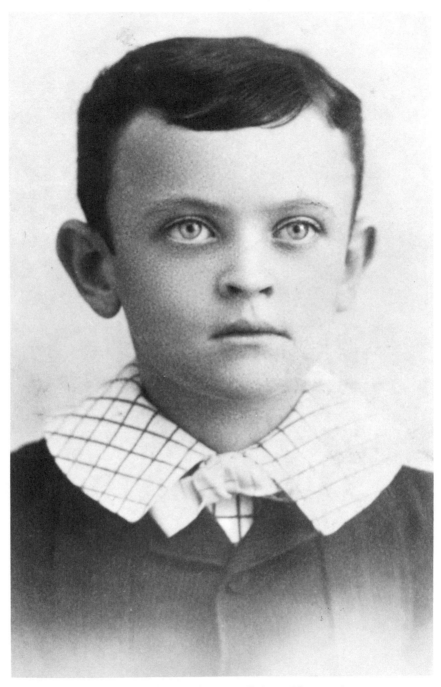

Julian S. Carr, Jr. (courtesy of Laura Noell Carr Chapman)

Albert Marvin Carr (courtesy of Laura Noell Carr Chapman)

Claiborn McDowell Carr (courtesy of Laura Noell Carr Chapman)

Charles Jones Soon (courtesy of Laura Noell Carr Chapman)

tures after he left his uncle's home contends that Soong Yao-ju joined the Coast Guard, shipping aboard the U.S. Revenue Cutter *Gallatin* at Boston Harbor, and that his name was entered on the muster list as "Sun" on 8 January 1879. For sixteen months he served as a cabin boy for the captain, Eric Gabrielson, who has been described variously as "a quiet, sea-wise man," a former Union soldier who hated the idea of slavery, "a salty, God-fearing Norwegian," and a dedicated Methodist. Gabrielson frequently took his cabin boy to church in Edgartown, Massachusetts, the *Gallatin*'s home port; in his off hours he "schooled the heathen adolescent in the ways of Christianity." The captain further endeared himself to the boy by cutting off his queue, buying him his first suit of American clothes, and calling him Charlie. Even if his uncle had ever seen him when the *Gallatin* docked in Boston Harbor, he probably would not have recognized him.[11]

In the spring of 1880 Gabrielson was transferred to the cutter *Schuyler Colfax*, based in Wilmington, North Carolina. His cabin boy requested and received a discharge, followed him to Wilmington, and reenlisted aboard the *Colfax* on 1 August 1880. Moved by this display of affection from a youngster whose bright mind and obvious potential already had impressed him, Gabrielson decided to help Charlie better himself; as a first step in that direction he introduced his charge to Dr. T. Page Ricaud, the pastor of Wilmington's Fifth Street Methodist Church. Ricaud, "a linguist of considerable ability" and an interpreter for the port of Wilmington, also was a visionary: If this Chinese boy could be educated to become a missionary to his own people, who knew how many souls he could bring to Jesus Christ? Inspired by his dream, the minister spent enough hours talking to Charlie to inspire him, too. On 7 November 1880 the Wilmington *Star* announced that, when the sacrament of baptism was administered that day at the Fifth Street Methodist Church, "a Chinese convert will be one of the subjects of the solemn rite, being probably the first Celestial that has ever submitted to the ordinance of baptism in North Carolina."[12]

A month later, at the North Carolina Methodist Conference in Winston-Salem, Dr. Ricaud approached Braxton Craven, the president of Methodist-affiliated Trinity College in Randolph County, about entering this recently baptized Celestial in the school's preparatory department. Craven, in turn, approached Julian Carr, one of the wealthiest and most generous laymen in the conference, about financing the boy. Carr, immediately intrigued by Soon's story, replied, "Send him up and we'll see that he gets an education."[13]

A far more imaginative and sentimental account of Soong Yao-ju's early adventures in America describes him as restless, unhappy, and given to roaming along Boston Harbor, where "the mystery of the sea and ships answered a strange urge in his soul" and eventually turned him into a stowaway on the *Schuyler Colfax*, a "second-class side-wheeler tied up at the Boston docks." According to this version, the captain of the *Colfax* was not Eric Gabrielson but Charles Jones, a pious Methodist whose understanding heart "went out to the friendly, ambitious youth who was discovered aboard ship after they were out of port." Jones made Soong his cabinboy, talked to him at great length about "the savior of all races and peoples," and apparently had him primed for conversion to Christianity by the time the *Colfax* docked at Wilmington in the autumn of 1880.

Jones, no stranger to Wilmington, made a special trip ashore to see his friend and minister, the Reverend T. Page Ricaud, and to talk to him about Soong Yao-ju, who wanted an education, was unlikely to obtain it without help, and seemed to deserve better than the life of an ordinary seaman. Ricaud, stirred by the captain's story, told him to bring Soong to the service on Sunday and promised to talk to the boy on Monday. The pastor and the skipper never dreamed their discussion would have such far-reaching consequences: the highly impressionable Yao-ju, moved by "the simple gospel message" he heard on Sunday and by his long conversation with Ricaud on Monday, became a Christian then and there. Before he left the pastor's study, he announced his intention of going into the ministry and taking the "good news" back to China.[14]

Supposedly at Dr. Ricaud's urging, he was baptized "Charles Jones Soon," in honor of the man who had led him to Christ. The fact that Coast Guard authorities have stated "no man named Charles Jones was on the *Colfax*" gives credence to the theory that Soong's own pronunciation of "Yao-ju" (which sounded more like "Charles Jones" than anything else) gave him his American first name. Charlie himself dropped the final consonant from his American last name, resuming it only after he returned to China.[15]

Whether Charlie Soon was a member of the Coast Guard or a stowaway on the *Schuyler Colfax* has never been proven. The most recent account of his life, which surfaced sixty years after Julian

Carr's death, contends that his name was not Soong Yao-ju, but Han Chaio-shun; that the "uncle" who brought him to America was a very distant kinsman; that his parents did not know he had left China; and that the Reverend T. Page Ricaud was a lapsed Catholic and a former revolutionary who picked the name "Jones" out of thin air. Nevertheless, a Chinese boy known as Charlie Soon did remain in Wilmington after the *Colfax* sailed and was befriended by Dr. Ricaud, who helped him find work in a local printery and encouraged him to sell the knotted rope hammocks that he had learned how to make while he was at sea. Finally, in the spring of 1881, the minister took him to Durham to meet the man who had promised to help him get an education, and that meeting marked a dramatic change in Soon's way of life.[16]

Although some of the Reverend T. Page Ricaud's detractors saw him as small, gaunt, and haggard, with an untidy beard and pale, hypnotic eyes, some of his admirers saw him as small, immaculate, cheerful, erudite, and saintly. Julian and Nannie Carr reportedly were "delighted" with Ricaud, and his obvious belief in the superior qualities of the fifteen-year-old Chinese lad who wanted to become a missionary to his own people convinced them that investing in Soon's future would further the cause of Methodism and promote the kingdom of God. But it was Charlie who inspired the Carrs to take him into their home "not as a servant, but as a son." His bright, inquiring mind and his extreme politeness impressed both of them, and his fun-loving, mischievous, affectionate nature completely charmed their children. Seven-year-old Eliza Morehead and her younger siblings, Lalla Ruth and little Julian, immediately were drawn to the short, sturdy boy whose tilted eyes were the color of their mother's jet beads and whose skin was the color of their father's gold watch. Even the baby, Albert Marvin, seemed to find Charlie Soon's arms more comfortable than most and his Chinese lullabies especially soothing.[17]

When the black servants at Waverly Honor and the white children in the neighborhood "marveled at the strange looking foreigner, the first Oriental they had ever seen," their stares, whispers, and giggles seemed not to bother Charlie. Necessity had taught him how to ingratiate himself with strangers of all ages, and, with Julian Carr as his sponsor, he was "cordially received by the leading people of the community."[18] Many of them bought the hammocks he continued to make in order to help support himself.

One of his first customers was James Haywood Southgate, the genial son of the founder of Durham's first insurance agency and, like his father, a close friend of Julian Carr. Southgate and his twenty-year-old sister, Annie, took a keen interest in the Chinese boy who regularly attended the Trinity Methodist Sunday School during the summer of 1881. In spite of his apparent adaptability, they sensed that he might be homesick and went out of their way to make him feel welcome in Durham. Charlie responded to their kindness with characteristic fervor, becoming a devoted admirer and keeping up a lively correspondence with both of them even after he returned to China as an ordained deacon in 1886. They were perhaps his closest friends in Durham; in one of his letters to "Miss Annie," written during his last summer in the States, he said, "I love you more than anyone in America."[19]

When Soon entered the preparatory department at Trinity College in September 1881, it was the school's policy to waive tuition for poor boys who planned to become ministers. Because members of Trinity Methodist Sunday School agreed to contribute to Soon's room and board, Julian Carr's expenses for the boy's first year were minimal. But Waverly Honor continued to be Charlie's home during vacations, and when he transferred from Trinity to Vanderbilt University in 1882, the man whom he had begun to call "Father Carr" footed most of the bills.

At Trinity, Soon lived with Professor W. T. Gannaway, the instructor in Latin and Greek, but he spent most of his free time at the home of Dr. Braxton Craven, the college president. Craven's wife, Irene, tutored him in English and tried to help him learn to study in what was, for him, a strange and difficult language. During the long evenings they spent together in her sitting room, she became increasingly fond of him, and before the year was out she, too, was treating him like a son and "giving him the moral and spiritual training which was to make him not only a great but also a good man."[20] When it was time for Dr. Craven to report on Soon's progress to Trinity College's board of trustees, he said the boy was "doing very well in every way, studies closely and will be successful."[21]

With twelve Cherokee Indians in the preparatory department that year, Soon was not the only nonwhite student on campus, but he remained something of an oddity until his persistent good nature and his ability to take teasing overcame whatever racial prejudice existed. Within a few weeks he was one of the most popular boys at school, and he even became a favorite with the six members of the faculty. Because he wanted to return to China as a Methodist missionary, they "took special pains to equip him for his high calling."

On the Sunday before Christmas in 1881, Soon joined the Methodist church in the little village of Trinity, where the president of the college often preached. When Braxton Craven announced that his text for that morning was "Go ye into all the world and preach the gospel," Charlie Soon convinced himself that Dr. Craven was speaking directly to him. He departed from the church fired with ambition, and during the Christmas holidays at Waverly Honor he told "Father Carr" that he wanted to finish his training as quickly as possible, so he could go back to China and spread the good news about God.[22]

There is speculation about Soon's next move, from Trinity to Vanderbilt, which was instigated by the Board of Missions of the Southern Methodist Church. Braxton Craven may have persuaded board members that in Charlie Soon they had a potential saver of many Chinese souls, and that his education needed to be broadened and, at the same time, accelerated. On the other hand, those same pious officials may have been galvanized into action by a rumor (never substantiated) of Soon's serious crush on the adolescent daughter of a Trinity faculty member. At any rate, the board did advise Dr. Craven to transfer Soon to Vanderbilt, where he could obtain better and faster training "through contacts with members of the board and returned missionaries in Nashville."[23] Despite his recently acquired religious zeal, Charlie did not want to leave his friends at Trinity, nor did he want to move so far from his supporters in Durham. The Cravens convinced him that Vanderbilt was better equipped to turn him into a bona fide missionary, however, and when Julian Carr assured him that he could still spend his vacations at Waverly Honor, Charlie accepted the decision with good grace.

Accounts of Soon's life at Vanderbilt are slight and (like those of his brief career as a sailor) vary considerably. University records show that he matriculated in the Biblical Department in 1882; took courses in English, mathematics, modern languages, systematic theology, moral philosophy, and church history for three years; and was graduated with a Certificate in Theology in 1885. Although most of his professors categorized him as "not a highly successful student," they acknowledged that this probably was because "he was not better prepared when he entered the University"; "for a foreigner, handicapped as he was by limitation in his command and use of English," he did well.[24]

One of Soon's fellow students, who later became a dean in Vanderbilt's School of Theology, described him as "a harum-scarum little fellow" who seemed to have no interest in religion "and even less in preaching." Another classmate said, "He had a fine mind, soon learned to use the English language with accuracy and fluency, and was usually bubbling over with wit and humor and good nature." Nevertheless, Charlie was not always as equable as he often seemed. He joined an especially zealous group that congregated on Sunday mornings in the chapel at Wesley Hall "for a sort of experience meeting," and on one occasion his cheerful facade crumbled beneath a wave of homesickness. "I feel so little," he confessed, with quivering lips. "I get so lonesome. So far from my people. So long among strangers. I feel just like I was a little chip floating down the Mississippi River. But I know that Jesus is my savior," he insisted. When he began to cry, at least a dozen boys came to his side to offer comfort and to assure him "that they loved him as a brother."[25]

This spontaneous show of support undoubtedly helped Charlie Soon through his orientation to Vanderbilt, and by the end of the semester he was taking a more philosophical view of the situation. In handwriting that was "like a copy-plate, with a hairline touch and the shading flourishing," he wrote in a classmate's autograph book: "How you live, not years, but actions tell / The man lives twice who lives the first life well."[26] Like the students at Trinity College, those at Vanderbilt began to change their minds about the "chunky" little fellow with the "good typical Chinese face," the kind of face they were used to associating with certain laundries and restaurants. Responding to his friendly and mannerly ways, they began to include him in campus social activities, and to those officials of the Methodist church who placed a high priority on missionary work in China, he became "a center of interest."[27]

These positive reactions to his protege were gratifying to Julian Carr, who became increasingly involved in the affairs of Trinity College while Soon was at Vanderbilt. Carr's first loyalty was always to his own alma mater, the University of North Carolina, but as a dedicated Methodist he felt a duty toward the little school in Randolph County. When a mortgage on the college property was threatened with foreclosure in 1880, he helped to prevent that disaster by cosigning a note with Robert T. Gray of Raleigh, another influential friend of the school.[28] This magnanimous gesture no doubt was one of the reasons for Carr's election to Trinity's board of trustees in December 1883, just a year after the sudden death of President Braxton Craven left the school with a debt of $6,000, a mortgage on its property, and a dwindling student body. The newly elected trustees and the Reverend Marquis L. Wood, who succeeded Craven, outlined their goal of "increased patronage and liberal financial donations" for Trinity. As a first step toward reaching that goal, John Wesley Alspaugh, chairman of the board, and Julian S. Carr attempted to start an endowment for the college.

Alspaugh, a successful banker from Winston-Salem, apparently was not affected by the economic depression that had gripped the country since 1882. He announced that he would be one of twenty $1,000 donors to Trinity if nineteen like-minded men would join him; one of fifty to give $100; and one of 100 to give $250, thereby enriching the school, one way or another, by $50,000. And if $100,000 could be raised, Alspaugh added, the North Carolina Conference of the Methodist Episcopal Church South could count on him for $5,000 of that amount.

Julian Carr, while admitting that "money matters are exceedingly tight just now and shows but little signs of improvement," rose to Alspaugh's challenge, agreeing to match his offer and also to be one of twenty to donate $5,000 toward a $100,000 endowment. It probably came as no surprise to either man when their offers were met with ridicule by some and sharp disagreement by others, who advocated paying off "every cent of the college debt before starting such a movement"; but the state's Methodists were either too hard hit by the depression or too indifferent to pay off that debt. Even the Conference pledge of $2,500 to cover "pressing bills" was not paid, and in 1884 Trinity College was in such precarious financial condition that many felt it should close its doors.[29]

Julian Carr, however, was not in the habit of giving up. Calling on Alspaugh and James A. Gray, another banker from Winston-Salem who was a Trinity alumnus, he suggested that the three of them become a "committee of management" and keep the college open for at least two years by guaranteeing $5,000 for that purpose, provided the Methodist Conference would guarantee a like amount. Alspaugh and Gray, like Carr, could afford to be charitable. Because they shared his enthusiasm for both the Methodist church and higher education, they joined him in drawing up a "Proposition to Relieve

Trinity College." Presented first to the trustees and then to the conference, it was accepted after due consideration by both bodies.

Marquis L. Wood soon resigned as president of Trinity, ostensibly because the demands of the office "were rapidly telling on his physical condition." Members of the relief committee promptly allocated many of Wood's duties to John F. Heitman, a professor of Greek and German, clergyman, editor, and the husband of Carr's sister, Emma. Heitman was appointed chairman of the faculty, and in that capacity he worked closely with the treasurer of the committee of management, who happened to be his brother-in-law.

The new administrators went about their duties in a businesslike fashion. After carefully investigating every department in the college, they repaired, cleaned, and painted the buildings, improved the appearance of the campus, and appointed four new faculty members in order to upgrade the curriculum. A later assessment of their accomplishments unequivocally stated that they guided the college through one of its most critical periods; "their policies were wise; their financial arrangements, businesslike; and their appointments to the faculty, discriminating."[30] One of the new faculty members was Horace Williams, University of North Carolina graduate who became a close friend of Julian Carr and played an important role in securing John Franklin Crowell for the presidency of Trinity College in 1887.

Unfortunately, the Methodist Conference did not fulfill its part of the financial agreement. Although it was "in honor and gratitude bound to raise the $2,500 promised," at the end of the 1885 academic year there was a deficit of $431.52.[31] Carr, Alspaugh, and Gray were outspoken in their disappointment, but they agreed to continue to administer the affairs of the college through 1886, as promised. John F. Heitman, as virtual president of the institution in everything but name, redoubled his efforts to increase enrollment and church support for the school, and to collect unpaid bills.[32]

Carr wrote frequently to Heitman, addressing him as "My Dear Sir and Bro." and often ending his letters with "Give my love to sister and kiss the children for me." Most of his correspondence was mainly concerned with recruiting students, prodding recalcitrant Methodists to support Trinity, and paying the faculty. "I shall write to Gray this evening and request him to make a payment to the faculty for their salaries," he told Heitman in October 1885. "Men who work can't live without money, and I shall request Gray to send you all a remittance, which I think you shall receive during the coming week."[33] But it was almost Christmas before Carr was able to tell Heitman that he was sending to James Gray, cashier of the Wachovia National Bank in Winston-Salem, a check for $1,000 "to be used in paying the Professors at Trinity their salaries so far as it will go."[34]

While Trinity struggled to survive, one of its former students struggled to stay in America. Charlie Soon wanted to study medicine before returning to China, and while Julian Carr agreed to underwrite him, Bishop Holland J. McTyeire, chancellor of Vanderbilt University and head of the Southern Methodist Mission in China, vetoed the proposition. After receiving his diploma in 1885, Charlie attended a meeting of the Methodist Conference in Charlotte, where he was ordained a deacon by Bishop J. C. Keener. He then went to see his "Uncle Ricaud," who had been transferred from Wilmington to Washington, North Carolina. From that small, quiet town on the Pamlico River, Charlie wrote to Annie Southgate, reporting that he was having "a very pleasant time. . . . They say there are seven girls to one boy. And some of them are very beautiful. I have fallen in love with Miss Bell. Don't you think that is too bad, for I have to leave my heart in Washington and I go to China. . . ." Apparently the young deacon also left a favorable impression with Miss Eula Bell, who later recalled that he dressed well, had beautiful manners, and was "much better looking than any of his photographs suggested."[35]

From Washington, Soon went to Wilmington, where he renewed old acquaintances and preached several times in the Fifth Street Methodist Church, the scene of his conversion to Christianity five years before. The Reverend D. H. Tuttle, Dr. Ricaud's successor, said Soon spoke "in good English, and to the spiritual edification of all who heard him," and Tuttle's praise may have mitigated the sadness Charlie must have felt as he traveled about the state, saying goodbye to friends he might never see again.[36]

While Charlie Soon was thus engaged, the man who had denied him the opportunity to study medicine was planning his future. On 8 July 1885, Bishop Holland McTyeire wrote to Dr. Young J. Allen, the director of all missionary activities of the Southern Methodist Church in China and a resident of Shanghai, saying,

> We expect to send Soon out to you this fall, with Dr. Park. I trust you will put him, at once, to *circuit work*, walking if not riding. Soon wished to stay a year or two longer to study medi-

cine to be equipped for higher usefulness, etc. And his generous patron, Mr. Julian Carr, was not unwilling to continue helping.

But we thought it better that the *Chinaman* that is in him should not be worked out before he labors among the Chinese. Already he has "felt the easy chair"—and is not averse to the comforts of higher civilization. No fault of his.

Let our young man, on whom we have bestowed labor, begin to *labor*. Throw him into the ranks: *no side place*. His desire to study medicine was met by the information that we already had as many *doctors* as the Mission needed, and one more.

I have good hope that, with your judicious handling, our Soon may do well. It will greatly encourage similar work here if he does. The destinies of many are bound up in his case. . . .[37]

Soon had known for five years that eventually he would go home, but taking leave of his friends, especially the Carrs and the Southgates, was far more difficult than he had expected. Indeed, it would have been even harder had he known the kind of "judicious handling" he would receive when he arrived in Shanghai during the winter of 1886. As soon as he reported to Dr. Allen, he discovered that his superior not only disliked native missionaries, but also considered it unnecessary to treat them "with ordinary human courtesy, let alone Christian charity." Allen's attitude came as a tremendous shock to Soon, and he wrote to the Southgates: "I am very much displeased with this sort of authority, but I must bear it patiently. If I were to take a rash action the people at home (my Durham friends especially) might think that I am an unloyal Methodist and a lawbreaker; so I have kept as silent as a mouse."[38]

Charlie continued to maintain his silence and to conceal his feelings about Dr. Allen for almost six years while he taught school and preached the gospel in Woosung, Soochow, and, finally, Shanghai. During those years he married a Christian girl, Ni Kwei-tseng, the intelligent, well-educated daughter of Chinese Episcopalians, in a match arranged by her brother-in-law. He also took a job as salesman with the American Bible Company in order to supplement his salary of fifteen American dollars a month. He joined the Hung P'ang, or Red Gang, a revolutionary brotherhood dedicated to the overthrow of the Manchu dynasty that had ruled China since 1618. Finally, he founded the Hua-Mei Shu Kuan, or Sino-American Press, which printed inexpensive Bibles and other religious literature for the masses—and, secretly, revolutionary tracts for the Hung P'ang. In 1892 he was successful enough to sever his connection with Dr. Allen. After resigning from the Southern Methodist China Mission, Charlie changed the spelling of his name fron Soon to Soong.[39]

Through his secret society Soong met Dr. Sun Yat-sen, an unsuccessful physician who had dedicated his life to freeing China from the Manchus and defending it against the Communists. Having lived in a democracy, Charlie was in complete sympathy with "the little doctor" who wanted to consolidate the many factions opposed to absolute monarchy into one Young China party, and, by peaceful revolution, to unseat the Manchus and establish a government by and for the people. The former missionary became secretary and treasurer of the former doctor's proposed political party; because Sun Yat-sen's revolutionary activities forced him to spend most of his time in hiding, Soong also became his cover-up man.

While surreptitiously serving the cause of freedom, Soong openly advocated the industrialization of China, something he was inspired to do after he saw how laborers were worked like animals but not treated half so well. Because he was already familiar with printing presses, it was not difficult for him to learn to install and operate machines used in the manufacture of flour and cotton. Once his mechanical proficiency became known, he was offered, and accepted, a job running a mill owned by one of Shanghai's wealthy merchant families. As manager and "English Secretary" of the Fou Foong Flour Mill, Soong was on his way to the financial success his associates attributed to the fact that "his mind had been moulded in America and was essentially Western."[40]

One of the most powerful molders of Charlie Soong's mind was Julian Carr. While living at Waverly Honor, Charlie could see for himself what business acumen, ambition, and charisma had done for his surrogate father. That he tried, either consciously or unconsciously, to emulate Carr seems evident, for after leaving the mission field, Soong became a successful businessman and an advocate of public education, as well as a philanthropist who built a Methodist church in Shanghai and established China's first YMCA. Like Carr, he also became the proud and loving father of six children.

Soong and Kwei-tsing brought up three daughters and three sons in an atmosphere of "devout Christianity, genuine culture and . . . gracious living" that reflected, in some ways, the climate of both

Waverly Honor and the Braxton Craven home at Trinity College.[41] Their house in the suburbs of Shanghai's Hongkew District had a second story, an unusual feature in a Chinese dwelling. It also had both an upstairs and a downstairs porch and two living rooms, one typically Chinese and the other unmistakably American. The latter had an open fireplace, book-lined walls, arm chairs, and a piano; and the upstairs rooms were furnished with American beds and mattresses. Sun Yat-sen often found refuge from his enemies in that house, where Soong's children called him "Uncle Sun" and grew up believing that his "Three Principles of the People"—nationalism, democracy, and socialism—would someday be the salvation of their homeland.

Convinced that his children needed American education and exposure to Western ideas, Soong sent his daughters to Wesleyan College in Macon, Georgia (the youngest also attended Wellesley, in Massachusetts), and his sons to Harvard. Eventually all of them came home and took part in governing the Chinese Republic, which was established in 1911, after several abortive attempts by "Uncle Sun" and his followers. T. V. (Tse-ven) Soong became minister of finance, minister of foreign affairs, and chairman of the Economic Council, with jurisdiction over public health, highway construction, and the improvement of agriculture. The middle son, T. L. (Tse-liang), was director of the Federal Bank and chairman of the Whangpoo Conservatory Bureau that controlled Shanghai harbor. T. A. (Tse-an) Soong "held a position analagous to First Secretary of the Treasury" and administered the Salt Gabelle tax that provided the government with one-fifth of its entire revenue. T. A. Soong later moved to America and managed the San Francisco branch of the Bank of Canton.

Soong's daughters, Ai-ling, Ching-ling, and May-ling, were intelligent, strong-willed women whose husbands, not surprisingly, played major roles in the political and military drama that was unfolding in China. H. H. Kung, the extremely wealthy seventy-fifth male descendant of Confucius, was a banker and an alumnus of Yale University; he was also, at various times, China's minister of finance and minister of commerce and industry, and Charlie was not displeased when Ai-ling married him. On the other hand, he was horrified when Ching-ling ran away with Sun Yat-sen, a married man old enough to be her father. Although the little doctor divorced his wife in order to marry Ching-ling, Charlie never forgave his former great friend. Nor would Charlie likely have forgiven May-ling when she staged her rebellion against his strong Methodist principles and accepted General Chiang Kai-shek, "an uneducated peasant whose only ability was the art of warfare" and a Buddhist who already had a wife and several concubines.

Death had already called Charlie to what he called "the garden of God in Heaven" when his youngest daughter married the general, but Kwei-tsing, Charlie's widow, suffered enough for both of them. Even though Chiang Kai-shek divorced his wife, divested himself of his concubines, and made May-ling the first lady when he became president of the Republic of China, Madame Soong did not regain peace of mind until her warlord son-in-law embraced Christianity and was baptized at her home on Seymour Road in 1930.

Almost twenty-five years before that historic conversion, when Charlie Soong was thirty-nine years old, he crossed the Pacific Ocean on a liner bound for San Francisco. A little later he crossed the American continent on a series of trains that brought him eventually to Durham, where he visited Julian Carr for several weeks.[42] Ostensibly, Soong had come to the United States to see his daughter, Ai-ling, at Wesleyan College; to arrange for Ching-ling and May-ling to attend a preparatory school in Summit, New Jersey; and to see the cherished friend who had given him his start in life. Some believe, however, that raising funds for the Chinese revolution was Soong's top priority and that the biggest American donor to that cause was Julian Carr. As no proof of this assumption has been found, it can only be viewed as an interesting rumor based entirely on Carr's fabled generosity and his never-ending sympathy for the underdog.

8. Losses and Gains

JULIAN CARR must have taken great pleasure in squiring around Durham the Chinese merchant prince whom he had once called "Son," and Charlie Soong must have been amazed at the changes he saw in the place he had once called home. The bustling little town he had left in 1885 had more than tripled its population, and although factories and warehouses still dominated the scene and filled the air with the smell of bright leaf, Durham no longer was merely a tobacco town. Among its 18,000 residents were doctors, lawyers, ministers, teachers, and businessmen of all kinds. Its corporate limits had been increased from one square mile to just under four square miles.

Within those limits were thirty-four churches, six grammar schools, five banks, four cotton mills, three newspaper offices, two hospitals, two hotels, two hosiery mills, two telegraph offices, and a telephone company with eight hundred subscribers. A police department, water department, health department, and fire department made life safer for Durham's inhabitants; a gas company, electric light company, ice plant, and street railway made it far more convenient than it had been in Soong's days. A county court house and a municipal building added dignity to the business district, and the new high school, the public library, and the conservatory of music proclaimed that Durham residents had developed an appreciation for learning and culture. As evidence that residents also were engaged in a serious battle against mud and dust, there were seventy miles of paved streets, sixty-two miles of streetcar tracks, and at least one mile of concrete sidewalks in the center of town.[1]

A few miles west of that center stood Charlie Soong's alma mater, Trinity College, which had been moved from Randolph County to Durham in 1892. Soong and his host may have discussed that move while they "renewed their old friendship and re-discovered the ties of affection which bound them together." If by chance Soong had failed to hear about Julian Carr's role in bringing Trinity to Durham from Carr himself, no doubt he heard the story at the Commonwealth Club on the corner of Main and Market streets, where "he spent long hours conversing with his old college mates" about business and church affairs, and also about "the promising future of the college in its new setting."[2]

When Soong had last seen Trinity, in 1885, its future had been anything but promising. Indeed, had not Julian Carr, John Alspaugh, and James Gray taken over the management of its affairs from 1884 to 1886, he might never have seen it again. Their contributions of time and money had enabled the college to survive, and on 9 June 1886, Carr was named chairman of a committee to select a president, which the school had lacked for almost two years.[3]

On the recommendation of philosophy professor Horace Williams, who had taught briefly at Trinity before joining the faculty of the University of North Carolina, Carr decided to interview John Franklin Crowell, who had been Williams's friend and classmate at Yale before becoming principal of Schuylkill Seminary in Fredericksburg, Pennsylvania. Williams assured Carr that Crowell, a divinity school graduate and Larned Scholar in Philosophy, was both a progressive educator and a skilled administrator. Because Carr felt that such a combination was exactly what struggling Trinity College needed, he arranged to meet Crowell in Philadelphia, possibly at the Bellevue-Stratford, his home away from home. After several lengthy conversations with the twenty-nine-year-old candidate, Carr returned to Durham full of enthusiasm for Crowell and convinced that he was, as Horace Williams had said, "the right man for the job."[4]

As might have been expected, there was opposition to the appointment of a man who was neither a southerner nor a Methodist. It took considerable detailed correspondence with the trustees before John Franklin Crowell persuaded most of them that he was deeply and sincerely interested in the South and that he was confident of putting Trinity "in the front ranks." Finally, on the strength of Crowell's letters and Julian Carr's unqualified endorsement, the board made an offer. Crowell accepted without ever having seen the college he proposed to place on a par with Davidson, Wake Forest, and the state university at Chapel Hill.[5]

When Crowell did see the "crude and almost featureless three-story brick structure doing duty as a college on a 10-acre sandhill in the Old North State of America," all he could manage to say was: "Is this Trinity?" Shocked almost to the point of resigning, Crowell spent a sleepless night wrestling with his conscience. He finally decided to stay, he said, because of "the spirit the Institution had engendered, and . . . the faith which the people had in its future—if I would consent to lead them." Having given that consent, he began his presidency by initiating a number of changes in the curriculum, by hiring six new faculty members, and by taking it upon himself to teach nine courses in history.[6]

Soon after Crowell was formally installed as president at the commencement of 1887, the trustees voted to establish an endowment of $100,000 by "persistently appealing" to every Methodist in the state and giving whatever contributions they collected to James Gray for investment. When Julian Carr became the first man to respond to the appeal by turning over to Gray $10,000 worth of stock in the Durham Cotton Manufacturing Company, the chairman of the endowment committee called it "a high day for Trinity."

But many low days were to come. After the enthusiasm generated by Carr's gift subsided, North Carolina's Methodists seemed to forget about the endowment. During the months to follow they virtually ignored the financial needs of their little college, and the president and the faculty often had to go without pay. Finally, in 1889, Crowell convinced the board of trustees and the North Carolina Conference that Trinity's only hope lay in moving from its rural setting in Randolph County to a city, "where the jobs, the money, and the activity were centered."[7]

Julian Carr initially opposed Crowell's proposition and spoke out against it, as did many influential Methodists who felt that students should not be exposed to "urban vices." Crowell argued successfully that sin could be controlled by law in a city, however, whereas nothing short of violence could banish "the harlots that stalk the streets of Trinity." Carr thereupon not only gave his support to the move, but also joined forces with his old adversary, Washington Duke, in an effort to bring the college to Durham.[8]

Until Raleigh offered $35,000 for Trinity College, which the North Carolina Conference accepted, Duke had not demonstrated much concern for the school beyond contributing $1,000 to the endowment fund that was established in 1887. But the seed of interest in Methodist-sponsored education had been planted in Washington Duke's mind when the Baptists of North Carolina decided to build a female seminary in Raleigh, even though they had been offered much more money by "pushy little Durham."[9] Duke, basically an unpretentious man, probably paid little attention to the fact that the cultured city of Raleigh had always "lifted an eyebrow" at the slightest mention of his hometown; but when the Baptist State Convention refused an offer of $50,000 from Durham because "it was no fit place for innocent girls to abide in," he became angry enough to outbid Raleigh for Trinity College.[10]

Julian Carr, who had offered "to add five dollars to every dollar subscribed by local Baptists" when Durham was bidding for the seminary, also had been offended by the snub, for he was a well-known benefactor of the Baptist-supported Wake Forest College.[11] Reaction to the insult made him more receptive to President Crowell's pleas for help. When Crowell told him that Duke had guaranteed to match Raleigh's offer of $35,000 and to "also provide an additional $50,000 for endowment," Carr responded to Crowell's request for land by offering his sixty-acre racetrack, Blackwell Park, as a site for the college. The North Carolina Methodist Conference immediately asked for, and subsequently received, a release from its prior commitment to Raleigh. John Franklin Crowell's dream of Trinity "as a university, with other Methodist colleges in the state in affiliation" then began its long journey toward reality.[12]

Blackwell Park was Carr's last major contribution to Trinity, for as the college began to come more and more under the influence of the Dukes, his interest waned. The united front that he and Washington Duke had presented to the public in 1890 dissolved a year later, when the recently formed American Tobacco Company, of which Duke's youngest son, Buck, was president, bought out two Baltimore factories in quick succession and became the nation's largest producer of smoking tobacco.[13] Alarmed by that serious and painful thrust at his Durham Bull, Carr vowed never to sell to the "unholy, unrighteous trust," but he was too shrewd and too seasoned in the dog-eat-dog tactics of big business to blind himself to the fact that he and Sam Austin and the McDowell brothers were in deep trouble.

Buck Duke was determined to gain control of the entire tobacco industry. Although Carr and his partners did not share the fate of many manufacturers who "watched their businesses slip into the hands of the American Tobacco Company or into bankruptcy," there is no denying that such happenings made them uneasy. Nor were they alone—even Richard Joshua Reynolds, one of the toughest and most knowledgeable tobacco men in the South, "feared that his well-organized and prosperous manufacturing interests would be acquired by the trust," which was effectively discouraging competition either by buying it up or by running it out of business.[14]

But competition did continue, at least for a time. In 1898, Thomas

Fortune Ryan, Peter A. B. Widener, William C. Whitney, and Anthony N. Brady formed the Union Tobacco Company and began to round up the last important manufacturers of smoking tobacco, plug tobacco, and cigarettes. These four powerful financiers, who seemed not to be intimidated by American's aggressive president, made substantial offers to Blackwell's Durham Tobacco Company, the National Cigarette Company of New York, and Liggett and Myers Company of St. Louis—so substantial that Blackwell's and National agreed to sell, and Liggett gave Union an option on the controlling portion of its stock.[15]

Like other outspoken opponents of the tobacco trust, Julian Carr no doubt was happy to hear that wealthy New York industrialists planned to "make it hot for Duke," but the fact that they paid almost $3,000,000 for Blackwell's Durham Tobacco Company did not ease all the pain of parting.[16] At a family gathering shortly after the transaction took place, the grace he pronounced before Sunday dinner was so packed with petitions to the Almighty to bless and sanction the sale to Union that the soup was cold by the time he said "Amen," and those who were at the table, hearing his voice break, looked up to see tears running down his cheeks.[17] Losing the business and the brand he had helped to make world famous was a traumatic experience for Carr; it was even worse when, in 1899, the Union Tobacco Company sold out to the trust for American Tobacco Company stock worth $12,500,000.[18] Many voices cried "foul," and a writer for the Raleigh *News and Observer* said, in 1900, "What force failed to do was afterward accomplished by indirection; a 'fake' opposition . . . was organized to which Carr was induced to sell in hope of producing a strong and healthful competition, and under assurance that 'Blackwell's Durham' never should pass under control of the American Tobacco Company."[19]

But if Carr was duped—and there were those who believed him the victim of a highly skilled maneuver—it never was proven. One of the hard facts he was forced to accept was that he and his partners had been bested by a younger man whose singleness of purpose was awesome to contemplate. Buck Duke, who since 1883 had "watched with envy the advance of the Bull," finally captured that legendary animal in 1899. Jule Carr, whose battle cry had been "Let buffalo gore buffalo and the pasture go to the strongest," was forced to admit defeat as gracefully as possible.[20]

Fortunately, Carr had staked out a claim on another pasture that would prove almost as fertile as the one his Durham Bull had roamed for sixteen years. On 17 February 1898, he established the Durham Hosiery Mill, a business he envisioned as "something for my boys." By 1905, when Charlie Soong came to visit him, Carr's dream of a family enterprise had begun to materialize. With Julian Junior and Marvin, he was manufacturing and selling "Durable Durham Hosiery," a product destined to become "only slightly less famous than Bull Durham smoking tobacco." It already had been decided that Claiborn and Austin would follow their brothers into the mill as soon as they graduated from the University of North Carolina.[21]

So the president of the Durham Hosiery Mill and the manager of Shanghai's Fou Foong Flour Mill probably avoided the subject of Buck Duke's tobacco trust, instead discussing the production of American socks and Chinese noodles during long conversations in the library at Somerset Villa. They may also have talked about Dr. Sun Yat-sen's need for money with which to continue his revolution. If Charlie Soong asked Julian Carr for a donation to that cause, it is more than likely that he received it. And it is very likely that, at some time during their reunion, Soong listened while Carr spoke volubly and happily about scientific agriculture, which he had been demonstrating at his model farm since 1892. Although there is no documented evidence that the two men visited the farm just outside Hillsborough in the fall of 1905, it would have been out of character for Julian Carr to have missed the opportunity to show Charlie Soong the wonders of Occoneechee, where he was raising Berkshire swine, Shropshire sheep, Holstein cattle, Belgian hares, Shetland ponies, thoroughbred horses, pheasants, peafowl, guineas, ducks, geese, chickens, parrots, birds of paradise, and even monkeys.[22]

Carr's desire for a home in the country, where he could escape with his family from the intense heat that blanketed Durham in July and August, undoubtedly influenced his decision to buy the estate in Orange County when it became available in 1891; his interest in scientific agriculture then prompted him to transform the place into a model farm. That interest had been sparked and sustained by the annual state fair, inaugurated in 1853 by the North Carolina State Agricultural Society and held in Raleigh each October. Originally designed to promote agriculture and industry, the fair very quickly became the most important social event of the year for many people, especially those who lived on remote farms or in isolated villages like Chapel Hill, Carr's childhood home.[23]

Being the son of a prosperous merchant who could afford the trip by special train to Raleigh, young Julian Carr probably accompanied his family to the state fair every year until the Civil War brought it to a temporary halt in 1861. There can be little doubt that he was dazzled each time by the opening-day parade, when officers of the agricultural society and fair marshals, all on horseback, led a procession of marching bands and military units from the courthouse to the fairgrounds.[24] And if, like so many small boys, he dreamed of leading such a procession himself one day in the distant future, that dream would eventually come true—not once, but twice.

After Carr became a partner in the W. T. Blackwell Company, he also became a highly visible member of the North Carolina State Agricultural Society. In 1877 he served on the executive board and co-chaired the department of mechanic arts, which exhibited stoves, copper stills, furniture, earthenware, many types of vehicles, and samples of woodwork and house paint.[25] The following year he again managed the display of mechanical arts, and in 1879 he was in charge of the poultry exhibit. In 1880 his duties as chairman of the department of dairy and garden products did not prevent him from planning and executing a W. T. Blackwell Company float that proved to be one of the most popular features of the opening-day parade. His mobile advertisement of the firm's famous product included "an immense Durham Bull ridden by a negro boy" and a six-horse bandwagon carrying "a number of colored employees putting up the fragrant weed while they sang the quaint songs peculiar to their race."[26]

Considering the amount of time, energy, imagination, and money that Carr contributed to the state fair each year, it is not surprising that his status in the agricultural society rose steadily. Except for a six-year interval from 1881 until 1887, he was a member of the executive board from 1877 until 1894, when he was elected president of the society and rode with the governor at the head of the opening-day parade. By then he had been "landed gentry" for three years, and at his farm in Orange County, which had become one of the showplaces of North Carolina, he was demonstrating his belief that innovative methods, resulting in superior products, could solve most of the problems of agrarian life.

On 25 April 1891 Carr paid $10,000 to James Hogg Norwood and Norwood's sister, Margaret, for an eighteenth-century farmhouse and 663 acres of land on the Eno River, just east of Hillsborough and along the North Carolina Railroad. Norwood, also a leader in the agricultural society, was a bachelor whose chief interest lay in raising and selling fighting cocks; he and his sister had been land poor long enough to welcome Carr's offer. Their maternal grandfather, James Hogg, an original trustee of the University of North Carolina, also was the original owner of the land, which had been part of an eleven-hundred-acre tract granted to him by Lord Carteret, earl of Granville, in 1754. Around 1790 he began construction of three homes on the river, one for each of his daughters. In his will he bequeathed the plantation he called Banks of the Eno to his daughter Robina, who married William Norwood. A woman of strong opinions, Robina did not care for that name; as she saw it, the seventeen giant poplars in front of the house had far more beauty and significance than the muddy Eno River, which was visible only from the backyard. As soon as she took possession of the place, she changed its name to Poplar Hill.[27]

The Norwood clan, as well as other long-time residents of Hillsborough, were shocked when Julian Carr announced that he intended to call his newly acquired estate Occoneechee, after an Indian tribe that once had lived in the vicinity. Carr apparently was oblivious to raised eyebrows and whispered innuendos about nouveau riche manufacturers with no regard for tradition, and he was determined to establish his ownership in name as well as in deed. Out on the highway, above a massive pair of gateposts that marked the entrance to a cedar-lined driveway, two red fieldstone posts supported a wrought-iron arch that spelled out "Occoneechee Farm." The posts were topped with jagged rocks reminiscent of tomahawks, and the palings of the heavy iron gates beneath the arch were pointed, like arrowheads.

For thirty years those gates would swing open to "the wealth and beauty of the State" whenever the Carrs entertained at a reception, a dance, or a barbecue. On sunny Easter Mondays, droves of chattering children from Sunday schools in Durham and Hillsborough would swarm down the driveway, eager to look at the animals in the barnyards and pastures and to picnic under the ancient trees.[28] But long before that unconventional gateway was completed, a succession of carpenters, bricklayers, stonemasons, tinsmiths, and other artisans came to expand and remodel the "big house" that would be the Carr family's summer retreat; to build a resident manager's home and an office for transacting farm business; and to construct, by degrees and at great cost, a number of elaborate dependencies. Among these were a sizeable barn for sheep; a large piggery with several breeding pens; a concrete-floored dairy barn with fifty-six stanchions; five poultry houses, each large enough to accommodate three hundred chickens; and an enormous three-story barn with a slate roof, oak floors, stalls for thirty-six horses, and a basement for mules.[29]

These were the necessities, in Carr's opinion, but there were luxuries, too. One was an outdoor living room, screened against insects and equipped with a shower bath; another was a "club house" designed especially for parties and dancing.[30] With its huge stone fireplace, gleaming hardwood floor, and wide, inviting porch, the club house appealed to Carr's two daughters, who were students at an exclusive boarding school in Washington, D.C., and who often invited roommates from "up North" to visit during summer vacations. For these young ladies and their carefully chosen escorts, a dance at the club house was a gala affair; but any kind of party at Carr's farm was a memorable experience, particularly for guests who lived above the Mason-Dixon line.

One young lady from Pennsylvania, feted by the Carrs at a Fourth of July picnic in 1893, rode "in a dray pulled by four spanking bays draped in flags" from Somerset Villa to Occoneechee, twelve hot, dusty miles away. There, with twenty-eight voluble Southerners, she celebrated Independence Day by eating barbecued pork, singing "Dixie," and watching a parade comprised of a hundred sheep, fifty swine, twenty cows, fifteen yearling colts, ten brood mares, ten Shetland ponies, ten two- and three-year-old horses, and one thoroughbred trotter named Miss Wandoo.[31] Had it been feasible to swell that caravan with the fifteen hundred chickens, ducks, geese, and guinea fowl that occupied Julian Carr's poultry yards, no doubt he would have done just that, for nothing delighted him more than showing off his livestock to wide-eyed, impressionable young people.

Carr never bothered to conceal his pride in Occoneechee or his pleasure in the fact that, except for the natural beauty of land, river, and sky, he was responsible for all of it. He had rescued Poplar Hill from the genteel decay into which it had fallen after the Civil War, and with imagination, money, and the knowledge of farming that he had acquired through the agricultural society, he created a miniature kingdom that retained much of the flavor of the Old South. At the same time, Occoneechee exhibited much that was modern: electricity, acetylene gas, running water, and sewerage disposal made life easier and cleaner than it ever had been for the aristocratic Norwoods.

Club House and Big House at Occoneechee Farm
(courtesy of Rufus Tucker Carr)

Their antebellum home, neglected, of necessity, for over twenty-five years, was transformed by Carr's eccentric friend, Jule Gilmer Korner, into an eight-room plantation house with white columns, a balcony over the double front doors, and three bathrooms.[32]

Korner, as Reuben Rink, had captured world attention in 1883 with his spirited paintings of the Durham Bull. In 1888, when he embellished the walls and ceilings of Somerset Villa with exquisite plaster moldings, he created an expanding demand for his talents. Shortly after the cornerstone-laying at Somerset, Korner established the Durham Manufacturers' Home Furnishing Agency, and by 1891, when Carr hired him to oversee the remodeling of Occoneechee's "big house," Korner was the state's foremost interior decorator. In return for the free rein Carr gave him, Korner provided Carr with an elegant country house "of Colonial design . . . furnished throughout with colonial furniture," and Occoneechee Farm, like Somerset Villa, became famous for its hospitality.[33]

Seven years prior to his work at Occoneechee, Korner designed and built prize-winning exhibits for Blackwell's Durham Tobacco Company at both the North Carolina state fair and the World's Fair in New Orleans. In 1894, when Julian Carr was serving his first term

Occoneechee Farm (courtesy of Rufus Tucker Carr)

as president of the agricultural society, the reproduction of "the great Ferris wheel at the Chicago World's Fair" that advertised Bull Durham tobacco probably was Korner's creation. The wheel, its passenger cars brimming with tobacco and its entire surface layered with bright yellow leaves, appeared as a revolving circle of gold that dominated the exhibition hall. The Occoneechee Farm display, housed nearby in three dome-shaped booths "handsomely furnished without regard to expense," was another eye-catcher. Large tubs filled with oats, hay, wheat, rye, soybeans, pumpkins, carrots, cymblings, and grains of corn "as big as the tooth of an ox" proclaimed the fertility of Carr's fields, and a three-foot-high American eagle made of Occoneechee butter advertised the superior quality of one of his best-known dairy products.

Elsewhere in the exhibition hall were specimens of iron ore from Carr's Bessemer City Mining Company, bolts of cloth from his Durham Cotton Manufacturing Company, and a variety of bags from his Golden Belt Manufacturing Company. According to the Raleigh *News and Observer*, these exhibits proved beyond a doubt that "Col. J. S. Carr practices what he preaches. He has been preaching a great big State Fair for 12 months and for 2 months has been working steadily in a practical way to make the fair big." One result of Carr's

*Boating on the Eno River behind Occoneechee Farm
(courtesy of Rufus Tucker Carr)*

campaign for the largest fair in the state's history was the arrival of thirteen carloads of "the finest and most magnificent stock, including the famous Holstein-Fresian bull which took the premium at the Great World's Fair at Chicago." This unprecedented influx of animals required the construction of one hundred extra stalls; carpenters also had to build two hundred additional coops for the twelve hundred fowl that constituted the poultry exhibit.[34]

For children of all ages, "Wombwell's Show of Trained Wild Animals," featuring lions, tigers, hyenas, wolves, monkeys, an elephant, and the "only specimen of a bovalupus in Captivity," was a special attraction. For adults who favored the sport of kings there was racing every day, with many out-of-state entries in both the trotting and running classes. Young and old alike watched with "wonder, admiration and astonishment" the Cyclorama of the Battle of Gettysburg, a spectacle that helped to attract 12,000 people to the fair on the final day.[35]

Carr's successful leadership in 1894 insured his reelection to the presidency of the agricultural society. In 1895, when he rode with Governor Elias Carr in a carriage that led the parade, his pleasure was increased by the fact that his seventeen-year-old son, Julian Junior, a sophomore at the University of North Carolina, was one of the marshals who followed on horseback. Beginning at the Yarborough House, Raleigh's leading hotel, the procession moved up Fayetteville Street, circled the capitol building to Hillsborough Street, and continued on to the fairgrounds. There the governor asserted, in a "brief and breezy" speech, that low excursion rates, fair weather, and fair women were the most important ingredients of a successful fair.[36]

Julian Carr knew that sunny skies, pretty faces, and penny-a-mile train fares were not enough to guarantee success. The public wanted entertainment. People no longer were willing to drive long miles in wagons and buggies or to ride trains to Raleigh simply to learn about improved methods of irrigation and tobacco cultivation, or how to grow indigenous and foreign grapes, or new ways to make cheese. Speeches about those very subjects were on the agenda in 1895, and interested farmers sat in the hall of the House of Representatives and listened to them. But many fairgoers preferred to watch the six-furlong dash for thoroughbreds, or the tournaments where "knights" on horseback attempted to gallop ninety yards in eight seconds for the privilege of crowning the Queen of Love and Beauty at the agricultural society's Coronation Ball.

Balls, parties, and plays performed by touring theatrical companies were an important part of fair week, especially for Raleigh socialites and their guests, who often spent the early evening in a darkened theater and the rest of the night in a brilliantly lit ballroom. Less sophisticated visitors enjoyed the carnival atmosphere of the midway, with its freaks, exotic animals, and games of chance; and country folk, as a rule, liked to listen to the impassioned speeches of well-known politicians. Those who came primarily to see purebred livestock, improved seeds and fertilizers, and the newest farm implements were not disappointed. In 1895 they watched the McCormick Harvesting Machine in action, and at the Occoneechee exhibit they saw samples of rye, wheat, and barley that measured over five feet in length, plus a life-size cow made of butter "as hard as a hickory nut." Julian Carr had been farming for four years, and in addition to marketing grain and dairy products, he was breeding and selling Shetland ponies, English setters, peafowl, Pekin ducks, Black Essex hogs, registered Jersey bull calves, and both thoroughbred and standard-bred horses.[37]

The owner of Occoneechee would continue to show his products at future state fairs, but he had decided, before the 1895 exposition opened, to decline a third consecutive presidency of the agricultural society. While he would give as his excuse "the press of business," several factors had contributed to his decision to step down. One was a desire for political office that had been kindled in 1892 by friends who envisioned him as the ideal governor of North Carolina. Another was his wife's health, which had been delicate since the birth of their sixth child, Austin, in 1894. Still another was his eldest daughter's approaching marriage.

Eliza Morehead Carr, who was always called Lida, had been courted successfully by Henry Corwin Flower, a prominent attorney from Kansas City, Missouri, who was the only son of a wealthy widow. Plans for a December wedding at Somerset Villa were in the making; as the day approached, it may have behooved Carr to curtail some of his activities and spend more time with his wife and children, who often inspired him to fatuous declarations of affection. He had always been a doting husband and father, on one occasion confessing to Cornelia Spencer of Chapel Hill that "Providence has been especially kind to me in the selection of my wife. I have *one of the best*. I married her for pure love, and we are still in love. You must excuse this little bit of family history, but I have such a handsome, lovable wife, and such dear nice children, and feel that they contribute so much to make life pleasant, and to them I am due such a large measure of my success, that I can never approach the subject without 'slopping over,' if you will pardon the expression."[38]

Carr's pride in his family must have been highly evident on the last night of his presidency of the agricultural society, when all but the two youngest boys accompanied him to the Marshal's Ball, one of the most important social functions of fair week. Most of those in attendance already knew that Bennehan Cameron, of Durham County, was to replace Carr as president of the society, but the general public was not informed until the following morning. Under a headline that proclaimed "THE KING IS DEAD, LONG LIVE THE KING!," the Raleigh *News and Observer* announced that "Col. Julian S. Carr, who has given to North Carolina the two best fairs ever held in the borders of the State, declined a reelection last night of the Presidency of

Julian S. Carr with Austin Heaton Carr
(courtesy of Austin Heaton Carr, Jr.)

the North Carolina State Agricultural Society and Col. Benehan Cameron, of Durham County, was elected to succeed him." The owner of Stagville Plantation, which had been home to over a thousand slaves before the Civil War, was a well-known and wealthy breeder of fine horses, and fair officials were hoping that his plans to upgrade the racing program would result in a substantial increase in revenues.[39]

Six days after the 1895 fair ended, Julian and Nannie Carr went to Philadelphia to engage the services of florists and caterers for Lida's wedding, to complete the trousseau she had begun to acquire the previous summer in Europe, and to outfit the rest of the family for the grand occasion, which was to take place on 18 December.[40] While conferences with dressmakers, tailors, decorators, and chefs consumed the days, leaving little time for rest and less for contemplation, there may have been nights when Carr, lying in his bed at the Bellevue-Stratford, looked back over the twenty-one years since Lida's birth and remembered some of the milestones—her first heart-catching smile, perhaps, or her first triumphant steps into his outstretched arms. And like any devoted father of a bride-to-be, he may have recalled the day when he took her to school for the first time.

Having two young daughters to educate had prompted Carr to join a group of his fellow churchmen in establishing the Methodist Female Seminary. The school began operations on 4 September 1881 under the aegis of a five-member board of trustees, of which he was president. Mrs. Julia R. Williams, who had taught at a similar institution in Staunton, Virginia, was the first principal. With the trustees' approval, Mrs. Williams offered five months of instruction in French, Latin, music, drawing, painting, and calisthenics to girls whose fathers could afford the tuition of fifty-five dollars a session.[41]

Housed in a frame building on the Trinity Methodist Church grounds, the seminary began each day with divine worship, dispensed knowledge from standard textbooks, and maintained firm discipline in a "high-toned and generous" manner. It also encouraged pupils to "emulate all that is lovely and beautiful in female character" and put special emphasis on the importance of duty and honor. Lida Carr and her sister, Lalla Ruth, were among the first Durham girls to attend; they continued to study there, under the shadow of Trinity Church, until they were old enough to be "fin-

Nancy (Nannie) Graham Parrish Carr (courtesy of Austin Heaton Carr, Jr.)

ished" at Miss Summers' School, a prestigious establishment in Washington, D.C., that later became Mount Vernon College.[42]

After Lida's graduation from Miss Summers' School, she experienced a hiatus that only the daughters of the rich were privileged to enjoy. Always properly chaperoned, she exchanged long visits with former schoolmates, met eligible bachelors, became a popular hostess and an equally popular guest at parties and balls, and was exposed to culture and high fashion in Philadelphia, New York, and Europe. It was while visiting a friend in Kansas City that she met Henry Corwin Flower, fourteen years her senior and "a gentleman of high culture, with a most lucrative practice both in this country and in Europe."[43] Flower was obviously a fine catch—and so was Lida Carr, an imperious beauty with a keen mind and a firm hold on her wealthy father's heart.

Lida's wish for a wedding of "simple elegance" was carried out, in so far as that was possible under the circumstances. Newspapers in both Kansas City and Durham covered it thoroughly, during the week before Christmas in 1895, and Durham citizens were still talking about it long after the holidays were over. Only family members and close friends of the couple were invited. Most of those who came from Kansas City, Richmond, Washington, Baltimore, Philadelphia, New York, and Chicago were lodged at Durham's newest hotel, one Julian Carr had built two years earlier after deciding that the town badly needed public accommodations "worthy of the rapidly growing influx of business men from all parts of the country."[44]

Carr located his three-story hotel directly behind his bank and just across the tracks from his tobacco factory; he named it, appropriately enough, "The Carrolina." Designed by G. L. Noorman of Atlanta, it was a classic example of the late Victorian style, with turrets, gables, hooded dormers, and a mansard roof that protected seventy rooms, all "handsomely frescoed by well-known artists" and boasting ceilings that compared "very favorably with those of the fine hotels of New York." Constructed and furnished at a cost of $85,000, the building was "equipped with modern appliances, heated and ventilated by improved methods, and had its own electric plant." Its stunning main lobby was decorated in the French rococo style, with a color scheme of "delicate shades of salmon and blue"; a gentlemen's reading room was in Louis XV style, and an Empire-style ladies' reception room opened onto the ivory and gold Louis XVI main parlor.[45] In the Old English atmosphere of the dining room, where paneled walls were

Hotel Carrolina, Durham, North Carolina (courtesy of Albert G. Carr)

hung with fine tapestries, one hundred customers could be seated comfortably. The bill of fare included not only the finest southern cooking, but also such delicacies as lobster mayonnaise, Lynnhaven oysters, and potatoes parisienne.[46] So the out-of-town guests for Lida Carr's wedding probably were pleasantly surprised to discover that Durham was no backwater, and by the time their visit was over, they may have concluded that the bride's father was largely responsible for that fact.

Well before eight o'clock on the night of 18 December 1895, carriages began to roll up the driveway of Somerset Villa through "a glittering maze" of electric lights provided by Hugh A. Graham, one of Philadelphia's outstanding decorators. Earlier that day, after Graham and his staff had studded the grounds at two-foot intervals with "tiny, welcoming flamelets of blue and red and green and white," they festooned the interior of Somerset with ropes and clusters of pink and white roses and carnations, improvising an altar in one of the parlor's bay windows. Another Philadelphian, Carl G. Essner, a former employee of the Waldorf-Astoria hotel in New York, catered the affair. With his own chefs and waiters, Essner arrived by train a day in advance, took over the kitchen and dining room of Carr's house, and transformed two boxcars of imported food into a wedding supper that was "rarely, if ever, surpassed on such an occasion."[47]

Lida Carr, whose trousseau had been created by dressmakers in Paris, Vienna, and Philadelphia, wore an ivory satin gown trimmed with pearls, point lace, and orange blossoms. Later in the evening she changed into a going-away dress of dark green broadcloth lined with violet silk that had been made for her by "Mlle. Charlotte, 47 Fauborg St. Honore, Paris."[48] A dazzled Durham reporter described the bride as "one of the lovliest young women North Carolina has produced" and placed the groom among "the best lawyers in the United States." The same reporter also noted that Adlai Stevenson, vice-president of the United States, had sent the young couple a handsome antique chair, and that the hundreds of wedding presents on display were "the most valuable ever seen in the State."[49]

At two o'clock in the morning, the newlyweds left for St. Augustine, Florida, on a private railroad car that had been "beautifully decorated with cut flowers and other ornaments." Although it was very late and Julian Carr was very tired, he went to his desk in the library and wrote to "Our precious dear darling Lida." Explaining that neither he nor her mother could go to sleep without bidding their "precious Angel child" good night, he continued: "Dear Sweet Mother and I are very sad tonight. As we sit and think of the Sweet Angel, our beloved first born leaving our home and going out into the world, unbidden the tears course down our cheeks."[50]

Although he knew that Lida and her husband would return within a week to spend Christmas at Somerset before going on to Europe, Carr mourned: "You have left us before, but your going has never burdened our hearts with a Shadow comparable to this. We shall both pray that you may ever be happy. While we feel that dear Mr. Flower is all that we could wish mortal to be & that you love each other & he will truly care for and love you, still in spite of all this, our hearts bleed, as they have never bled."

Carr's lament undoubtedly was sincere, but his reaction to this first break in the family circle may have been due more to fatigue than to grief. Daughters, after all, were meant to grow up and marry, and Lida had married extremely well. Henry Flower not only had a brilliant legal mind, he had a talent for finance, too, and his background

Eliza Morehead Carr in her wedding gown (courtesy of Ruth Flower Lester)

Lalla Ruth Carr (courtesy of Ruth Flower Lester)

was impeccable. Carr may have paused to consider these undeniable facts, for the tone of his letter then brightened: "Remember, My Angel, that our Home is always yours and Harry's home. . . . We shall take your Harry into our hearts and he shall be our Harry, and we will love him My Darling with the same pure love with which we have and always will love you. And in our devotions we will link the two names, Lida & Harry, in our petition to our Heavenly Father and commend you both to his loving care. . . ."[51]

Having thus cast his burden onto a higher power, presumably Julian Carr went to sleep with a peaceful mind and awoke with his usual eagerness to begin another day. According to Durham's morning newspaper, Lida's wedding was "one of the most notable functions of the State's history."[52] The presence of Governor Elias Carr and his uniformed staff consisting of one general, two colonels, and four majors had added a nice touch of military glitter to the scene. Everything had gone smoothly, and now Christmas was on the way. Little Austin, not yet two years old, would rekindle the whole family's belief in Santa Claus; and, best of all, Lalla Ruth had completed her course of study at Miss Summers' School and was home to stay for a while.

Lalla Ruth Carr, a striking girl of nineteen, had intense blue eyes, her Grandmother Eliza's square, determined jaw, and an easily triggered, infectious giggle. Friendly, outgoing, and endowed with a keen sense of humor, she very quickly became a popular member of Durham's younger set when her school days were over. The pursuit of pleasure did not top her list of priorities, by any means. In 1896 she acquired a budding sense of social consciousness through membership in the town's first literary organization, the Canterbury Club, which included a number of Trinity College professors on its roster. When an English professor, Edwin Mims, suggested that the club might inject a much-needed dose of culture into the community by sponsoring a public library, Lalla Ruth transmitted her enthusiasm for the project to her father, who not only shared her love of reading but also yearned to erase the North Carolina Baptists' condemnation of Durham as a town lacking in refinement and "unfit for young women in their formative years."[53]

On 30 April 1896, Carr addressed a town meeting that had been called to gather support for Mims's proposal, concluding his speech by saying, "We cannot flatter ourselves that we approach the full measure of what we ought to be as a Christian community until we can boast of a public library." Then, in the name of Lalla Ruth Carr, he donated a building site valued at $2,500, one ideally located at the western end of Main Street in a section known as Five Points. When it was suggested that the pie-shaped piece of property might not be wide enough for a building designed to house a great many books and to provide space for readers, Thomas H. Martin, a prosperous tobacco broker who owned the adjacent lot, agreed to donate the necessary additional footage. These two initial offerings sparked individual subscriptions amounting to over $1,300.[54]

Because that sum fell far short of the estimated $4,000 needed to build an adequate library, a group of Durham women, including Lalla Ruth Carr, formed themselves into a Board of Lady Managers and staged a house-to-house campaign to solicit funds. Their drive was successful, and in 1897 construction began. When it opened on 11 February 1898, the library had the distinction of being the first in the southeast to make books available to the public without payment of dues or fees; because it had been given a stipend of fifty dollars a month by the town council, it also became the first library in North Carolina to receive municipal support.[55]

While Lalla Ruth Carr was helping to improve the cultural and educational climate of Durham, Lida Carr Flower was adjusting to her role as wife, mother, and Kansas City socialite. On 24 January 1897, Lida made Julian Carr a grandfather for the first time when she produced a son, Henry Corwin Flower, Junior; in September 1899 she presented him with a granddaughter whom she named Ruth. Acknowledging the honor, Lalla Ruth wrote to Lida: "You cannot imagine what a proud aunt I am now, nor how happy I was to get the glad message. . . . Although I had determined if this little one had been a boy I should love it devotedly, yet you have no idea how proud and delighted I am that I have such a dear little namesake. It is my most sincere wish that Ruth's pathway in life may be ever filled with sunshine and happiness, and that her old maid 'Auntie' may ever be able to add some pleasure to her life.[56]

"Old maid Auntie" was then twenty-three and possibly already engaged to William Foley Patton, a young lawyer from Curwensville, Pennsylvania, whom she married in 1901. Will Patton, whose sister, Honora, had roomed with Lalla Ruth at Miss Summers' School, was from a family "prominently identified with the best interests of . . . the State of Pennsylvania," and his father, like Lalla Ruth's, had been a highly successful businessman, banker, and promoter of railroads. As a Republican congressman, John Patton also helped to put Abraham Lincoln in the White House, and in 1864 he was "one of the Presidential electors who placed Lincoln at the helm of the government for the second time."[57]

Julian Carr did not allow political differences or his devotion to the beautiful lost cause of the Confederacy to interfere with what one Durham newspaper called "a love affair that binds together North Carolina and Pennsylvania . . . in closer ties of love and affection." With commendable magnanimity, he gave Lalla Ruth a wedding that surpassed even Lida's in grandeur. "One of the most elaborate affairs in the history of the state," according to the local press, it was attended by "the elite of the south." For the second time, Hugh Graham came down from Philadelphia to decorate Somerset Villa and Trinity Church. In order to do a proper job for one of his wealthiest and most generous clients, Graham used 1,400 Easter lilies, 2,500 carnations, 500 yards of asparagus fern, 200 American Beauty roses, 1,000 sweet peas, 2,500 double violets, 800 white roses, 1,000 lilies of the valley, 2,000 white and yellow daisies, 100 spires of japonica, 200 potted palms, and 50 azalea plants. Maintaining his reputation as "a decorator with a lavish hand," Graham also brought along enough electrical equipment to light Carr's church, as well as his home, with "thousands of fairy lamps." He set a new record for ingenuity by designing Lalla Ruth's bouquet of white violets and lilies of the valley in such a way that, when she threw it from the top landing of the stairway, it separated into eight smaller bouquets—one for each bridesmaid, and one for her mother.

That astonishing bouquet and Graham's elaborate decorations elicited a great deal of animated discussion among Durham's citizens. Carr also had engaged a famed Fifth Avenue caterer to feed his guests and a band of Russian musicians to entertain them; while Louis Sherry and a corps of twenty-seven assistants served such delicacies as terrapin and Nesselrode pudding to the assembled company, the Russians played "entrancing music throughout the evening."[58] One small neighbor, too young to accompany her parents to the wedding reception at Somerset but old enough to watch and listen from a nearby porch, remembered throughout a long lifetime "all the lights, like a million fireflies twinkling in the dark, and the ladies and gentlemen in their fine clothes going up the walk to the big house, and the sound of music whenever the door opened."[59]

When the music had ceased and the double front doors had closed on the last guest and the bride and groom had departed, Julian Carr probably suffered the same sense of loss he had known when Lida married Harry; but at the age of fifty-seven, he was more philosophical than he had been at fifty. He had learned, in those seven years, that the pain of a loss eased after a while, even when you had lost what you thought was your heart's desire. He had discovered this when he realized he would never be a governor or senator from North Carolina. He had come close to both offices, but the Populist party had blocked his path to the governor's mansion in 1892, and in 1896 his own wife had used her influence to keep him out of that house.

To tell the truth, it wasn't much of a house compared to Somerset Villa (sparsely furnished, no central heating, and, of all things, outside privies!), but the power of high office was there. Had he possessed that power in 1900, could he have been defeated in the race for the senatorship?

He liked to think not.

9. Adventures in Politics

H AD it not been for a widespread agricultural depression that began during the Panic of 1873 and finally resulted in the formation of a third political party, Julian Carr's supporters—and he had many—might have elected him governor of North Carolina in 1892. Unfortunately for Carr, however, the People's party, which held its first convention in Omaha, Nebraska, on 2 July 1892, had a serious impact on American politics. In North Carolina the Populist party, as it came to be called, was the catalyst for a reorganization of the Democratic party that resulted in a Democratic victory in 1892. In 1894, however, the Populists helped Republicans seize control of the North Carolina legislature for the first time since Reconstruction. Two years later they were instrumental in electing a Republican governor.[1]

Backed by western and southern farm organizations and a limited number of eastern industrial workers, the Populists endorsed, among other issues, the free coinage of silver at a ratio of sixteen to one; government ownership of railroad, telephone, and telegraph facilities; a graduated income tax; an eight-hour work day; restricted immigration; popular election of United States senators; and a secret ballot. Some, if not all, of the planks in the Populist platform appealed to certain elements in both the Democratic and the Republican parties. One of the first North Carolina Democrats to support the Populists was state senator Marion Butler of Sampson County, the president of the Farmers Alliance and owner of a weekly newspaper called *The Caucasian*.

In the state senate, in his newspaper, and in his frequent dealings with agrarian leaders, Butler espoused the cause of populism, especially the issue of free silver, which most farmers equated with hard times. By 1892, enough Farmers Alliance men had defected to the new party to strike fear into the hearts of the ultra-conservative, old-line Democrats who had controlled the legislature since 1875.[2] Having two enemies to fight, and facing the possibility of collaboration between Populists and Republicans, Democratic leaders decided that reorganization of their party was essential. The man for the job was Furnifold McLendel Simmons, a former congressman from North Carolina's Second District and one of the state's most astute politicians.

Unprepossessing in appearance and definitely no orator, Simmons was a seasoned campaigner and fund-raiser and a master strategist. Skilled in the art of "compromise and conciliation," he was not above using stronger tactics when necessary. One of his first steps as chairman of the North Carolina Democratic Executive Committee was to round up a group of young, intelligent, politically ambitious party workers. Under his direction they canvassed the state, making speeches, raising money, and persuading disgruntled farmers and laborers that defecting to the Populists would not solve their problems.[3]

While these political maneuvers were going on, Julian Carr was keeping quiet about the fact that he had been approached by friends who wanted to submit his name as a Democratic candidate for governor at the state convention in May 1892. Some newspapers already were speculating about his intentions, however; on 16 March 1892 the *Durham Daily Globe* reprinted editorials from the *Wilmington Messenger* and the *Atlanta Journal* advocating Carr for governor of North Carolina and extolling his virtues: he was rich, intelligent, talented, liberal, benevolent, and highly moral—a true North Carolinian and a gallant Confederate soldier.[4]

The next morning a *Charlotte Observer* scribe, after defining the governorship as essentially a business office, recommended Julian Carr because he was "the most successful of all our businessmen." Two days later the *Raleigh Signal* said, "Mr. Carr . . . has a host of friends in the Republican Party who would hesitate a long time before they would oppose him. In fact, there are several thousand Republicans who would openly and boldly support Mr. Carr."[5]

One month before the Democrats met in Raleigh, Al Fairbrother, the editor of Durham's *Daily Globe*, asked Carr if he was a candidate for governor. Carr replied, "Fairbrother, when I want to be a candidate, I will let you know . . . just keep your shirt on. If the people want me, I know my duty, but just now I have so much to do I would rather vote the straight ticket than run on it."[6]

Many North Carolinians did want Julian Carr, who had served the state well, in many capacities, for seventeen years. But Furnifold Simmons was running the Democratic show in 1892, and Simmons already had decided that Elias Carr (no relation to Julian Carr), a wealthy farmer from Edgecombe County, was the man most likely to defeat Republican David Furches and Populist Wyatt Exum. As a prime mover in the establishment of the North Carolina College of Agriculture and Mechanic Arts and a leader of the Farmers Alliance movement, Elias Carr would be able "to unify farmers behind the Democratic ticket," Simmons believed.[7]

On 18 May 1892, the day before gubernatorial nominations were to be made at the state convention, the *Durham Daily Globe* ran a front-page story in which Julian Carr denied the accusation by Benjamin Newton Duke, an official of the American Tobacco Company, that Carr had tried to connect himself with the tobacco trust. Alleging that typewritten copies of a letter written by Duke were being distributed for the purpose of injuring his reputation on the eve of the nominations, Carr said:

> During the year 1891, without my knowledge, Messrs. M. E. McDowell, Samuel Austin, and J. M. Duncan, all of Philadelphia and owning three-fourths of the stock of Blackwell's Durham Tobacco Company, began private negotiations with certain directors of the American Tobacco Company. After negotiations had been pending for a week, I was summoned to Philadelphia by a telegram to attend a meeting of the directors of Blackwell's Durham Tobacco Company, of which I was president. At that meeting, I was informed of the pending negotiations, whereupon I declared emphatically to my associates that if they effected a sale, it must permanently sever my connection with the business lock, stock, and barrel. I would not under any circumstances have any connection with the American Tobacco Company, in any capacity.[8]

Although Carr admitted that his board of directors asked him to visit the American Tobacco Company with Samuel Austin "to give certain information about the company's business," and that he had complied with their request, Samuel Austin confirmed the veracity of Carr's above-quoted statement. "My recollection, also Duncan's, is exactly as you state," Austin declared. "Not only then, but at other times, you have expressed exactly the same decision."[9]

Whether Ben Duke intended to smear Carr's reputation is a matter of conjecture, but Duke's letter did not prevent Carr's friends from presenting him as a candidate for governor. Nor did it prevent Carr from making a surprising showing against Thomas M. Holt,

George Sanderlin, Elias Carr, and Sydenham B. Alexander, whose names also appeared on the first ballot. Although he never surpassed the incumbent Governor Holt, he led Elias Carr until the fifth ballot; then the man whom Furnifold Simmons had drafted in order to secure the farm vote outdistanced Julian Carr by 117 votes, and Holt by forty-nine. On the sixth ballot, Elias Carr, who had never aspired to the office, was nominated for governor, and Furnifold Simmons became, in the eyes of most of his fellow Democrats, "the man who knew how to win."[10]

Knowing how to win in the tough, dirty, and often brutal political game required a certain kind of mentality that Julian Carr lacked. As a businessman, he had the touch of genius; as a politician, he was naive. He believed that the voice of the people was more powerful than any party machine, and it took him eight years to learn otherwise.

A month after Elias Carr's nomination, the Democrats met in Chicago and nominated Grover Cleveland for the presidency. Cleveland, an outspoken advocate of the gold standard, had served as president from 1884 until 1888, when he was defeated by Benjamin Harrison. During his tenure Cleveland made many enemies in the South and East because of his pro-business policies and his firm belief that the unlimited coinage of silver would be dangerous to the national economy. As far as western silver miners and southern farmers and factory workers were concerned, the national economy already had deteriorated to the point of collapse by 1892. In North Carolina, thousands of unhappy Democrats chose to follow Marion Butler into the Populist party, rather than to vote for Grover Cleveland.[11]

During Cleveland's first term, Julian Carr, like so many wealthy businessmen, was solidly behind the president. After buying Occoneechee Farm in 1891, he began to have more sympathy with men who made their living from the land, and by 1892 he also had changed his thinking about the silver issue. Zebulon B. Vance, the junior senator from North Carolina, had altered his own views on the matter; Carr was a great admirer of Vance, and when the senator responded to pressure from his constituents by speaking out for free silver, Carr also became an advocate of what he called "White money . . . the people's money . . . the Dollar of our Daddies."[12]

The Panic of 1893, for which Grover Cleveland and his Democratic congress received most of the blame, further increased the strength of the two-year-old Populist party. In 1894, the event that most North Carolina Democrats had been dreading occurred: Republicans and Populists combined their votes and took control of the legislature. The following year, Marion Butler ousted Senator Matt Ransom, a Democrat who had held his seat for twenty-three years, and Republican Jeter Pritchard defeated Thomas J. Jarvis, who had been appointed by Governor Elias Carr to fill Zebulon Vance's unexpired term when Vance died in April 1894.

In 1896 William Jennings Bryan became the Democratic presidential nominee, and Julian Carr again emerged as a possible candidate for governor. The North Carolina Democratic Executive Committee, whose seal of approval usually guaranteed nomination, also considered Walter Clark, an associate judge of the state supreme court, and Charles D. McIver, a noted educator; because Clark chose to remain on the bench and McIver preferred to devote his entire time to public education, Carr became the committee's choice. His loyalty to the party, tangibly expressed by large contributions to its coffers, assured him of strong Democratic support, and as a farmer and a silverite, he appealed to a certain segment of the Populists as well. According to the Raleigh *News and Observer*, many Republicans declared they would support Carr rather than Daniel L. Russell, the GOP candidate who allegedly had promised that, if he was elected, "the Negroes who put him in office should have all the oats and fodder there was to give." That allegation obviously was an attempt to frighten white voters, for while Russell believed that Negroes should be educated to handle equal opportunity, he definitely felt that their political activity should be "limited and subject to white domination," and the editor of the *News and Observer* probably was well aware of that fact. But Josephus Daniels's newspaper, which rarely missed an opportunity to lambast Republicans, made much of Russell's so-called promise.[13]

Thus the political climate was highly favorable for Julian Carr in 1896. At the age of fifty-one, he was either president, vice-president, a director, a leading stockholder, or a trustee of over thirty organizations connected with the business, educational, and religious life of North Carolina. Like Zebulon Vance, he was a man of great charm. Nor was there any doubt about his enthusiasm for the venture. His appetite for politics had been whetted by the 1892 campaign, when he had made a more than creditable showing at the state Democratic convention; since that time he had been "looking toward the governorship and was ambitious to hold that office."[14]

Julian S. Carr (courtesy of Austin Heaton Carr, Jr.)

Unfortunately, Carr's wife did not want him to run. According to Josephus Daniels, the Raleigh editor who was becoming a power in the Democratic party, Nannie Parrish Carr summoned him to Durham and begged him, in the name of their friendship, to persuade her husband to turn down the nomination, which had been "virtually tendered to him, and if he had been willing to accept it, he would have obtained it by acclamation." Daniels admired Nannie Carr for her level head and strong character, but because he knew Carr's heart was set on being governor, it made him extremely uncomfortable to hear Nannie say,

> You know Mr. Carr and you know what politics means. He cannot say no to anybody and if he runs for governor the politicians will bleed him to death ... his inability to say no is his greatest virtue and his greatest weakness. He ought not to go into politics and I know it. I want him to have anything in the world he wants, but I feel his entrance into politics would not bring him happiness, but the contrary, and I want you and his friends to dissuade him from accepting the nomination.[15]

Just how many of Carr's friends were placed in a similar position is not known, but it is a matter of record that his partners in Blackwell's Durham Tobacco Company "strenuously objected" to his entering politics. They, along with Daniels, added their voices to Nannie's and persuaded him to abandon what he wanted more than anything else at the time. It may have been the biggest sacrifice of his life, but the so-called virtue that was also a great weakness prevailed in the end, and he bowed to his wife's wishes.

Dropping out of the gubernatorial race did not keep him from campaigning for the Democratic party, and when William Jennings Bryan headed for North Carolina on a speaking tour, Julian Carr, Josephus Daniels, and several other prominent Democrats met Bryan's train in Knoxville, Tennessee, and rode with him to Asheville, Hickory, Statesville, Charlotte, Salisbury, Greensboro, Durham, and Raleigh. It was extremely hot, and Bryan, exhausted from making speeches, accepted Carr's invitation to stop over at Somerset Villa long enough to take a bath. When he emerged refreshed from one of Somerset's palatial bathrooms, the staunch silver man refrained from commenting on the solid gold faucets in his host's tub and basin, but he was not unimpressed.[16]

After his appearance in Raleigh, Bryan toured Virginia, Maryland,

Delaware, and New England before going to the Democratic convention in Chicago; by the time he arrived there, in July, he had traveled 18,000 miles and made 600 speeches. North Carolina, which was strong for Bryan, was the first state to nominate him for president, and it was one of the most disappointed when William McKinley won in November. But McKinley's organization had "both hands full of money," as well as "the full power of the press," and dissention among Democrats, which had led to the establishment of the Populist party, considerably reduced their voting power.[17]

A similar situation occurred in North Carolina that year. Republican Daniel L. Russell, Democrat Cyrus B. Watson, and Populist William A. Guthrie competed in the race for governor; Russell won, not only because of the third party and the consequent reduction in the Democratic vote, but also because the extremely well-organized Republican campaign resulted in an extraordinarily large Negro vote. All sixteen counties in the so-called black belt went for Russell, but when he did not reward the Negro voters with "all the oats and fodder there was to give," he alienated a number of influential black Republicans, who also accused him of appointing too many whites in towns where blacks predominated. He did not deny the charge; on the contrary, he stated publicly that "of 818 gubernatorial appointments to civil office a grand total of eight had gone to Negroes."[18]

While that statement was made to refute the Democratic accusation that North Carolina, with eleven black legislators and a black congressman, was under Negro rule during Russell's administration, it carried no weight with readers of the *News and Observer*, who were reminded almost daily of the horrors of Reconstruction. However, the Democratic press was not entirely to blame, for even the Populist Marion Butler's *Caucasian* and J. L. Ramsey's *Progressive Farmer* spoke out against a situation that the Populist party and the Farmers Alliance had helped to bring about. On 7 February 1897, *The Caucasian* said that "the Legislature is a damnable disgrace to the State." A few weeks later the *Progressive Farmer* lamented: "There is some talk of an extra session of the Legislature. Please don't, Governor Russell. We can endure famine, pestilence, drouth, war; but don't inflict any prolonged agony on the State, such as an extra session."[19]

In a desperate effort to recapture the legislature from the Republicans, North Carolina Democrats again appealed to Furnifold Simmons, the political wizard who had put Elias Carr in the governor's office in 1892. Shortly after his candidate's inauguration, Simmons had resigned as party chairman in order to become U.S. collector of internal revenue for eastern North Carolina, but apparently it was not difficult to persuade him to leave his federal post.[20] Once more, Simmons agreed to reorganize the Democrats and to direct the campaign to regain control of the General Assembly. Realizing the value of emotional appeal, he made white supremacy the chief issue, although free silver was still an important party plank. The first thing he did was to revive his old machine of 1892, and then he began to promote Charles Brantley Aycock of Wayne County for governor. Simmons also secured the aid of Josephus Daniels in publicizing the alleged scandals of Russell's Republican administration, and the Raleigh *News and Observer*, which Daniels had bought with Julian Carr's help in 1894, became "the printed voice of the campaign."[21]

By October 1898, Furnifold Simmons and his bright young workers had molded the Democrats of North Carolina into "one solid mass, organized like an army." Later that month he instigated a "white supremacy convention" at Goldsboro, where speakers contended that Negro officeholders under Governor Russell had endangered white women, paralyzed business, reduced the value of property, encouraged lawlessness, and caused the invasion of private homes. Race relations became extremely strained throughout eastern North Carolina. In Wilmington, after the Negro editor Alex Manly asserted in the Wilmington *Record* that it was "no worse for a black man to be intimate with a white woman than for a white man to be intimate with a colored woman," Alfred M. Waddell, a prominent Wilmington Democrat, swore publicly that he and his fellow citizens would drive out the Republican administration even if they had to "throw enough dead Negro bodies in the Cape Fear to choke up its passage to the sea." Not surprisingly, the Red Shirts, a militant organization that had originated in South Carolina during Reconstruction, reappeared in some North Carolina towns for the express purpose of frightening Negro voters away from the polls. These red-shirted men, riding on horseback and brandishing shotguns and rifles, succeeded in striking terror into the hearts of many Republicans, both black and white. A rumor that Governor Russell and Senator Jeter Pritchard had asked for federal troops to police the coming election proved false; but the Democratic press, using the story for its own purposes, reported that Russell and Pritchard were afraid to ask

Washington for help because white supremacy advocates were so fired up "it would have taken Grant's army to have held them back."[22]

The November elections resulted in a sweeping victory for Democrats, who regained a two-thirds majority in the legislature and almost immediately went to work on a proposed constitutional amendment that would disfranchise the Negro voter by requiring a literacy test and a poll tax. The literacy test was not to apply to whites if they had been qualified to vote on or before 1 January 1867; nor would it apply if they were lineal descendants of such voters. This "grandfather clause" was to remain in effect for ten years, during which, the Democrats promised, enough aid would be given to public schools, both black and white, to do away with illiteracy. By 1 December 1908, they said, the grandfather clause would no longer apply because it would be possible for all men of both races to vote.[23]

This, then, was the political scene in North Carolina when Julian Carr began to receive letters urging him to run for the Senate in 1900. As early as October 1899 a spokesman for the Richmond, Virginia, *Christian Advocate* said:

> From all sections of Carolina and from all classes there is the one desire that Carr represent his native state in the Senate at Washington. He is without question the most popular citizen. The Commonwealth never had a more loyal son. He has poured out money without stint for the State. The University, the charity institutions, the colleges, have received munificent aid from his purse. No citizen is classed with him in public spirit. In politics, he is the Democrat of Democrats. The State was lost to the Party some years ago. He never lost heart. He planned, labored, cheered, paid. When there was an empty treasury and despair everywhere, one man never gave up or closed his purse. His contributions to the camp chest ran up into the thousands of dollars. . . . He is in his prime, of noble presence, cultured, gifted in speech, and "without spot or wrinkle on his character."[24]

The Raleigh *News and Observer*, after reprinting the *Christian Advocate*'s editorial about Carr on 1 October, made what could be seen as an apology on 3 October:

Col. Carr is very much worried that he is reported as having announced himself as a candidate for the U.S. Senatorship. He feels that for the future, as in the past, the Democratic Party has known his whereabouts and how to avail itself of his services should they be needed and that he is entirely content to let it go at that. In a note to the editor, Carr said the paramount question was not who was going to be the next U.S. Senator, but that the proposed Constitutional Amendment be adopted . . . that every true and loyal Democrat should lend himself to the success of the Amendment . . . [and] that he does not now or in the future propose to join a scramble for office. He never has, and he never will.[25]

Despite that public protest, Julian Carr's political ambition, smoldering for seven years, definitely was rekindled. This time his wife made no overt attempt to put out the fire. Somehow Carr must have convinced her that being a senator would not jeopardize his health, his pocketbook, or their relationship, and that Washington would be a wonderful place to live for part of each year. At any rate, on 8 April 1900, when the Durham County Democratic Committee met in the courthouse and endorsed him as Marion Butler's successor, he replied that he expected to come home from the state Democratic convention "with that grand word victory emblazoned on my banner." He also promised Durham Democrats that "North Carolina's slogan shall be the White man shall rule the land or die."[26]

The convention, reported as being "the greatest and most enthusiastic political convention that men of that generation had ever seen," met in Raleigh the next day and, following the dictates of Furnifold Simmons, nominated Charles Brantley Aycock for governor. Julian Carr was elected a delegate at large to the national convention, and when that body convened in Kansas City on 4 July 1900 and nominated William Jennings Bryan for president, Carr was offered by the North Carolina delegation as a candidate for the vice-presidency. (The fourteen votes he received were later switched to Adlai Stevenson.) Bryan subsequently told reporters that, next to his home state of Utah, North Carolina gave him more support than any other.

In August, after North Carolina's constitutional amendment was passed by a majority of over 50,000 votes, Julian Carr formally announced his candidacy for the Senate. He promised to support the industrial, educational, and agricultural interests of North Carolina and to protect them from "hostile legislation"; he also pledged himself to fight "Federal interference in our new Constitutional Amendment."[27] Opposing Carr were Furnifold Simmons, the acknowledged Democratic party boss; Alfred M. Waddell, the mayor of Wilmington; and former North Carolina governor Thomas J. Jarvis. For the first time in the state's history, the contest was to be decided by the people in a primary, rather than by a convention. The campaign was exceptionally bitter, and after both Jarvis and Waddell realized they had no real organizations behind them, they withdrew.

Again Josephus Daniels went to his friend, Julian Carr, and warned him against running, but this time it was not because of pressure from Carr's wife. Daniels knew that most Democrats were going to support Simmons simply because he had been responsible for returning the party to power in 1898, and for securing the passage of the constitutional amendment in 1900. Although Simmons had created his machine primarily to battle Republicans and Populists, he could also use it to fight Carr. Many so-called regular Democrats were afraid a split in the vote would mean victory for Populist-Fusion forces led by Marion Butler; many ultra-conservatives opposed Carr because he favored electoral reform, free silver, and state-supported higher education.[28]

Carr, however, chose not to withdraw from the race, mainly because he had received "thousands of letters from people all over the state urging him to run."[29] He believed that, in the primary, the voice of the people would ensure his election; he said as much in a campaign speech at Mount Holly, declaring that he had no machine behind him and asking only for "a fair count of the ballots." Angry Simmons forces retaliated immediately and accused Carr of attacking the means by which white supremacy was attained in 1898. One eastern North Carolina newspaper, *The Windsor Ledger*, hotly defended the machine, saying it was composed of state, district, county, township, and precinct committees; that officers and members of various Democratic clubs throughout the state also were part of it; and that together they represented the virtue, worth, intelligence, and patriotism of the white race. "To be denounced . . . by one asking office at their hands, is an affront they are likely to resist with vigor."[30]

The editor from Windsor was right about the resistance. Carr was charged with ingratitude for the hard work done by party regulars to secure the victories of 1898 and 1900; he also was accused of supporting Populists and Republicans against "good Democrats." To reinforce their accusations, Simmons supporters constantly brought up memories of the alleged "Negro rule" that had resulted from Populist-Republican fusion in 1896. Simmons himself said very little, but he was the symbol of recent Democratic victories, and some newly elected Democratic officials were told that they would be seen as blatantly disloyal if they voted for Carr, who only wanted to prove that poor people could not win against a man of wealth.

Carr supporters argued that "having used every opportunity that North Carolina's resources furnish for the acquisition of wealth, [Carr] has in turn faithfully employed that wealth for the improvement of North Carolina," and that, as a successful businessman, he was better equipped to successfully administer government affairs. They cited his benefactions to both public and private schools, his close connections with the agricultural life of the state, his identification with its manufacturing interests, and his unswerving loyalty to the Democratic party. They reminded the public that, as a member of the state party's executive committee for over eighteen years, Carr had put his checkbook "largely at the command" of its various chairmen; that he had "paid out of his personal funds for the success of the [party] more than all the other candidates combined"; in spite of all this, he never had received any compensation for his services. Furnifold Simmons, they said, had been sent to Congress and had been made a director of internal revenue; Thomas Jarvis had been made a legislator, a governor, a minister to Brazil, and a senator; Alfred Waddell had been rewarded by several terms in Congress and a district attorneyship. Julian Carr had never received any reward, even though for over thirty years he had been "a worker in the ranks."[31]

Letters to the editor poured in to the *News and Observer* office. Although Josephus Daniels had refused the request of Carr's campaign manager to "throw all the weight of its influence" to the man who had helped him buy the paper, he did print more signed statements for Carr than for Simmons "simply because more were sent in." Daniels was frank enough to say that Carr was no politician, and that although he yearned for high office, "he was so agreeable he didn't like to run against anybody anyhow."[32]

In sharp contrast to Julian Carr, Furnifold Simmons was a man whose political sense and organizing capabilities were the envy of both his admirers and his detractors, a man who knew how to make "a virtue of necessity" and who did not hesitate to promise favors "which later became somewhat embarrassing" in order to gain votes.[33] Having led the successful movement to disfranchise Negroes, Simmons felt that he should have any office he wanted, and he made party loyalty the issue of the 1900 senatorial campaign. He pointed to Carr as a villain backed by liberal forces that would split the Democrats, allow a renewal of Republican-Populist fusion power, and put black men back in office.

Simmons's scare tactics worked. Carr supporters doggedly maintained that their candidate would carry fifty-eight of North Carolina's ninety-seven counties, but Simmons won with a 60,000-vote majority and carried eighty counties. Although the outcome was a terrible blow to Carr, he wired Simmons: "Accept my heartiest congratulations. In all your efforts to promote the welfare of North Carolina and the Democratic Party I pledge my loyal support." Simmons immediately replied: "Accept my thanks for your wire of congratulations. It is my earnest desire that any dissentions in our party may be speedily healed. I trust that the spirit of your telegram may meet a universal response from our party friends and that we may all work together for the success of Democracy and the welfare of the State. Surely nothing shall be left undone on my part to accomplish this much desired result."[34]

The day after the election, Carr was "on the street early, shaking hands with friends and not at all depressed, as good a Democrat today as he ever was," according to the *News and Observer*. That newspaper carried an open letter from Carr to the Democratic party which said, in part,

> You have at the ballot box stated your choice for United States Senator. Your will is my pleasure. I assure you my devotion to the welfare of North Carolina is unabated, and my loyalty to the great Democratic Party unshaken. My defeat leaves no bitterness. In the future as in the past, I will be found fighting the battle of Democracy. I am deeply grateful to my friends throughout the State who have stood so loyally by me. Surely it is the privilege of few to be honored by the support and confidence of so many good and true men. I shall never forget their loyalty, and may Heaven's richest blessing abide with them.[35]

Most of the friends Carr asked Heaven to bless came from the Piedmont, an area of industrial and urban growth and of large-scale production. Those friends felt, as he did, that businessmen rather than "small politicians" ought to run the state on "broader lines," and that it was not impossible for a candidate to dissent from party policy and still be loyal to party principle.[36] Such was not the case in North Carolina at the time, however; nor was there any appreciable change in the situation as long as the Simmons machine held sway, as it continued to do for the next thirty years.

But Julian Carr, who did not give up easily, rearranged his private dream of high office by casting his oldest son in the role he had hoped to play himself. After four years at the University of North Carolina and a year at Harvard Law School, Julian Junior was working as secretary and treasurer of the Durham Hosiery Mill. When he had learned everything there was to know about the business, he would take over his father's duties as president, but there was no reason why he should not have a political career as well.[37]

That fantasy may have helped the elder Julian Carr through the initial throes of disappointment following his defeat at the polls. Returning to the comparative sanity of the world of business, where his expertise was unchallenged, was an even more powerful restorative. Like time, work helped to heal all things, and major projects on Carr's agenda would provide him with an abundance of work in the months to come. Already under construction were new quarters for his Golden Belt Manufacturing Company, which had produced muslin bags for tobacco and other commodities in a section of the Bull Factory until that landmark was sold to the American Tobacco Company. As soon as those quarters were finished, he would build a bigger and better Durham Hosiery Mill directly across the street from the Golden Belt. Finally, he would surround both companies with "superior housing" for the employees.

It was an exciting prospect that would leave no time for looking back. Best of all, Carr would be working closely with his son and namesake.

10. "Four Dear Good Boys"

JULIAN SHAKESPEARE CARR, Junior, was a freshman at the University of North Carolina when the business that was to make him "hosiery king of America" experienced its inception, no doubt in the dignified atmosphere of his father's office at the First National Bank. There a man with the unremarkable name of John Smith joined the bank's president as a partner investing in what would eventually be the largest hosiery mill in the world.

One historian claims that the Golden Belt Hosiery Company, "promoted by Julian S. Carr and John W. Smith," was established in December 1894, but company records state that the formal organization occurred on 13 December 1895, and that Thomas M. Gorman, Carr's private secretary, and William A. Guthrie, Carr's brother-in-law, also were present at that meeting.[1] The company was capitalized at $10,000, divided into 100 shares "of the par value of one hundred dollars," and it was agreed that capital could be increased "at any time to any amount not exceeding $50,000." Smith and Carr, each holding forty-nine shares of stock, were president and vice-president, respectively; Gorman, with one share, was secretary-treasurer, and Guthrie, with the remaining share, was the firm's attorney.[2]

It was not the first such firm in Durham. Washington Duke's oldest son, Brodie, had supplied most of the capital for the Commonwealth Cotton Mill to produce yarn and "a moderate quantity" of hosiery in 1893, and a year later George Mordecai Graham, a Hillsborough native, had established the Durham Hosiery Company. Julian Carr, however, was not intimidated by competition. He believed that the hosiery market eventually would expand southward, as the tobacco market had done. He meant to corner that market in North Carolina and to compete successfully with northern knitting mills.

Carr's Golden Belt Hosiery Company set up shop in a small building located at the western end of Main Street. Three months later, on 13 March 1896, the four stockholders agreed to increase their capital to $25,000.[3] The fact that business was by no means booming may have discouraged John Smith; the following spring he sold out to

Carr, who could afford to await better times. Ten months later, times were indeed better. On 17 February 1898, after Congress passed the Dingley Tariff Act and placed hosiery on its protected list, Carr bought out George Graham's Durham Hosiery Company. Moving the machinery and raw materials from his own plant to Graham's building on Morris Street, Carr then hired a skilled New England mill man to manage the new business, which he capitalized at $46,000 and renamed the Durham Hosiery Mill.[4] To facilitate wholesale distribution of his product to hosiery dealers who would retail it under their own brand names, he established the Carolina Hosiery Commission at 43 Leonard Street in New York City. Under the management of A. T. Bloomer, this firm acted as agent not only for Carr's mill, but also for other North Carolina plants specializing in knitted goods.

Whether thanks to luck or premeditation, Carr's timing could not have been better. Spain and the United States were on the brink of war, chiefly because Spain's policies in Cuba were detrimental to American investors and proponents of United States expansion into Latin America. Every day the "yellow journalism" of William Randolph Hearst and Joseph Pulitzer aroused American sympathy for Cuba's struggle for independence. Lurid stories of Spanish concentration camps, where Cubans allegedly died of starvation and disease, appeared in the *New York Journal* and the *New York World* and were picked up by other newspapers across the country, and after the U.S.S. *Maine* was sunk in the Havana harbor, Spain received the blame, although it never could be proved that Spain actually did the deed. But the public was clamoring for revenge, and on 22 April 1898, two months after the *Maine* went down with 250 men aboard, Congress authorized the enlistment of volunteers for the army. Two days later Spain declared war on America; the following day America declared war on Spain, retroactive to 21 April.

These events paved the way for the president of the Durham Hosiery Mill, who had important connections in Washington and a commission agent in New York, to apply for and receive substantial government orders for that most necessary part of a soldier's equipment: socks. Though the Spanish-American War lasted only about four months, that brief conflict, coupled with the Dingley Tariff, gave a tremendous boost to Julian Carr's career as a manufacturer. By 1900, when Julian Junior came into the business, it had outgrown the Morris Street quarters, and the senior Carr was planning to build a handsome new mill on a large tract not far behind Somerset Villa.[5]

The photograph of Julian Shakespeare Carr, Junior, that went into Somerset Villa's cornerstone box portrayed a small, solemn-faced, ten-year-old boy with a prominent forehead, very large light blue eyes, dark hair, and flaring ears. He wore a dark jacket over a checkered shirt with a wide white Eton collar; his expression was wistful, as if he already had begun to feel the heavy responsibility of being his father's namesake. A few years after the cornerstone laying, Little Jule, as he often was called, left home for the first time to attend the Horner Military School in Oxford, North Carolina. In 1895, at seventeen, he entered the University of North Carolina.

Before the son departed Durham for Chapel Hill, his father cautioned him to be a gentleman under all circumstances, and never to forget that the world contained only two classes of men: those who led and those who followed. "My son, never follow," his father told him. "Always lead."[6] How many additional exhortations Julian Junior received can only be imagined, but we know that Julian Senior had taught Sunday school at Trinity Methodist Church for over twenty years; he often urged his "young gentlemen" to let conscience and reason and love of God control their bodies and govern their minds, instead of letting passion and appetite dictate. He urged them to close their hearts against evil thoughts and evil suggestions just as they would bolt their doors against robbers. He also informed them that a thousand experiments had already settled the fact that "a cold water drinker can do more work, do it better, stand more fatigue, march further, endure heat and cold better, and be far less liable to disease and contagion than one who uses intoxicating liquors," and that the use of such spirits was "wholly evil and without apology."[7]

So it is hardly surprising that Julian Junior vowed privately that, while he was in college, he would never retire without first reading his Bible and saying his prayers; nor would he smoke, drink, gamble, or have sexual relations.[8] He said nothing about this resolve until the beginning of his junior year, when he learned from university president Edward Alderman that Julian Carr, Senior, had been "mortified" because the name of Julian Carr, Junior, had not appeared on the sophomore honors list at the 1897 commencement. Stung by the rebuke, young Julian wrote his father to say that "If it had not been for my sickness last Spring I would have made honors," and that talking to Dr. Alderman "made me realize more your unbounded ambition for me." It was true, he admitted, that he had not always led his classes; but he had always been "up among the first," and "you have not a child that tries to please you more than myself. I will now try to show this to you," Julian declared. After listing the resolutions he had made as a freshman, he stated unequivocally, "These I have carried out for two years, and you never would have known about it unless this matter had come up. I guarantee you cannot find two more men in my class, or any other class, that can say the same. So you see when you do not know it, I am trying to do those things I think would please. I think if Dr. Alderman or anybody else knew these things, they would say I am a deserving son."9

Despite his high standards, this deserving son was neither a "religionist" nor a "goody-goody" in the eyes of his classmates, nine of whom were coeds who agreed that "He can make you think what might be" and who allowed that confession to be quoted in the college yearbook.10 As a student of Latin, Greek, French, English, mathematics, chemistry, geology, and political science, Julian earned his highest grades in math and chemistry and his lowest in geology; although he usually ranked among the top performers in his classes, he was not a "grind." On the contrary, he found time to take an active part in the Zeta Psi fraternity, the Order of Gimghouls, the German Club, the Horner School Club, the YMCA, and two honorary fraternities, Theta Mu Epsilon and Alpha Theta Phi. He also went out for baseball during his sophomore year and played well enough to make the team.11

In September 1898, Julian was elected president of the senior class and of the general athletic association. The following June, shortly before his twenty-first birthday, he was graduated cum laude.12 As salutatorian, he gave the welcoming address at the commencement of 1899, and he made a second speech when he presented to the university, on behalf of the senior class, a bust of "our great War Governor, Zebulon B. Vance, likewise an alumnus, a Trustee and warm friend of the University."13 There can be little doubt that the elder Julian Carr was one of the proudest fathers in Chapel Hill that day. If he was perhaps less than happy about his son's intention of going to Boston to study law, instead of coming directly into the hosiery business, the public was not aware of it.

Young Julian may have thought that studying the law would help him in the business world, but whatever his reasons, he remained at

Julian S. Carr, Jr. (courtesy of Julian S. Carr III)

Harvard Law School for only one year; in the summer of 1900 he moved back to Somerset Villa and became treasurer of the Durham Hosiery Mill. In that capacity he played a major role in the construction of Edgemont, the village that would be home to employees of both the mill and the bag factory that his father had established.

The first fifty houses in Edgemont, located on streets that the elder Carr had named Carnation, Goldenrod, Marigold, Hollyhock, Sunflower, Dandelion, Red Rose, and Rhododendron, were three-, four-, and five-room dwellings underpinned with "good hard brick" and constructed with "good #2 lumber and #1 shingles of sawed pine." Carr's contract with the builder, Andrew C. Mitchell, stipulated that each house was to be "finished in good workmanlike manner," protected by two coats of the best lead and oil paint, and plastered and trimmed inside. Every room was to have a fireplace and a mantel "of late Victorian style," and the chimneys were to be constructed so as not to smoke. Each house was to have a front porch and, in the back yard, a shingle-roofed privy with two seats. Outside maintenance, as well as water and electricity, would be furnished by the company. Tenants would pay weekly rent of twenty-five cents per room.[14]

Like most mill owners, the Carrs had what amounted to total control over the lives of their employees. All workers understood, from the moment they were hired, that "if you lived in a company house, you had to behave." Company houses were so far superior to anything the tenants had previously known that infractions of the rules against drinking, gambling, and fighting were practically nonexistent. Julian Junior especially "made an effort to construct a pleasant living and working environment for employees," a group composed, for the most part, of entire families—father, mother, and every child past the age of six.[15] Little Jule was opposed to hiring children under the age of twelve, but, had he made that a rule early in his career, he would not have been able to staff the mill.[16]

Employment of children was not considered exploitation as such by their parents, who knew that no father could support a family on his wages alone. Babies kept their mothers at home only until they were old enough to be farmed out, often to older relatives. By the time the last child was six years old, everyone in the house was up at five o'clock in the morning, to do the chores before going to work for twelve hours a day, five and a half days a week. It was a long, hard week, but not as long or as hard as a week of farming. The same family might work as many hours, or more, on a poor dirt farm and not have anything like the good living at Edgemont.

Even if they did have to breathe lint all day, and to squint perpetually in order to keep track of the fine thread that tangled and broke so easily, it was easier to work in a mill than on a farm, all things considered. They sweltered in the mill during the summer, with all the windows and doors closed to prevent the slightest breeze from blowing the lint around or breaking the thread. The only water they had was from a bucket, with everyone using the same dipper. But it was better than sweating in the scorching-hot fields and never knowing whether they'd make a crop or not, on account of hail or bugs or mold or wilt or floods or drought.

The children, as a rule, were eager to work. They liked being sweepers, or toppers, or packers, or working with the spools or the bobbins. It gave them a little money of their own—something they'd never have had on a farm. And it wasn't lonely the way a farm was lonely. They could talk while they worked, and help each other when the thread got tangled. They made friends that way, friends they could play with on Saturday afternoon, if they weren't too tired. Some of the littlest ones became so tired that they would sometimes lie down on a pile of stockings and take a nap, but the foremen in the Carr mill didn't seem to mind.[17]

In 1902 the new Durham Hosiery Mill, described as "one of the finest examples of mill construction in the country," was completed. In that year Julian Carr's second son, Marvin, entered the business after graduating from the University of North Carolina with a bachelor of science degree and an enviable reputation as a star athlete.[18] Like his older brother, Marvin joined the Zeta Psi fraternity and the German Club, of which he was president in his senior year; he also was tapped into the Order of Gimghouls. Unlike Julian, however, Marvin never made the honors list. Football was Marvin's forte, and what he lacked in the classroom he more than compensated for on the gridiron, which lured him from the beginning of his college days and held him to the end. He was captain of the freshman team in 1898; he made the varsity squad and served as assistant team manager in 1899; he played fullback on the varsity team and was vice-president of the General Athletic Association in 1900; and in the fall of 1901, as captain of the team that won seven out of nine games for Carolina, he impressed serious sports fans and was named to the All Southern Team.[19]

Fortunately for Marvin, prowess on the playing field was not his only attribute. Just under six feet tall and weighing 165 pounds, he was a good-looking young man with exquisite manners and a flair for ballroom dancing—a combination of virtues that endeared him not only to young ladies, but to mothers and chaperones as well. He was "a real charmer and a good dresser," and his naturally sunny disposition, so like his father's, enabled him to accept with equanimity the fact that his future had long since been planned for him. Those plans included learning all phases of the family business before going on the road as a salesman. He was to travel between New York and Chicago, marketing Durable Durham Hosiery, "good, comfortable, long-wearing hosiery for the whole family." Marvin was to convince the public that socks and stockings with reinforced toes, heels, and soles were "strongest where the wear is hardest." After experience had ripened him, he would be named vice-president in charge of sales, with headquarters at 43 Leonard Street in New York.[20]

While Marvin Carr was being oriented to the business, his brother Julian was spending every spare minute in hot pursuit of the affections of a young woman with an exquisite face and figure, a lilting, musical voice, and a highly successful father. Margaret Cannon was the daughter of James William Cannon of Concord, North Carolina, a contemporary of Julian's father and, like Carr, a gifted businessman. Cannon was a textile baron whose cotton towels were fast becoming as familiar to the American people as Bull Durham tobacco had been in its heyday. He and Carr were pleased when the romance between their children culminated in marriage on 18 December 1902.[21]

Shortly after Julian and Margaret Carr moved into a house two doors away from Somerset Villa, Julian decided that the cotton ordinarily sold as waste could be used instead to knit cheaper socks for a less discriminating clientele, and that Negroes could be trained to do the job. The only work available to blacks in North Carolina, other than farming and domestic service, had traditionally been in tobacco factories; blacks usually served as stemmers because they were not considered intelligent enough to run machines. Julian Junior disagreed with that premise. Blacks could be taught, he maintained, and once they had learned not to be afraid of the formidable-looking contraptions that knit socks and stockings, they would be as efficient as whites.[22]

Julian's father, seeing the advantage of tapping yet another supply of abundant, cheap labor, endorsed the idea and proposed that they ask John O'Daniel, the family butler, to recruit the needed manpower. O'Daniel, who considered himself a member of the Carr clan, was pleased to be part of the organization of Mill Number Two, as it was called; but Durham's white laborers were far from pleased when they learned that the Carrs intended to "take bread out of their mouths" by paying black men and women to operate the proposed mill. Resentment blossomed into anger, and then into threats to blow up or burn down the building. Little Jule and his father "went ahead to see the thing through" in spite of local censure. As a result of their persistence, they were able to claim that the fifty workers selected by John O'Daniel were the first Negroes in America to staff a white-owned cotton mill.

At first, it was slow going for both management and labor. On that historic Monday in 1903 the Negroes turned out only 108 pairs of socks, an average of two pairs each. They seemed fascinated and, at the same time, intimidated by the machines; but gradually they lost their fear, as Julian Junior had predicted. Within six months they were averaging 360 pairs, the standard output for a nine-hour day. They achieved this in spite of the fact that they rarely, if ever, let work interfere with their attendance at funerals, weddings, church meetings, and circuses. The Carrs, realizing the futility of trying to prevent sporadic absenteeism, "managed to get on without many rules," and they got on well enough to see Mill Number Two go on a paying basis within eight months of its inception.[23]

That same year, William Frederick Carr, the oldest of Dr. Albert Gallatin Carr's three sons and one of Julian Carr's favorite nephews, was taken into the firm. After a period of indoctrination similar to that experienced by his cousins, Julian and Marvin, Will Carr was given the title of second vice-president. Company by-laws stated that his job was to act for the president and the first vice-president, should both of these officers be absent or incapacitated at the same time, and to "perform such other duties as the President of the Board of Directors shall prescribe." Because he had been an outstanding baseball player at the University of North Carolina, one of those additional duties was managing the Durham Hosiery Mill baseball team.[24] Steady and reliable, Will Carr eventually became secretary of the company, although that position went first to Julian Carr's third son, Claiborn McDowell Carr, following his graduation from the University of North Carolina in 1905.

Named for Doctor Claiborn Parrish, his maternal grandfather, and Marcellus E. McDowell, one of his father's partners in Blackwell's Durham Tobacco Company, Claiborn often was called the best-looking member of the family. A popular student at Chapel Hill, he followed family tradition by joining the Zeta Psi fraternity, the Order of Gimghouls, and the German Club; he also became a member of the Sphinx Club and the Order of the Golden Fleece. An active social life did not prevent him from serving on the University Council, or from managing, at various times, Carolina's football, baseball, and track teams. Even with these extracurricular activities, he maintained a B average and demonstrated an aptitude for mathematics that was to serve him well in his business career.[25]

First as secretary and later as treasurer of the Durham Hosiery Mill, Claiborn Carr took an active role in the company's expansion. Success, in some instances, resulted from other men's failures. The tremendous surge of growth in the textile industry that occurred in the late 1890s and early 1900s produced a number of North Carolina mills whose owners lacked Julian Carr's manufacturing experience and ready access to capital; in the face of stiff competition, some of these would-be cotton barons either went bankrupt or sold out. A textile plant that failed in High Point became Durham Hosiery Mill Number Three in 1906. In 1909, after the Carrs bought the Blanche Hosiery Mill Company and the Alberta Cotton Mill, both located just west of Chapel Hill, they consolidated the two plants and thus created the fourth link in their growing chain. From Isaac W. Pritchard, William F. Lindsay, and J. J. Pritchard they purchased the Blanche Mill for $9,800. Thomas Lloyd, whose illiteracy masked an innate shrewdness, received $130,000 for the Alberta Mill, which he had built in 1899.[26] Before the year was out, a fifth unit of the Durham Hosiery Mill was established in Goldsboro. Julian Senior then decided to step aside and let his three sons and nephew run the business.

On 5 January 1910, Carr called a special meeting of the board of directors and resigned as president, whereupon Julian Junior resigned as treasurer and was elected president; Claiborn resigned as secretary and became treasurer; and Will resigned as second vice-president and assumed the double duty of secretary and assistant treasurer. Marvin Carr, who was living in New York and absent from the meeting, was reelected first vice-president and sales manager. Sixteen-year-old Austin Carr, a student at Hotchkiss School in

Lakeville, Connecticut, was taken into the firm and given the title of second vice-president. The board of directors now was comprised of Julian Carr, Senior, his four sons, his nephew, and his daughters' husbands, Henry C. Flower and William F. Patton, at last making the Durham Hosiery Mill the family business its founder had envisioned in 1898. Four months later, when the company increased its capital stock from half a million to a million dollars, Julian Carr felt a justifiable sense of accomplishment.[27]

Having Lida Carr Flower's husband on the board of directors made it convenient, as well as mutually profitable, for the Durham Hosiery Mill to do business with the Fidelity Trust Company, which Henry Flower had established in Kansas City in 1899. On 1 June 1911, Julian Junior secured a loan of $30,000 from his brother-in-law's bank for the purpose of constructing a new office and a finishing plant in Edgemont. In March 1912 the board of directors voted to increase the capital stock again, this time to $1,750,000, and to spend $200,000 on enlarging and improving its five mills. The board also decided to adopt the new president's "Co-operative Profit Sharing Plan with the Employees," a plan that Julian Junior had been contemplating for at least a decade.

Reduced to its simplest terms, the president's plan advocated extending the boundaries of the family business to include the employees, thereby convincing them "that we are all together in an adventure which has boundless opportunity." Julian readily admitted that it was not an easy idea to put across, but he wanted to go beyond the usual paternalistic attitude of "blind loyalty to the employer [and] payment in kind words instead of money."[28] He dreamed of true cooperation between management and labor, and in the hope of achieving it, he established his cooperative plan in the five units that comprised the Durham Hosiery Mill.

The plan, which later became known as "industrial democracy," was similar to the system under which the federal government operated. The constitution's stated aim was "service . . . the result of justice, cooperation and energy"; there was a senate, and a house of representatives, and a cabinet. The cabinet, consisting of officers and directors of the mill, often met in joint session with the house and senate; these two bodies, comprised of workers, met twice a week to discuss how to improve production and working conditions, as well as to iron out grievances "in their incipiency." These meetings led to better sanitation and lighting, better care of the machinery, less in-equality in pay rates, and more satisfactory adjustment of grievances.

Critics of the plan said it was designed to prevent unionization, but Little Jule Carr insisted that its purpose was, rather, to manufacture more and better hosiery at a reduced cost, so that all employees could be paid higher wages. To stimulate interest, he offered the workers an equal share of whatever money was saved through more economi-cal production. The result was what he had hoped for: decreased waste, increased production, and raises in pay.[29]

During his first five years as president, Julian Junior instigated the addition of two new links to the Durham Hosiery Mill chain. He built a second mill in Goldsboro and bought one on the outskirts of Chapel Hill from the widow of Thomas Lloyd, who had sold his first mill, the Alberta, to the senior Carr in 1909. Adding Mill Number Six and Mill Number Seven did not relieve the overcrowding in Mill Number One, so young Julian built a new plant and several ware-houses in Edgemont. These proved invaluable when, in 1914, the Durham Hosiery Mill contracted to deliver 200,000 pairs of socks to the U.S. Army, 300,000 pairs to the Navy, and 100,000 pairs to the Marine Corps. Again war was booming the Carrs' business, and by 1915 they had accounts with twelve banks in North Carolina, three in New York, and one each in Boston, Philadelphia, Kansas City, and Richmond.[30]

In June 1915, Austin Carr graduated from the University of North Carolina. As a chubby freshman he had acquired the name Billy Bounce, but after his weight dropped from 185 to 160 pounds, his Zeta Psi brothers instead began to call him Doodlebags, for reasons that remain obscure.[31] His jovial disposition was disarming, and the fact that he became the first Carolina student to successfully ignore the rule banning cars on campus displayed a daring that greatly in-creased his standing among his contemporaries, who voted him the best-dressed man and "biggest social bull" in his class.[32]

While maintaining a B average, Austin also indulged his appetite for extracurricular activities, as had his brothers. He played fresh-man football and managed the freshman baseball team; was elected to the YMCA cabinet; became assistant manager of the Glee Club and business manager of the Student Directory; and joined the Zeta Psi fraternity, the German Club, the Gorgon's Head Lodge, and both the Coop and the Oasis, two clubs designed to provide their members with a more convivial atmosphere and better food than could be had in the university dining hall. But Julian Carr's youngest son was not just a "social bull." He had "a tendency for business and philosophy," and his more than average interest in geology may have had its roots in the fields of Occoneechee Farm, where arrowheads, tomahawk blades, and fragments of Indian pottery were unearthed at every spring plowing.[33]

Occoneechee had provided a testing ground for Austin's latent business talent during the summer of 1909, when his father allowed him to bottle water from the farm spring and to sell it in Hillsborough and Durham. No doubt with his father's help, the budding entrepreneur secured an endorsement from Dr. John Musser of Philadelphia, "an eminent and world-recognized authority" who had the water analyzed at the University of Pennsylvania and proclaimed it to be some of the purest in the world, "good for malaria, rheumatism, dysentery, typhoid and teething children."[34] Offering five gallons of this remarkable elixir for one dollar, and daily deliveries of same, Austin advised the public: "Phone 75 and I do the rest." When he was not bottling and hauling water that summer, he was busy building a new spring house to protect the purity of his product.

Six summers after his first commercial venture, Austin went to work at the Durham Hosiery Mill. The elder Julian Carr saw a cherished dream become reality three months prior to his seventieth birthday: his "four dear good boys" were in business together at last. "Don't separate," he told them. "In unity there is strength. Carry the Golden Rule into your business, and especially in your relations with each other. You good boys are of the same bone, the same flesh and blood. . . . Let the interest of one be the interest of all. . . ."[35]

Carr continued to advise his sons periodically on how to run their business, just as he continued to keep a weather eye on what now was his main interest, the First National Bank. However, that institution was being run so efficiently by its cashier, W. J. Holloway, that Carr had ample time for other pursuits. One that afforded him special pleasure was the United Confederate Veterans of America, an organization dedicated to preserving the South's "glorious" past and one that gave its members a yearly opportunity to mourn "the beautiful lost cause."

Several years before the association was formed, Carr told a newspaper reporter that while in the Confederate Army he had refused two commissions because he did not want to be separated from "the boys." Then he added: "I don't deserve any credit for this because the boys made a pet of me and wouldn't let me do any of the hard work. Do you know I only had to cook once during the whole time I was in the service. That was when I was on detail duty and alone. With me soldiering wasn't much of a hardship, and I was young enough to thoroughly enjoy myself."[36]

That reminiscence, voiced in 1883 and blurred, perhaps, by time and wishful thinking, has the mythical quality often found in yarns spun by veterans long after their particular wars are over, but it also has a disarming ring of truth. In 1864 Carr was nineteen years old, small for his age, and eager to please, so he probably fell easily into the role of company mascot. The fact that he preferred remaining a "pet" to becoming a junior officer, at the mercy of weary and embittered superiors, is understandable. Given the circumstances he described, it is not surprising that he enjoyed soldiering, and when the United Confederate Veterans of America was founded in 1889, he began to enjoy it even more.

Many veterans' organizations cropped up after the Civil War, but Union soldiers were the first to benefit from them. The South, primarily engaged in fending off starvation and coping with Reconstruction, had neither the time, the will, nor the money to pay special attention to its old soldiers or to commemorate its dead. As prosperity gradually returned, however, concern for Confederate veterans and their widows and orphans began to surface in the form of local and regional groups that were not only benevolent, but also literary, historical, and highly social. Their aims were to care for the disabled and needy, to preserve records and relics, and to gather data for a history of the Civil War—one written, presumably, from a southern viewpoint. The groups appeared first in South Carolina, Georgia, Virginia, and North Carolina, but their growth was steady. In 1889 they merged into one unit that was divided into three districts and included sixteen southern states and the Indian Territory.[37]

As soon as Julian Carr joined the organization, he took it upon himself to act as a one-man veterans' administration for fellow members less fortunate than himself, and there were many. He gave them money and encouragement; he lobbied on their behalf for government aid; and, on innumerable occasions, he footed the bills to send them to Confederate reunions by the train carload. The first reunion of the United Confederate Veterans of America took place in Chattanooga in 1890, and except in 1893, when the country was in a severe economic depression, the association met annually. Carr was always in attendance, and more often than not he was a featured speaker.

11. Confederate Veteran and Gentleman Farmer

ONFEDERATE reunions were grandiose affairs, with speeches, parades, dramatic entertainment, dancing, and dining more prominent on the agenda than was attention to business. Ladies also played an important part as sponsors and "maids of honor" whose main function was to entertain the veterans. They appeared at grand balls, exquisitely gowned, to dance with old soldiers; they enhanced receptions with the kind of light-hearted chatter that put the veterans at ease; and they rode on elaborately decorated floats in colorful parades, smiling and waving at men who were unable to march but by no means unable to appreciate beautiful women.

The parades were a popular feature of every reunion. In addition to spectacular floats, there were many brass bands interspersed with bunting-draped automobiles whose occupants frequently startled onlookers with assorted versions of the Rebel yell. In 1914, at Jackson, Mississippi, 2,000 cars swelled the ranks of the final parade, which always featured the old soldiers themselves. Some were amazingly spry for their years, but many lacked an arm or an eye or a hand, and a few stumped along on peg-legs.[1] Marching to the strains of "Dixie," they seemed happy for a few heart-stirring moments, at least. Most of the North Carolina delegation usually had Julian Carr to thank for that happiness, because he made it his business to transport them to the event if they could not go at their own expense.

Whenever Carr was asked to speak at reunions, he obliged with flowery orations full of quotations from statesmen, writers, and warriors of the past. Mindful of posterity, he often had his talks printed and bound into pamphlets, as he did when he addressed the 1894 reunion in Wilmington, North Carolina. Calling the occasion sacred and declaring himself hesitant to speak, he said, "I would vastly prefer to sit silent in this presence today and hear some of your distinguished townsmen." Despite his professed reluctance, his comments filled twenty-three typewritten pages. Beginning with a hymn of praise for southern women, he said that history had recorded noth-

General Julian S. Carr in parade at Confederate veterans' reunion in New Orleans (courtesy of Austin Heaton Carr, Jr.)

ing equal to their "patience under unparalleled hardship, courage in the face of peril, and hope in the darkest hours of misfortune"; in his opinion, Confederate soldiers would have found it easier "to face Northern bullets than the scorn of the matchless daughters of the South."[2]

Had Carr been confronted with the fact that many southern women deplored slavery and were glad to see it abolished, he might have denied it.[3] Slaves had been an integral part of his childhood, and those he had known before the war had appeared to be not only contented, but also proud of their connections with the university. At one time John Wesley and Eliza Carr had owned four Negroes, and their son never apologized for that fact. Nor did he ever relinquish his feelings about slavery, which he believed had made "a Christian people out of a pagan people." In the course of elaborating on that belief before an audience of Confederate veterans in 1899, he said:

> I am greatly in love with the civilization that obtained in the old South prior to the Civil War. My mother was a slave owner, and I remember how we of the South went forth to battle, with what confidence we committed our dear ones and our homes to the watchful care of our slaves, and we were never disappointed. No finer testimony to the righteousness of that civilization could be afforded . . . [for] they kept themselves true to their trust until the last days of their bondage.[4]

A surprising number of Chapel Hill Negroes "kept themselves true" long after their bondage was over. As late as 1869 the village population was almost equally divided: 483 whites and 453 blacks, with most of the blacks still working for their former owners. In spite of the Emancipation Proclamation and the Freedmen's Bureau, there were few opportunities for ex-slaves to earn a living anywhere, north or south, and many may have reasoned that it was better to stay with an impoverished white family than to starve. White families in Chapel Hill wore ragged clothes, and their shoes were fashioned out of wood or old leather gloves; but most of them still had a few fruit trees and a garden and a smokehouse, and they shared what they had with their servants.[5]

So Julian Carr, a product of his time and place, did not believe that slavery was wrong. Nor could anyone persuade him that the South was not superior to the North or, for that matter, to any other section of the United States. In the address at the 1894 Confederate reunion in Wilmington, he used statistics to prove his point: the southern states had "guided and protected the Republic for nearly a century prior to 1861" by giving it fifteen presidents and eighteen Supreme Court justices, while the North had provided only six chief executives and eleven justices during the same period. There had been fourteen attorneys general from below the Mason-Dixon line, but only five from above it; and the eighty-six foreign ministers from the South obviously overshadowed their fifty-four northern counterparts.[6]

Most army and navy officers were southerners, Carr asserted, and they, assisted by southern statesmen, "led in acquiring the National

Territory and placed on the flag of the Union thirty of the forty-two stars that glittered there." Furthermore, "the fathers of American liberty and the architects of her institutions" had been George Washington, Thomas Jefferson, James Madison, John Marshall, and Patrick Henry, all from the South.

North Carolina in particular inspired Julian Carr's rhetoric that day in Wilmington. Because he felt that his home state was far too reticent about recording her patriotic deeds, he considered it his duty to "set forth her glories with tongue and pen" so that future generations could know what her dead and living heroes had done during the Civil War. "North Carolina loved the Union!" he cried. "The last Southern state to secede, she only took that step when Mr. Lincoln demanded that she draw her sword against her Sisters."

After taking that step, North Carolina furnished more troops to the Confederacy than any other state. One of her citizens, Henry Lunsford Wyatt, became the first casualty of the war on 10 June 1861 at Bethel Church, in Hampton, Virginia. "When he gave his young life for us . . . his name was surrounded by a halo of glory," Carr told the old soldiers who had gathered in Wilmington for their fourth reunion, and he implored them: "Let his name forever live! Let us teach it to our children and wreath it with that sublime sentiment, 'died on the field of honor and duty'!"

Lovingly, and at great length, Carr cited further facts about North Carolina's performance in the Civil War. He emphasized that 125,000 of the 600,000 soldiers comprising the Confederate Army had been North Carolinians; that Tar Heels who died at Chancellorsville comprised half of the entire Confederate loss; and that the soldiers from the Old North State who gave their lives at Gettysburg outnumbered the combined casualties of Virginia, Mississippi, and South Carolina.

Carr also noted that a North Carolina division, Cox's Brigade, made the last charge at Appomattox. He exhorted his audience to "teach it to our posterity that North Carolina furnished the most men, laid upon the altars of Southern liberties the first victim, led the last charge, and fired the last gun in defense of Southern homes." That particular audience undoubtedly shared his sentiments about Robert E. Lee, "the peerless soldier," and his approbation of Joseph E. Johnston, Jubal Early, J. E. B. Stuart, and all the other Confederate officers he mentioned. But when they heard him say that his highest praise was for the man who was "clad in the simple uniform of the private, with the old slouch hat and glistening bayonet," they must have felt what he intended to make them feel—that they, too, were heroes "inspired by the loftiest principles and a sublime patriotism."

It was a feeling they needed to experience occasionally, those aging survivors of one of the bloodiest wars in history, those men who had seen the annihilation of everything they valued. Ragged and starving, they had limped home to find their world destroyed and the nightmare of Reconstruction awaiting. Having somehow lived through all of it, they needed to believe, at least once a year, that it had not been in vain. And because Old Jule, as they called him, made them believe that whenever he spoke at one of their reunions, they loved him. Although the cause they had fought for was lost, when he told them that "success is not the test of honor and merit," and that their devotion to principle was "a priceless legacy to civilization," their spirits soared, however briefly, and again they felt like men, instead of relics.

Carr told the veterans to have no regrets for the past, which he defined as "a sacred treasure," but he also urged them to "dedicate themselves henceforth to the perpetuation and glory of this Union." If they took his words to heart, it was because, in spite of his wealth and prestige, he was one of them, part of the rank and file. Because he was proud of that and said so publicly, they could be proud, too.

Thirty-four Confederate reunions occurred during Carr's lifetime, and he figured prominently in all of them either as a speaker, an organizer, or an active and colorful addition to social gatherings, especially where ladies were present. In a letter to a friend shortly after his return home from the 1919 meeting in Atlanta he said, "I had a very large part of the Reunion exercises dependent upon me. . . . I sat upon the platform at the auditorium until I looked like I was an old fixture and was part of the stage trappings. Then when Saturday a.m. came and we were leaving at eleven o'clock, every woman that was in town and some of them that were not were nagging at me to get to say good-bye."[7] This letter was written four years after Carr's wife died and only a few days before his seventy-fourth birthday. He was still handsome, energetic, and courtly. Women were greatly attracted to him; he returned their admiration enthusiastically, sending them his photograph upon request, going to see them if he happened to be "in the area," and writing them extravagantly flattering letters, which he often signed: "Your Sweetheart General."

General Julian S. Carr and General Lewis S. Pilcher clasp hands at Zeta Psi Chapter House in New York before Major James T. Pilcher (courtesy of Austin Heaton Carr, Jr.)

That strictly honorary title of "General" was conferred on him first in 1915 by the North Carolina division of the association; in 1919 the survivors of his old outfit, the Army of Northern Virginia, promoted him to Lieutenant General. Finally, in 1921, he was rewarded for thirty-two years of devotion to, and support of, the old soldiers of the South: he was elevated to the position of Commander-in-Chief of the United Confederate Veterans of America.[8] By then he had been both addressed and referred to as General Carr for over six years, and he frequently dressed the part in a magnificently tailored uniform emblazoned with stars and braid and embellished with a scarlet sash of heavy silk. His picture, taken in that custom-made regalia, found its way into the parlors and boudoirs of many female relatives, friends, and Confederate maids of honor. To one maid who complained that her request for that particular photograph had been ignored, he wrote:

My dear Beulah dear, you are a real queen and I make an honest confession when I say I thought you had my picture. I directed my former stenographer that the picture be framed and sent to you a month ago, and I really thought it had gone. When I saw you looking so handsome in Atlanta, I thought it was because you had received my picture and were smiling at me with your eyes. I do not see otherwise how you could have looked so pretty and handsome. . . . But Beulah dear, you shall have that picture. I have a new stenographer and I am going to put her on her metal and see that you get my picture all nicely framed and "dolled up" right. I enjoyed seeing you in Atlanta. You never looked prettier, more attractive, and more handsome. I wish you belonged to me.[9]

Following a Confederate reunion that took place in Louisville, Kentucky, after he had been made commander-in-chief, Carr wrote to a young lady he had met there:

My very dear sweetheart Hillary, I remember our association at Louisville with great pleasure. You were exceedingly kind and sweet to me and I shall not forget you. I hope you have a very happy and delightful Easter, and I am sending you, with my love and a sweet remembrance of our association in Louisville, a string of nice beads, which wear always with my love.

> Affectionately,
> Your Sweetheart General.

On the same day, 17 April 1919, he wrote to another "dear sweetheart" (whom he did not address by name):

I'm glad you enjoyed so thoroughly our few days at Louisville. They were a perfect delight to me and there was no break in my happiness except for the evening you "paced out" and left me in the hands of that little Hillary girl, but that was explained all right afterwards and we forgot it. It looks now as if the next Confederate Reunion will go to Savannah. As soon as something definite is arrived at, I will let you know.

> Affectionately,
> Your Sweetheart General.[10]

Like the bulk of Carr's correspondence, these letters, and many more in the same vein, were dictated to a stenographer; carbon copies were filed at his office in the First National Bank of Durham. He made no secret of his feelings for pretty women, or of his re-

sponses to the overtures of the "sweet little queens" he met at reunions after his wife's death, but he remained elusive. On one occasion he told his Sunday school class at Trinity Methodist Church that
Solomon, with 700 wives and 300 concubines, "must have had wheels
in his head." He then went on to say, "Not that I have any criticism to
offer respecting a good wife, the noblest, greatest gift of God to man,
but it is possible to get too much of a good thing."[11]

Regardless of that pronouncement, Julian Carr never seemed to
get too much of the Confederate Veterans of America. Like Trinity
Methodist Church and Occoneechee Farm, the organization reminded him, after he retired from business, that he was still needed,
and he gave it the same enthusiastic support that he gave to those
other good things in his life.

It was a rare Sunday when Carr was not in his pew at Trinity
Church, surrounded by his family and demonstrating, in a lusty bari-
tone, that he knew the Methodist hymnal "almost by heart."[12] He had
joined the church when he came to Durham in 1870, and when the
congregation agreed to renovate the small wooden meeting house in
1872, he helped to repair its leaky roof "with his own hands." Three
years later, "with his own means," he bought two acres of land for a
burying ground; then he arranged to have the remains of members
who had been laid to rest in the churchyard exhumed and transferred to Maplewood, Durham's first cemetery.[13]

By 1878 Carr was one of the leading laymen of the Methodist
Episcopal Church, South, and in that year he was a delegate to the
Robert Raikes Sunday School Convention in London. He returned to
England in 1881 and attended the Methodist Ecumenical Conference; in 1887 he represented the North Carolina Conference at the
Methodist Centennial in Baltimore. In the meantime, he had not
neglected the home front. In 1879, having "collaborated with his
fellow members in building a new church—the brick church—with its
far famed high steeple," Carr had the satisfaction of seeing his son,
Julian Junior, become the first baby baptized there. Fourteen years
later, when that church no longer could accommodate its congregation and Sunday school, Carr, who taught the men's Bible class and
superintended the Sunday school, led the drive to enlarge the existing structure. He offered $25,000 for that purpose, provided his
fellow members, together, would match that amount.[14]

For fifty-two years Carr sat on the board of stewards that governed
Trinity church, for forty-four years as chairman. As a frequent dele-

gate to both the North Carolina Methodist Conference and the General Conference of the Methodist Episcopal Church, South, he had a voice in shaping church policy, and he enjoyed being on familiar terms with bishops and other powerful clergymen. But he also enjoyed, and often expressed a need for, "some good preaching" of the hellfire-and-damnation sort that was the backbone of many revivals that took place in Durham during the 1880s and that were "as catching as smallpox."[15] In 1885 he told his brother-in-law, John Heitman, "We have just gone through a gracious revival of religion in our community, and as a consequence everyone feels better. We had, I suppose, in the neighborhood of 100 conversions, besides a great many who had at one time been members of the church and had lost their membership. Our town has been very greatly benefitted by the effects of the meeting. . . . We have a Gospel Tent that will seat, I suppose, 2000 persons."[16]

The following year, when Trinity Church sponsored a revival, Carr reported to Heitman that fifty-five penitents had come to the altar and that there had been several conversions. But he was worried about how his thirteen-year-old daughter, Lida, had reacted when "the spirit moved upon the troubled waters very powerfully." It had distressed him when Lida admitted that she believed all the "essentials" but could not bring herself to believe that she herself was a Christian. Explaining Lida's dilemma to her Uncle Franklin, who was both a minister and a professor at Trinity College, Carr said:

> She believes she is a sinner, and she believes that Christ died for her. She believes that Christ is able, willing and ready to save her, but she just can't some how appropriate Christ personally to herself; fails to grasp Him, or to trust Him. . . . I have attempted to lead her, pray with her and talk to her, and yet she fails to get relief. . . . Her mother talks to her, and a great many friends have had a good deal to say to her, and a great many express the deepest interest in her, but somehow she is not quite satisfied, and at other times, seems badly befogged, and says at times she is sorry she made any effort at all, having done all, believed all and yielded all and still she fails to receive satisfaction.[17]

If Lida Carr got no satisfaction from the revival in 1886, she may have had another chance at salvation in 1889, when the Reverend Sam Jones held a protracted meeting in her Uncle Ed Parrish's warehouse, "transformed into a delightful tabernacle" for the famous evangelist. Jones and his daughter, Annie, were Julian Carr's house-guests at Somerset Villa while the revival went on. After a week of Jones's electrifying sermons, Carr announced that he was going to give the preacher $500 because of the spiritual benefits he had received; he then offered to cash all subscriptions made to Jones in good faith. After the "deafening applause" that followed his offer had died down, grateful Durham citizens pledged $2,260 to the evangelist. Sam Jones, thanks to his host, received the money that same night.[18]

As a child, Carr had been trained "in the way he should go" by devout Methodist parents, and he did not depart from that training. For over fifty years his support of Methodism in general, and Trinity Church in particular, went far beyond tithing and consumed much of his time, thought, money, and physical effort. But he was no zealot. The world was too full of interesting things for him to devote every spare moment to the church.

Carr's farm in Orange County played an important role in his life as well. Operating a plantation the size of Occoneechee was a twenty-four-hour-a-day job, and Carr, a perfectionist, had difficulty finding and keeping an efficient overseer with whom both he and the hands could work harmoniously. Farm managers came and went, for a variety of reasons; but in 1910, the year when Carr retired from the Durham Hosiery Mill, he hired Charles Spurgeon Brown, who, after one false start, for twelve years demonstrated both capability and loyalty to "the good owner and his good wife."[19]

A native of Happy Valley, near Lenoir, North Carolina, Charlie Brown came to work for Carr with the endorsement of Rufus Lenoir Patterson, who had perfected the automatic packing and labeling machine for Blackwell's Durham Tobacco Company in 1895. Brown had gained his experience in large-scale farming by working at Rufus Patterson's ancestral home in Happy Valley; during those years he also gained the friendship and respect of the inventor, who recommended him to Carr after the Patterson farm was converted into an Episcopal school for mountain boys.[20]

When Brown arrived at Occoneechee on 13 September 1910, Carr took pains to point out that his predecessor, W. B. Cheek, had left the farm in a virtual shambles. Most of the silage was spoiled. Several fences needed mending. Many stones and tree stumps had been left in the fields. The runs beside the roadways were washing badly, and "extravagance and waste seems to be the rule."[21] Carr expected things to improve under Brown's management, and he recorded that expectation in the plantation diary, which was one of the main avenues of communication between owner and overseer. "Mr. C. S. Brown, the new manager, reached the farm at 5 o'clock this afternoon," Carr wrote in the diary on the night of 13 September. "We are going to give him every opportunity to 'make good' and trust sincerely that he will." The following day Carr added, "Mr. Brown takes charge of the farm today as manager on a salary of $800 per year, provided he can 'make good.'"

Brown was conscientious about keeping his part of the diary. A few days after he assumed his duties, he wrote, with apparent enthusiasm, "Fine day. I started the hands out this morning on time, cutting corn with harvester and hauling with three teams. Plowed with disc plow in spring field bottom. The ground is verry dry, too dry to do 1st class work. I deposited $10.20 in bank at Hillsboro this morning. Two sheap came to the farm by express this evening. We broke the sparker to gasolene engin, was stopped 2 hours. I had the hands to pile some rock near dairy barn while we fixed engin. Getting on verry well filling silo."

The next day was beautiful, according to Brown, and again he got the hands out on time, to plow, to haul hay, and to cut corn and take it to the silo. Seemingly bent on making good, he continued to record his accomplishments: "Started three teams in the Railroad Field harrowing and using the drag. Rained verry hard beginning about ten o'clock. We trimmed the mules and measured oats and moved back a lot of hay in the barn to make room for more. Had the hogs brought up for Gen. Carr to see. Had a box made around the pipe in lot by barn so horse could not turn water out. . . . Dairy report, 83 lbs. butter, 11½ qts. cream, 16 qts. milk."

Apparently satisfied with his new job and eager to please his employer, Brown nevertheless missed his wife and children, who had stayed in Happy Valley because Maggie Brown, a victim of chronic kidney disease, had not been well enough to travel when her husband left for Hillsborough. The new manager of Occoneechee had little time to dwell on his loneliness, for Carr had filled several pages of the diary with a list of things he wanted done and detailed instructions for doing them. The hogs, shoats, and pigs were to have skim milk and buttermilk every day, as well as corn, soybeans, forage, and charcoal, which Brown could make by burning corncobs and sprinkling them with brine. "The hogs love them," Carr added, but he cautioned Brown to provide "only so much as they eat up clean. There must be no waste, and you must see to it with your own eyes."[22]

There was a heavy mast of beechnuts, acorns, and chestnuts that year, and "The Manager of Occoneechee Farm, if he does his duty, will see that the Occoneechee hogs get their share," Carr stated. He also cautioned Brown to "see that our pear trees are not robbed and our walnuts carried away." Fruit and nuts were to be gathered and stored in a room next to the office, where they would be safe from the petty theivery that went on each day, it seemed, unless a close watch was kept on the hands.

Carr insisted that Brown "have a place for everything and everything in its place. Then when you need anything you will know where to find it and not have to waste time running all over the plantation looking." Iron pipe, for instance, belonged under one particular shed, with "sizes and lengths put to themselves—not allowed to lay in heaps and piles." There was a definite need, too, for a junk pile; discarded plow points and broken castings could be thrown there, instead of being left in the fields. "Then some rainy day haul into town and sell," Carr said, "Money from junk is as good as money from corn."

Although Brown refrained from commenting on Carr's list of orders, his next entry in the diary displayed irritation. "I had all the hands cutting Johnson Grass and I am going to burn it," he wrote. "I wish it was all Dead." On the following day, however, his spirits rose when his family arrived from Happy Valley and joined him in the manager's house, which Carr had christened The Wigwam. That night Brown wrote "My wife and children came this evening. I am verry glad to have them with me. I think I can get on better with the work now."

A few days later, Carr stopped by Occoneechee on his way from Greensboro to Durham and made a note of the new arrivals. "Reached the Farm this morning and was glad to welcome Mrs. Brown and her six nice children. I hope all of them will have their health here, keep well and be happy and contented." Having thus observed the amenities, Carr reminded Brown to give more attention to the poultry. "Report to me any loss by death or thieves of any fowls of any kind," he ordered. "Also, watch closely the boy you appoint to do the feeding and see that he makes no waste. I will try to get you a good man soon."[23]

Brown, his loneliness alleviated and his general outlook improved by the prospect of an assistant, worked diligently for the next few weeks. He kept a sharp eye on the Negro boy he had assigned to the poultry yards and made sure that the chickens were counted every other day, but he gave most of his attention to one of the largest fields, which was not draining properly. During the first week in November he was rewarded with an enthusiastic note of congratulation from Carr: "The Kirkland Field looks improved. I compliment you on the job. Now that we are about to get this field in hand, let's keep at it and improve it every time. You can't do too much deep plowing and ditching for me. Put in any new ditch, or straighten out any ditch or change any ditch you please. It appears to me that you are taking care of Occoneechee Farm and I want to encourage you by saying I think you are doing first rate."

Carr further encouraged Brown by hiring a Mr. Wilbur to take over the duties of poultryman, and Brown expressed his pleasure in the diary. "I think Mr. Wilbur is a good man," he wrote. "I like his appearance verry much and I think he will be a great help to me in taking care of everything here. I hope he will be satisfied and stay a long time and prove to be the kind of man we want." Carr echoed Brown's feelings when, directly beneath Brown's seal of approval, he inscribed his own: "I have an idea that Mr. Brown and Mr. Wilbur will make me two good men."[24]

Brown's spirits were dampened during December, when one of the goats broke a sheep's neck, and a cow died for no apparent reason; but he was too busy to brood over the losses because it was time to cut ice from the pond and store it in the ice house. Before he and the hands could rest up from that back-breaking labor, it was time to slaughter hogs—a bloody, gruelling job that had to be done in bitter cold weather. Scraping bristles from a scalded hog's hide wasn't easy; nor was rendering fat into lard; nor was removing from the carcass those parts that could not be preserved (liver, brains, feet, backbone, tail, ears, snout, and chitterlings) and parceling them out to the hands. Once the butchering and cleaning up were finished, any pork not earmarked for Occoneechee and Somerset Villa had to be hauled to Durham and sold, and by Christmas Eve everyone was dog tired. But Brown and Wilbur and the hands continued to work, scrubbing the stalls in the dairy barn, cleaning the pony lot, shucking corn, gathering rocks and old horseshoes from the fields, and hauling wood.

Then, on Christmas Day, the farm was quiet. Unfortunately for Brown and Wilbur, it remained quiet for the next three days—none of the hands showed up for work, and the two men had to manage alone.

Five days after Christmas, Carr came up from Durham, went into the office, and added another entry in the plantation diary: "One more day and the year 1910 has passed into history forever. Time is short, but Oh, Eternity how long! Our chief purpose in time should be to prepare for eternity. *Think on these things*."

Charlie Brown must have taken his employer's admonition to heart, for on 1 January 1911 he wrote:

> I have been thinking of the past year and I wonder what is before us for the next 12 months. I feel to-night like there is a great responsibility on me here, so many hands to keep at work and to keep at something that will pay, and so much stock to be cared for and so much good judgment needed to run everything right. To think of all this makes me feel so small for the place, but I want to write here in this diary tonight and say that I am going to do my best while I stay here, and I pray God to help me understand what is right with the hands, and I want them to have all that is promised them and no more, and I want them to earn their money, so I do hope and pray that everything on Occoneechee Farm may prosper and the crops do well and pay back the expense of making them and more than the expenses, and I wish the good owner and his good wife good health and prosperity through this year.

The next day, still fired with resolution, Brown put the hands to work shucking corn, cleaning out stalls, and hauling hay. For the next two months he kept everybody who worked at Occoneechee busy from first light until dusk. They cleared the hickory woods, raked leaves, cleaned gutters, hauled manure and corn to Durham, and pruned the fruit trees. They cut briars and cleaned the poultry pens and hauled lumber and plowed the orchard and the garden; then it began to snow. They killed forty-two rats in one corncrib, mended gates and fences, cut down trees, pulled Johnson grass, blasted stumps, chopped wood, and shucked corn. Brown sold two cows, two calves, and two pigs, which pleased his employer; and he also supervised the construction of a new fence around the Railroad Field.

Suddenly it was spring, and Brown recorded the births of four pigs, three kids, and a lamb. Then things took a turn for the worse. He began to write that his wife was not well. One after another, his children came down with the chicken pox. On 7 March torrents of rain, snow, and hail killed all of the early fruit. Despite crazy weather and a ruined crop and a sick family, life had to go on, work had to be done, and Brown had to keep the farm record up to date.

Julian Carr, checking that record intermittently, was delighted when three Occoneechee cows sold for ninety-five dollars each and one sow brought twenty dollars. He also rejoiced when the black pony and the strawberry roan pony dropped two fine colts, but he was distressed when the bald-faced pony dropped a deformed colt, and he was shocked when several sheep died for no discernible reason. He ordered Brown to put the rest of the flock in another pasture, to give them wet, salted tobacco stems, and to dose them with sulphur every two weeks. Stock losses worried him, and he began to insist that every mare, cow, and sow on the farm be bred immediately. "*Breed Everything,*" he told Brown. "Give old Jack something to do, and I want you to be present and see what sort of performer he is and let me know."[25]

Brown was in no mood for breeding stock. He was too worried about his wife, who continued to ail until finally, toward the end of March, she had to leave the farm. Taking the children, she went back to Happy Valley. On 25 March, Brown received a letter from her physician that must have prompted him to give notice of his resignation, for on 11 April he wrote, with obvious emotion:

Mr. Skinner . . . came to the Farm . . . to take my place. I think he is a verry fine man and a first class gentleman. I do say and tell the truth that I wish him good luck and hope he will be successful with everything here as long as he stays at Occoneechee. I want everything at Occoneechee to do well, and I hope and pray that the good owner and his good wife may live long and be happy and prosperous as long as they live, and I do thank them for their kindness to me during my short stay at Occoneechee, and as this is my last line in this diary, I will say God bless the owners of Occoneechee.

The lanky mountaineer from Happy Valley had not seen the last of Occoneechee's "good owner," nor had he made his final entry in the diary. He had no way of knowing that he would be back a year later, saddened by the death of his wife but eager to make good again as Julian Carr's farm manager. Nor did he reckon that one day he would be known to the people of Hillsborough and Durham as Occoneechee Brown.

Although Julian Carr was genuinely fond of Charlie Brown and sorry to see him go, he felt fortunate in securing the services of Benjamin Smith Skinner, a well-born native of Hertford County and a widower who had recently resigned as superintendent of grounds and gardens at the North Carolina College of Agriculture and Mechanic Arts, in Raleigh.[26] Tall, blue-eyed, bald, and only a few years younger than Carr, Skinner was a dignified gentleman of strong opinions, and his entries in the Occoneechee diary reveal that he was not easily intimidated.

On his first day at Occoneechee, Skinner wrote that he found the place attractive but was "impressed with what seems to be a great deal of misdirected energy" and surprised to find "no hay on the place and limited pasturage." He could see that expenses were going to be very heavy: many farm implements needed to be repaired and many more needed to be replaced. "I cannot make any promise as to what I can accomplish," he wrote on that first day. "I shall do what I can . . . and trust to luck."[27]

Luck, apparently, was not kindly disposed toward the new manager that spring. During April and May the diary bristled with complaints. The woodpile was disreputable, the well was dirty, the water supply inadequate. Skinner could not understand why the sows were brought to the boar for servicing, instead of vice versa. One of the goats died, and the rest were so infested with lice that the whole herd had to be clipped and dipped. A new Shetland pony arrived by express "in bad shape, half starved," and two of the three pigs born to a prize sow died. The sinks used for cleaning milk vessels in the dairy barn were in such terrible condition that a tinsmith had to be brought from Durham to repair them. A Durham veterinarian, called in to castrate a pony, arrived drunk and botched the operation, causing the pony to die.

After a violent electrical storm blew down seven large oak trees on 26 May, some of Occoneechee's twenty-one farmhands failed to show up for work, and the angry manager wrote:

I find the labor here disposed to lay off for the slightest provocation and without making any excuse. They seem to think that it is all right. They evidently lose sight of the fact that they are under obligation to this farm for their living. They certainly have no just grounds for complaint, for everything is done for them and they give in return as little as possible. Seven men out this morning for one cause or another, just failed to show up. A most unsatisfactory way of doing business.

Skinner's irritation was contagious, and when Carr became likewise afflicted, manager and owner began a series of written skirmishes. Contending that the Percheron stallion did not get enough exercise, Carr wrote: "Exercise will make him vigorous. Work him! Work him! Give him exercise. It is essential. He stagnates from lack of work. Work him! Exercise him! Have Jesse drive him."

Skinner did not comment on the stallion's lack of vigor, but he did complain about the lack of hay. "Hay is very light," he said, "owing to the fact that the land needs tile draining the *worst in the world*. Can never produce until it is *drained*." Stung by criticism of his beloved land, which was always at the mercy of heavy rains that washed it away, Carr countered with a formal letter to Skinner concerning the matters of chaff and corn cultivation:

Colonel Skinner:

I feel that the chaff that was stored in the barn that the tree crushed ought to be taken care of. I am aware that you do not place much value on chaff, but I do. Then again, I believe very strongly in saving what you make. Saving is the wisest management. . . . Now, the corn as you enter the field going to the Race Track on the left appears to be suffering for work. Not hoeing. I don't believe in hoeing corn. In place of the Hoe we have substituted the Cultivator. This particular piece of corn, in my judgment, should have had the cultivator at least three times, and then have the cultivator every few days. I believe in giving corn the cultivator *Early and Often*. This piece of corn surprised and astonished me.

Yours very truly,
J.S. Carr[28]

The next day the colonel, with considerable heat, made a formal reply to the general's complaint:

General Julian S. Carr
Dear Sir:

I have read your criticism carefully and with some surprise, I must confess. The old chaff stored in the barn that the tree crushed was soaked with the only rain we had, and I have been using it for bedding. But I will store it, as you suggest. I am surprised at your criticism of condition of corn. It has been cultivated *frequently* and in *my* judgment enough. As a farmer, I have a reputation at stake and shall do my utmost to live up to it, and also to carry out your ideas if possible. . . . I do not profess to know it all.

For the rest of the summer, Carr observed the farm and Skinner's management of it closely; then, in the middle of September, he used several pages of the diary "to correct a few little things." He prefaced these corrections by saying that he knew Skinner to be a gentleman, that he wanted Skinner to remain in charge of Occoneechee, and that he wanted to retain Skinner's respect, services, and friendship. Having said these things, he continued: "I believe it is to be found in the Scriptures where it says, 'It is the little foxes that spoil the grapes.' The little foxes, the little things spoil life. . . . You must bear with me, because I am endeavoring to speak in great kindness and with the earnest, honest desire to cement our relations closer, and more lasting. I want to kill the little foxes."

Nevertheless, Carr's first blow at the little foxes appears to have been aimed directly at Skinner. "You and I went over the Kirkland Field early in the summer to inspect the corn crop," he said. "You drove the buggy right through the corn. The buggy did not touch my body, but the incident hurt me as bad as if I had fallen out and the buggy had run over me." Another thing that had hurt the owner of Occoneechee was the fact that his grapevines were suffering from Skinner's neglect. Declaring that grapes were "almost a household necessity" and that he had paid a professor from the agricultural college to come to the farm and locate the vineyard and put in a suitable species, Carr said: "I would not have done so if I had supposed the little foxes were going to get them."

Skinner's failure to get a fall crop of Irish potatoes was one more little fox, and the appearance of breaks in several iron gates was still another. "It would distress me to see these rents [in the gates] grow any larger," Carr said, and he suggested that "some wire of the proper size . . . and a pair of pinchers will do the work NOW that it won't do later on." Moving from the gates to the roads in and around the farm, Carr continued: "I would be glad if more use was made of our drag, and our roads kept constantly dragged and the side ditches kept open. The little foxes are out on our roads in plain view, to be seen by everybody, and they are doing serious damage."

Benjamin Skinner, who had held his position as farm superintendent of the state agricultural college for fourteen years, was a proud man who must have had to struggle for composure as he continued to read what Julian Carr had written:

> No person hates to have a tooth pulled more than I do, but the toothache never hurt me half as much as the washes and galded places on the Farm. The Kirkland Field, considering we have had a dry year, has surprised me the way it has washed, and unmolested. I said to Mr. Brown on page 33, "The Kirkland Field looks improved." But I don't feel I can repeat it. . . . If the rolls of wire resting in the hog runs have not been removed, they ought to be, and keep the little foxes out. And a clean-up of the lane running along side the hog pens would drive the little foxes further away. I won't, but I could say more. What I have said I have said hoping to improve conditions, and with the hope that it will make us better, stronger, and more lasting friends. Listen, there are a lot of little foxes I have not mentioned. I hope you will find them and drive them out. I will wait to see. I confess, they annoy me.
>
> Very respectfully,
> Julian S. Carr

That this diatribe did little to make Skinner and Carr better, stronger, and more lasting friends seems evident in the manager's reply:

General Carr
Dear Sir:

I waited some time before writing a reply to your severe arraignment of my management for fear I would say too much. Now, after mature thought, I want to tell you that I do not appreciate what you have said because it was unnecessary and uncalled for and I believe both of us would feel better if what you have written had been left off. I, too, could "say much more," but I will not, for what's the use? Life is too short and the State too big for us to exhange pleasantries of this sort. It would please me much better if, when you have anything to say to me, you would do so face to face, and not get behind my diary.

Very respectfully,
B.S. Skinner

There was undoubtedly a coolness in the atmosphere at Occoneechee following these exchanges. Skinner, jealous of his reputation as a conscientious and knowledgeable practitioner of scientific farming, seemed determined to erase the slur Carr had made on that reputation, and for the rest of the year Occoneechee hummed with activity. Skinner recorded that the hog lots and chicken runs were repaired, and that concrete water troughs for the cows were installed in the dairy barns. New floors were laid in the big house and in the office. The concrete bridge across the creek was reinforced. Rotting fences were removed, as was a rock wall Skinner described as "an eyesore lo these many years."[29] A large amount of swampy land was reclaimed by the installation of tile drainage, which also was used in the offending Kirkland Field and in the Gum Spring Bottom. Almost gleefully, Skinner noted that great quantities of field rock were removed, that it took three cases of dynamite to blast the rock, and that it gave him more pleasure than anything else he had done all year.

If dynamiting Carr's fields gave Skinner pleasure, spending Carr's money may have given him even more. Stating that the rolling stock he found at Occoneechee was "the limit," he proceeded to replace it, buying two new wagons, three John Deere disc plows, one pulverizer, and one smoothing harrow. He also had three old wagons repaired and made new wagon beds and hay frames for the rest. On the last day of December he wrote in the diary:

The year 1911, with all its pleasures and pains and ups and downs is a thing of the past and also brings to a close my first year (8 months and 2 days) as manager of Occoneechee Farm. I have found General Carr to be a gentleman, fair-minded, kindhearted. Sometimes a little irritable. Upon the whole, we have gotten on very nicely, and so far I do not regret coming here. On account of coming so late in the Spring, it took some doing to get in shape for planting crops, which was further aggravated by severe drought that continued all summer. But still, the corn crop was fairly good. Hay a complete failure, owing to the drought. I have sowed this Fall to wheat, oats and rye, about 12,500 acres, which is looking good. All things considered, I am very thankful for what we have. It could have been worse.

Although Benjamin Skinner's New Year's Eve remarks lacked the emotional fervor of those penned by Charlie Brown on the preceding January, their general tone was positive, even where Julian Carr was concerned. The fact that Skinner had no regrets indicates that the white flag of truce waved over Occoneechee Farm on the last night of 1911.

12. Patriarch

FOR Julian Carr, as for Benjamin Skinner, 1911 had been a year of ups and downs. After retiring from the Durham Hosiery Mill, Carr had responded to pressure from some of his Democratic cronies and agreed to run for office. Victory at the polls in November 1910 sent him to the North Carolina House the following January. Carr enjoyed the machinations of politics and the responsibility of being Durham County's only representative, and in his personal diary he kept a meticulous record of his involvement in the 1911 General Assembly. It was to be his only legislative session.

In addition to serving as chairman of the state banking commission, he introduced bills to increase the pay of Durham County and Orange County commissioners; to authorize the city of Durham to issue bonds to pay its floating debt; to establish a special criminal court in the city and county of Durham; and to regulate the pay of members of the Durham County Board of Education. Other bills affecting his constituents dealt with chartering a new railroad from Durham to Danville, Virginia; changing the boundary between Durham and Wake counties; prohibiting the sale of fireworks within half a mile of Durham; amending the Durham city charter to change the time for holding elections; and authorizing the Durham County Board of Education to provide funds for the erection of school buildings. His concerns were not exclusively local, however. He also supported acts to authorize sheriffs and special officers to break up unlawful distilleries; to secure state aid for the construction and maintenance of public roads; to regulate and control the banking business; to tax dogs and encourage sheep husbandry; and to promote more efficient municipal government.

Carr also introduced legislation designed to promote the welfare of North Carolina's Confederate veterans, that steadily diminishing group so dear to his heart. He asked the legislature to appropriate funds to cover the deficit at the Soldier's Home in Raleigh, and to purchase marble headstones for the graves of veterans who died at the home. And he proposed, with particular eloquence, that the General Assembly enshrine the "Noble Women of North Carolina and of the Southern States" by erecting a suitable monument to their memory.[1]

When the legislature adjourned in March, the tired Carr came down with what he called "the Grippe" and took to his bed, as did his wife, Nannie. By April they were well enough to spend their customary two weeks at the Bellevue Stratford, in Philadelphia; and in mid-May Carr traveled to Little Rock for the Confederate reunion. From there he went to Kansas City to visit Lida and Lalla Ruth. Shortly after his return to Durham he noted in his diary: "Will Patton operated upon at University Hospital Phila[delphia] Pa."[2] Nine days later he recorded the arrival of Will and Lalla Ruth's eight-year-old daughter, Ruth, who came to stay at Somerset Villa while her father recuperated from surgery.

In July 1911, an exceptionally hot, dry month, Carr bought an automobile for Nannie. They cooled off by taking late afternoon chauffeur-driven rides around the countryside. Then, when it was time to move to Occoneechee, they "motored to the Farm" instead of "going up on the Cars," as they had done for many years. That summer they enjoyed frequent visits from young Julian's daughters, Margaret Louise and Nancy. In August, Marvin came down from New York. Lida and Harry Flower, accompanied by their three children and a nurse, reached the farm on 14 September, in time to see Austin before he left for Chapel Hill to begin his freshman year.

Except for the sad fact that Will Patton was a very sick man, it was a happy time for Carr, who loved family gatherings. He was looking forward to a real reunion in November, when Claiborn was to marry Margaret Jordan Boylan, the granddaughter of William Boylan, a wealthy Wake County planter, journalist, and banker who "at one time owned most of southeast Raleigh."[3] Carr was delighted with the match, and if Lalla Ruth and Will had been able to come to the "beautiful pink and white ceremony in Christ Church in Raleigh"[4] on 15 November, his cup of joy would have brimmed over. But Will was no better, and Lalla Ruth would not leave him.

On 27 November, while Claiborn and his bride were still on their honeymoon, Carr received a telegram containing "Alarming news from Mr. Patton, who is in hospital at Phila[delphia]." Julian Junior left immediately for that city. Carr followed on 10 December, and for a week he spent part of each day with his grieving daughter at the University of Pennsylvania Hospital; when Lida and Harry arrived from Kansas City to give their support to Lalla Ruth, he returned to

Nancy (Nannie) Graham Parrish Carr with namesake Nancy Carr, daughter of Julian S. Carr, Jr. (courtesy of Austin Heaton Carr, Jr.)

Margaret Boylan Carr (courtesy of Rufus Tucker Carr)

Claiborn McDowell Carr (courtesy of Rufus Tucker Carr)

Durham. Three days later, on 20 December, he wrote in his diary: "Mr. William F. Patton, the husband of dear Lalla Ruth, died today at 1 o'clock in the University Hospital at Phila[delphia] Pa." It was the first break in the family circle, a tragedy that came at the worst possible season—Christmastime.

Lalla Ruth Carr's happiness with Will Patton had been marred only once, to her father's knowledge, when their second daughter, Nancy, named for Nannie Carr, died in infancy. Patton, "a polished gentleman" who loved golf, tennis, dancing, and traveling abroad, was wealthy enough to spend more time enjoying his hobbies with his wife than he did practicing law; and because they had been almost inseparable for eleven years, Lalla Ruth was devastated by Will's death. After a sad Christmas in Kansas City, she and young Ruth came to Somerset Villa for two weeks early in January. Carr noticed then that his widowed daughter's hair was rapidly turning white.[5]

Durham was gripped by bitter cold in January and February, and Carr's diary was peppered with gloomy comments about the weather. His spirits rose in March, when he learned that Claiborn and Margaret were expecting a baby. Carr was convinced that he could never have too many grandchildren. The six he had been blessed with thus far were paragons in his eyes; he had pronounced each one, as it arrived, "the finest baby ever."

While he was still congratulating himself on becoming a grandfather for the seventh time, more good news arrived in April. Marvin wrote that Aurelia Blassingame Fitzpatrick, whose grandfather, Benjamin Fitzpatrick, had been governor of Alabama and also a United States senator, had agreed to marry him on 12 October, his father's sixty-seventh birthday. From all reports, the exquisite Aurelia was the perfect match for the handsome, debonair Marvin, who had fallen in love with the well-born beauty while visiting his sister, Lida Flower. Marvin told his parents that he was "quite sure she is the woman for me or I would not love her as I do"; he added, "I have a very bad case, and don't care how much worse it gets, the more the better for my happiness and hers."[6]

Aurelia's first letter to Julian and Nannie Carr indicated that she, too, had "a very bad case." "Loving Marvin as I do," she explained, "it will be very easy for me to win, I trust, the faithfulness of your love. . . . It makes me very happy to feel that you approve Marvin's selection of a soul mate . . . and I shall feel very proud, indeed, to gain his dear mother and father for mine."[7]

Albert Marvin Carr (courtesy of Albert Marvin Carr, Jr.)

Aurelia Fitzpatrick Carr (courtesy of Mary Evelyn Carr Quisenberry)

Carr lost no time in assuring Aurelia that, although he and Nannie had never seen her, they already loved her because Marvin loved her. Aurelia replied that she knew she would love them; that she could see where Marvin got his sweetness; and that she hoped she would measure up to their expectations. Letters flew back and forth from Durham to Kansas City and New York, each one exuding declarations of love and crackling with plans for the wedding, which was to be large and, from all indications, very grand. Because Julian, Claiborn, and Austin were to "stand up" with Marvin, their father fully expected his sixty-seventh birthday to be his happiest.

Suddenly life was sweet again and Carr was on the move. In his various roles as director, trustee, officer, board member, and stockholder, he attended many meetings having to do with business, politics, education, and philanthropy. He seldom refused to mount a podium, and invitations to speak at reunions, conventions, commencements, dedications, unveilings, political rallies, and church conferences drew him like magnets. In 1912 he was rarely in Durham for more than a few days at a stretch. From February until August, he journeyed to Florida, Cuba, New York, Pennsylvania, Georgia, Mississippi, Tennessee, Maryland, South Carolina, Virginia, and Washington, D.C. The few weeks he did spend in North Carolina were punctuated with junkets to Raleigh, Wilmington, Chapel Hill, Greensboro, Winston-Salem, Maxton, Fayetteville, Charlotte, Kanuga Lake, and, of course, Occoneechee and Hillsborough. Although there were several automobiles in Carr's former carriage house, and a chauffeur to drive them, he preferred the train, even for short trips. Red caps, spotting him immediately as a man of means and a generous tipper, invariably added to the fanfare of his arrivals and departures; and those major domos of the train, the pullman porter and the dining car steward, never failed to provide Carr with excellent service. They also knew the proper responses to his good-natured banter, which was an essential part of his traveling equipment and, he believed, as necessary as luggage.

His wife, who was not strong, rarely accompanied him. They went together to Philadelphia each spring and fall, to Kansas City occasionally to see their daughters, and to Occoneechee every summer, where they usually stayed until October. They were there when their second grandson, Claiborn McDowell Carr, Junior, was born on 14 August 1912. Carr's joy over the safe arrival of another baby boy was clouded by concern for his wife's oldest sister, Annie, who had married his brother, Albert. Annie Parrish Carr had been taken to the Johns Hopkins Hospital in Baltimore for an operation that would not prolong her life for more than a few weeks at best. Carr grieved for Albert's widow, who stood high in his esteem; she was "a good true noble Christian woman," and it was "a very very sad day" when she died during the first week in October. He confided to his diary that "Sister Annie died beloved by the multitude" and that "her sweet spirit rests in Heaven." Despite what must have been keen disappointment, he refrained from mentioning that her death meant he and Nannie would have to miss Marvin's wedding.[8]

Out of deference to Marvin's mother, Aurelia called off the reception, but the cancellation failed to dim the happiness of the bride and groom. On the morning of 12 October they sent Carr a telegram: "Today doubly happy for us / Your birthday our wedding / Many happy returns to you and love to Mother." Immediately, Carr replied: "Earth holds no fortune too good or sacred that we would not ask to be your dowry on this your happy wedding day and not only for this day but for all the days of all the years / Our home our hearts and our prayers are yours without stint / A long life and a happy one/ Third John one four."[9]

His message, with its biblical reference to the necessity of being born again, apparently did not strike Carr as adequate. In less than an hour he sent a second telegram, addressed to Aurelia: "On this our anniversary I am most happy to dedicate to your loving care the finest young man in all our glorious American Union and I am delighted to know that I get in exchange the one only and onliest fine young woman / God bless you both." Two days later, the honeymooning couple wired from Asbury Park, New Jersey, "Watch out for bridal bouque / Had same shipped when leaving Kansas City to show you we were thinking of you and regretting that you were not with us."

Carr put great stock in such overt demonstrations of affection from his children, especially his sons. Their burgeoning business ability was another source of vast satisfaction to him, and he was highly pleased when Julian Junior told him they were making arrangements to buy the T. F. Lloyd Manufacturing Company, near Chapel Hill, which Lloyd had built shortly after he sold his Alberta Mill to the Carrs in 1909. If negotiations with Lloyd's widow proved successful, the business she had inherited would become Mill Number Seven in the Durham Hosiery Mill chain. The surrounding village of Venable, so called for the president of the university, might then be renamed Carrboro.[10] The fact that a mill town called Duke had existed in Harnett County since 1903 probably made the prospect of a similar memorial to the Carr family doubly pleasing to the head of the clan.[11]

The pleasures of 1912 seem to have outweighed the pains, and when the first day of 1913 dawned bright, clear, and balmy, the first thing Carr wrote in his new diary was a quotation from Thomas Carlyle: "Blessed is he who has found his work; he need ask no other blessedness." Other blessings of a special order were in the offing, however, and on 4 February he recorded their arrival: "Born to Julian and Margaret last night, Twins. A Boy and a Girl. Praise the Lord."[12] The advent of Mary Ann and Julian Shakespeare Carr III brought a flood of congratulatory telegrams, letters, and phone calls to Somerset Villa. The twins' paternal grandfather clipped and pasted in his diary the Raleigh *News and Observer*'s announcement of the event, which concluded with the editor's personal opinion that "There cannot be too many Jule Carr's in North Carolina."

The twins were followed, six months later, by Marvin and Aurelia's daughter, Mary Evelyn, born in New Rochelle, New York, on 12 August 1913. Ten days later Carr went to New York to see the baby, pronouncing her "a very fine baby indeed"; within six months he was calling her "the dearest of the dears, our sweetest dearest love."[13] To the baby's mother he confided, "Aurelia my dear, this is your first, but listen, you may try *a thousand years*, but you will never better Mary Evelyn." Carr's heart was a highly flexible organ that easily accommodated each new addition to the family, and when Albert Marvin Carr, Junior, was born on 9 December 1914, the infant's grandfather was equally enthusiastic about Mary Evelyn's "dear little brother."[14]

Carr was blissful in his role of patriarch, especially when the family gathered at Occoneechee. There, with Nannie beside him on the porch of the big house, he could watch the youngest grandchildren enjoying the sandboxes, swings, and sliding boards he had installed in the yard, while the older ones chattered and squealed and laughed and played the piano in the Club House, as his own children had done years before. But mealtimes were the best times. From the head of the long table in the dining room "Pa Pa" could beam on his progeny as they feasted on Occoneechee's bounty, "delightful vegetables, fried chicken and spring lamb, fresh buttermilk and rich sweet milk by the gallon ... the finest Irish potatoes that ever grew ...

Julian S. Carr, James W. Cannon, Julian S. Carr, Jr., Nancy (Nannie) Parrish Carr with Julian S. Carr III, Mary Bost Cannon with Mary Ann Carr, and Margaret Cannon Carr (courtesy of Paul W. Sanger, Jr.)

and eggs served so fresh on the table that they have the cackle on them."[15]

None of that bounty would have reached Carr's table had it not been for the farm's black population, which swelled and diminished according to the seasons, often numbering between forty and fifty, sometimes dwindling to fifteen or twenty, and occasionally shrinking to fewer than a dozen hands, depending on the weather. One small boy, whose bright mind and good manners won Julian Carr's approval and led to a paying job, never forgot "old times" at Occoneechee, when he drew a salary just for playing with Carr's grandson, Claiborn, while his own father worked in the fields. When he was over seventy, Clarence Walker of Hillsborough remembered those days:

> I knew Mr. Charlie Brown, but first I knew Mose McCown, a big man, used to drive a two-horse wagon to General Carr's farm to thresh the wheat. Then there was George Ferribault. We called him Ducky. He was the yard man and garden man, and Grace Hughes was the cook. Ducky, he made peach brandy every year, and then there was George Morgan and Jones Bradsher, they worked there, too, along with my Daddy. And Carl

Burke and Lorena, his wife, they took care of the cows. There was two cow barns, beside the horse barn, and when the cyclone came it killed ten cows. It blew off tin roofs and wrapped them around trees. Tore up a whole line of cedar trees and uprooted don't know how many fruit trees. General Carr had every kind, pear, apple, peach, plum, and it just took 'em all up.

In the horse barn, the horses had their names on the stalls, and there were great big iron horse shoes on each side of the doorway to the barn, and it had an oak floor and a basement where the mules stayed, and hay was on the third floor. Had a slate roof, too.

Sooner Torain was the name of the man took care of the horses, and the General had a white horse named Mamie that Sooner had to wash every day, wash down with soap and water. The General had four carriages and a buggy, and one time he had three automobiles. There was a green and white Franklin, and a Marmon that was maroon with a black top, and a green Buick roadster. But the funny thing was, the General mostly rode the train.

There was two mules named Rhoda and Bill. Bill got drowned in the river, and Rhoda, she always went home at twelve o'clock whether anybody liked it or not. Be in the field, twelve o'clock come, Rhoda went back to the barn. There was eight mules when I remembered it, and the General had twenty-eight people working for him then, six in the house and the rest outside. He had two horses he kept in Durham named Dan and Charlie, and when Dan died, Charlie came out to the farm and everybody treated him like one of the family.

And they had plenty ponies. I remember one, particularly, a little black one. We used to ride him, me and Claiborn. Claiborn was one of the grandchildren, and the General used to pay me two dollars and a half a week in the summertime to come play with Claiborn. Yeah, they sure had ponies, and monkeys, too. Kept them in cages, but there was one bad monkey that got out when he got ready, and you could see him almost anywhere sometimes.

I remember the General had a picnic every year for the hands, every summer. And it was just like the ones they had when visitors came. Seems like they had a picnic most every Sunday, and there was lots of folks coming up from Durham, and all around. They were good times back then, and plenty to eat. Ice cream they made with their own cream and their own ice they cut off the pond in the winter and covered up with straw.

Now the Wigwam was where the manager lived. All the managers lived there with their families, and I reckon the General called it that because he liked Indian names. But the Club House was where they had a good time, the children and everybody. Had parties there, and dances.

Now the Bungalow was where the General moved after Miss Nannie died. He didn't sleep in the big house anymore after Miss Nannie died, just moved out and had him a little narrow bed there at the Bungalow, and I brought him a pitcher of water every night and every morning. That was my job for him, that and shining his shoes. He had little bitty feet, and he liked his shoes to be so shiny you could near 'bout see yourself in them. And he gave me twenty-five cents for every shine, and that was fifteen cents more than you could get up town in Hillsborough.

But he was a generous man. He was good and kind, always giving things to folks. Used to send them vegetables and fruit, melons, eggs, and buttermilk and sweet milk. The hogs, they got buttermilk, but there was plenty more. The hands got all the milk and butter and vegetables they needed right there at the farm. All they had to buy was sugar and coffee and meal. They even got flour, the Occoneechee Flour that was made right yonder in Durham at the Austin Heaton plant.[16]

The plant that furnished the Occoneechee farmhands with flour originated as the Carrolina Roller Mill, established by Julian Carr on 21 April 1902. Capitalized at $49,000, the mill produced "a moderate amount of flour, about two hundred barrels a day, for family consumption." Families in Durham and Hillsborough were the first to consume it; gradually, however, Carr's Occoneechee Flour began to appear on the shelves of grocery stores in other parts of the state, and eventually it was marketed in neighboring South Carolina and Virginia.[17]

Occoneechee Self-Rising Flour accounted for approximately 80 percent of the Carrolina Roller Mill's production, but Peerless Flour, a plain variety that Carr named for "the peerless soldier, Robert E.

Lee," was also a popular brand. These two outsold a silkier, more expensive flour called Bon Ton, which was the company's finest grade. In 1910 Carr renamed the mill for his son Austin, and by 1917 business was good enough to warrant the construction of a new five-story brick building on McMannen Street, just south of Durham's main thoroughfare. At that location, the Austin Heaton Company, equipped with "the most modern milling machinery to be found," manufactured 800 barrels of flour a day, using "choice winter wheat" imported from Pennsylvania, Maryland, and Ohio.[18]

As in many of his entrepreneurial ventures, Julian Carr never assumed the presidency of the flour mill, although he and his sons controlled the stock and sat on the board of directors, and very few directors' meetings took place without him.[19] Regardless of his so-called retirement, monthly board meetings of the various business, educational, and religious organizations with which he was connected remained on Carr's agenda, as did daily visits to his office, weekly appearances at Sunday school and church, and semi-annual trips to Philadelphia with his wife.

The fact that Nannie Carr had been "a great sufferer for several years from failing health" may have desensitized her husband, who showed only a mild concern over the severe cold she developed shortly after their return from Philadelphia in May 1914. Carr noted the illness in his diary, along with the information that he was conferring with architects about new quarters for the First National Bank and was going to have to "examine some Washington bank buildings," which meant a two-day journey. He left Durham on 14 May, and although his wife was not much better when he got back, he left town again on 20 May to deliver the commencement address at Weaver College, near Asheville. He had long since filled his calendar with engagements for the next three weeks, so it was fortunate that his daughter Lida had come to Durham for an extended visit.[20]

While Lida was at Somerset with her mother, Carr flitted in and out of town. He spoke to the graduating class of Catawba College, in Salisbury; attended three days of commencement exercises at the University of North Carolina; made a second trip to Washington to consult with the architectural firm of G. A. Fuller and Company about the new bank building; returned in time to attend the Confederate reunion in Raleigh; and went to his sister Emma's funeral four days later. Emma Carr Heitman, who had lived her last years in High

Point, was "one of the best women I ever knew," Carr wrote in his diary. "Cultured and educated, beloved and respected by everybody. God bless her tender memory. I loved her very much."[21]

By the end of June, Nannie Carr was well enough to move up to Occoneechee for the rest of the summer, but during the fall she became increasingly dependent upon her physician and her personal maid, Annie. The following spring, she went to Kansas City to see Lida and Lalla Ruth, who persuaded her to consult a group of medical specialists. These doctors found that "she was suffering from a complication of diseases that could not be cured." Whether or not she was informed of her condition is debatable. She went to Occoneechee, as usual, during the summer, dying there on 18 August 1915, "after three weeks of serious illness."[22]

If Carr kept a diary in 1915, he may have destroyed it. His journals for the four years preceding his wife's death, as well as for the two years immediately following it, are extant, but no record of 1915 has been found. Perhaps he became too concerned about Nannie's condition to attach much significance to other matters. Apparently he could be glib about his affection for his sister-in-law, Annie Parrish Carr, and for his own beloved sister, Emma, but could not bring himself to write about his feelings for the woman who had shared his life for forty-two years.

In the parlor of Somerset Villa, Nannie Carr's body lay in state "amid thousands of roses and other flowers." A choir of six sang her favorite hymns, and two Methodist ministers eulogized her at great length. The house and grounds were packed with mourners, most of whom followed the horse-drawn hearse, which was driven by her coachman, Tom Charleston, from the house to Maplewood Cemetery.[23] It was common knowledge, at least in the family, that the ex-slave who had come from Granville County to work for the Carrs in 1880 had long ago promised his mistress "that, if I outlived her, I would drive her funeral coach; and if she outlived me, she would look after my funeral." On the day when he fulfilled that promise, Tom Charleston was a commanding figure dressed in a brass-buttoned coachman's uniform and a "tall silk hat with a large silver buckle at the side."[24]

The streets were lined with people, and although it was Saturday, the busiest day of the week for Durham merchants, every store closed its doors and suspended trade while the cortege passed. The First National Bank, as well as all branches of the Durham Hosiery

Mill, remained closed for five days. The *Morning Herald*, claiming that "Mrs. Carr has endeared herself to the whole city," described her as "Modest and retiring, but withal exerting a sure and strong influence for the good . . . a woman who seldom graced the public prints, who did her work in an unassuming and conscientious manner . . . and aided her distinguished husband in all his variegated business and philanthropic activities."[25]

Other descriptions of Nannie Parrish Carr depict her as petite, extremely well groomed, consistently pleasant, and rather reserved; a woman of taste and refinement, with a talent for hospitality and a penchant for large, beautiful hats. Those fabled hats, contrived of velvet, satin, felt, or straw (depending on the season) and adorned with plumes, flowers, veils, or egrets (depending on the current style), struck admiration and envy into many a female heart when Mrs. Carr, riding behind Tom Charleston, took the air in her open carriage on fine afternoons.[26] Her amiability ensured her popularity with both sexes, and she was a natural choice for charter membership in Durham's first literary group designed for ladies only, a select band organized by Mrs. Brodie Duke in 1899. Members of the Up-to-Date Club enhanced their pursuit of culture with elaborate teas and always looked forward to meeting in the opulence of Somerset Villa, where the finest food was served in grand style and the hostess's husband sometimes joined them for refreshments. Carr, in fact, enjoyed the ladies of the club so much that he encouraged Nannie to entertain them al fresco at Occoneechee. On one such occasion he presented each member with a live chicken in a box designed to keep it alive until it could be transferred to a coop in Durham.[27]

Although Nannie Carr enjoyed her book club and rarely missed a meeting until she became ill, she never let it take precedence over her church, which she attended faithfully as long as she was well enough to leave the house. She was active in the women's auxiliary, and for many years she supplied the elements for holy communion and arranged for flowers from her greenhouse to be placed each Sunday on Trinity's altar.[28]

Like many southern women of her day, Nannie Carr was placed on a pedestal by her future husband as soon as she agreed to marry him. That lofty perch, designed to protect her from the more sordid aspects of the masculine world (and also to keep that comfortable world safe from female interference), never lessened her strong but infinitely subtle control over her husband, nor did it reduce his un-abashed love for her. That she was equally devoted to him is obvious in what is thought to be the last letter he received from her. She wrote it while he was on his way to Philadelphia, either in 1914 or 1915, and he put it in his Bible for safe keeping:

My dearest Papa:

I am distressed over your legs hurting you so badly. I would see my doctor as soon as I got to Phil[adelphia]. Well Mrs. Erwin's party came off beautifully. My "Up to Dates" in the boxes looked just fine. After the play I brought them down home & gave them some refreshment & of course I have been in bed all today, but am feeling very well, am going out this afternoon. The play was very nice except it was too long, it was nearly 12 o'clock when we all got to the house, but they seemed to enjoy it very much. I had the house looking as prettie as could be, & everything passed off nicely, but I am very tired from it today. Our home looked beautiful, the dearest place on earth to me, & my table was a dream. I had on my black eve-ning gown & all had so many nice things to say about every-thing that I felt very glad about it all. Of course I missed you very much. Your not being here was the only draw back. I send you one of my invitations Julian got up for me, everyone thought they were very nice.

I hope you will not suffer *any more* with your dear legs. I always want my darling to always be well. This leaves us all very well, all the dear babes are fine, little Julian is nearly over his cold. I hope this will find my dearest one well. Austin is home, got through all right, & seems happy over his examinations coming out as they did. I am just so proud of our dear children, they always make me happy.

Do hurry on home. I do miss you so much. God bless you & make you well is always my poor prayer.

Devotedly,
Nannie[29]

Unfortunately Carr could not immerse himself in business in or-der to combat the loneliness he suffered after his wife died; by 1915 he had put all such ventures in other hands. His sons were running the Durham Hosiery Mills, William Holloway was running the First National Bank, and Charlie Brown, who had returned to Carr's employ in 1913, was running Occoneechee Farm. Thomas Gorman, his private secretary, was running everything else that Carr no longer found exciting or challenging. Young Julian and his family moved into Somerset Villa to take care of him and keep him company, but Somerset without Nannie was a different place.

Perhaps because he found it hard to adjust to that difference, Carr spent the first five months of 1916 traveling. Early in January he arrived in Honolulu. His pleasure in that tropical city was spoiled by an ear infection that required treatment from hotel doctors, a ship's surgeon, and, after his return to the mainland, a registered nurse who attended him for over a week at the Palace Hotel in Los Angeles.[30] February had almost come to an end before he was well enough to travel to Whittier, California, to see his nephew, Edward Parrish Carr, who was growing oranges on a recently acquired ranch in Santa Fe Springs.

Ed Carr, brother to Will Carr and son of "Brother Albert and Sister Annie," had worked briefly at the Durham Hosiery Mill and had replaced Will Patton on its board of directors in 1912. Being the fifth man in the family textile business evidently held no appeal for him, however, and by 1916, having followed Horace Greeley's advice on going west, he was in California, happily married and busy developing the acreage he called Carrancho.[31]

Ed and his wife, Fanny May, were camping "in good rough style" when word came that Uncle Jule was on the way. His uncle's visit was sufficiently memorable for Ed Carr to recall it in some detail thirty years later. To his cousin, Claiborn Carr, he wrote:

> A friend of ours drove him down to see us in our tent house, & I told Fanny May we would fix up the best dinner on the place for him, & that then he would have enough & be ready to say goodbye. When it got dark he said he thought he would stay overnight, so we gave him our bed and took our blankets (unknown to him) & slept on the porch of a neighbor. He stayed a week, & then decided that he wanted to stay on, so I built him a separate tent house, we moved back into our own, & he stayed with us . . . smoking his big pipe, & playing dominoes to his heart's content.
>
> We took an auto trip to the nearby Mexican border, & I had an awful time keeping him from putting on his *Vet uniform* and

crossing the border way back in the brush to visit one of the *rebel* chiefs allied with Pancho Villa. We finally packed our own grips in the car, paid the hotel bill, & told him we would have to return to the ranch. I then said I had to go to the post office (some distance) before leaving, & when I returned he had his own grips and was ready to go back with us. Just as I thought he would do, but the thing was not to argue with him any more, & make him decide.[32]

Carr did not decide to leave California until late in April, and he appeared in no hurry to get home. He stopped in Kansas City en route, visiting Lida and Lalla Ruth for two weeks, and then proceeded to the Confederate reunion in Birmingham, Alabama. He reached Durham during the last week in May, just in time to attend commencement at the University of North Carolina before going on to Washington and Lee University to deliver an address commemorating the birthday of Jefferson Davis. Then he managed to see his granddaughter, Ruth Flower, graduate from the Madeira School in Washington, D.C., before he left for St. Louis and the Democratic national convention, which began on 10 June. Following that week-long political rally, he returned to Washington to watch the unveiling of Gutzon Borglum's statue of North Carolina's wartime governor, Zebulon Vance. It was late June before he moved from Somerset Villa to Occoneechee and settled down in the small dependency he had converted to his own use and christened The Bungalow.[33]

As Clarence Walker said, Carr never slept in the big house after Nannie died. It was from the Bungalow, on the night of 18 August 1916, that he wrote a letter to his sons, addressing them as "My Four Dear Good Boys":

> Today one year ago our precious, dear Mother left us and went to Heaven to live with the Angels. It has been and is a great joy to me to witness the genuine respect you have manifested toward her sweet memory. It truly can be said of her, "Gone but not forgotten," and I am greatly rejoiced thereat.
>
> My approaching birthday, October 12th, and I will be 71 years of age. One year beyond the Biblical mention of three score and ten. It can't, therefore, be long before I go to join dear Mother—only a few years at best. But before going away I want to leave you a few messages, and I am not going to deliver

a lecture on Character, Duty and Right Living. These virtues were inculcated in you by our dear Mother. These were some of the virtues her life stood for. . . .

Carr's first message to his sons was: "DON'T GO INTO DEBT. . . . I know of no combination that can be made with any four letters in the alphabet that spells more trouble than D.E.B.T. IT IS AN ENEMY TO BE GREATLY FEARED." The second message, "DON'T ENDORSE PAPER for anyone, not even for each other," he reinforced by a lengthy discourse on why it was dangerous to sign notes, plus a standard answer to any would-be borrower: ". . . say NO SIR, under no circumstances, because my father who served his day and generation, specially charged me NEVER TO DO IT." A third warning was: "DON'T SCATTER YOUR INVESTMENTS." Although Carr approved of investing in life insurance, he cautioned against paying excessive premiums. Perhaps a $250,000 life insurance policy "might not be a burden if your interests are very large and very prosperous," he wrote; then he added, "Another and safe source of investment is State and National Bonds. The rate of interest it's true is lower than one hundred other propositions that will likely be brought to your attention, but one hundred times safer. Make SAFETY FIRST your motto."

Entreating Julian, Marvin, Claiborn, and Austin to "stay together in business" and to "go to Church at LEAST ONCE each Sunday," Carr ended his letter by saying, "Father loves his four good boys. Your precious dear mother poured her life into your lives, and that accounts largely why you have been so successful. Always honor your mother's memory with your lives, and may God bless you."[34]

Carr had honored Nannie's memory with a bound volume containing an account of her funeral, tributes to her exemplary character from a number of religious and secular organizations, and a copy of the telegram of condolence he had received from President Woodrow Wilson. He distributed the handsome little book among relatives and friends; later he gave a swimming pool, in his wife's name, to her alma mater, Salem College, in the hope that the school could "blend collegiate training with the best physical development." A Winston-Salem newspaper expressed gratitude "for his interest in one of the city's most beloved institutions."[35]

Still he was not satisfied. He wanted a memorial to "dear Miss Nannie . . . that will make the world sit up and take notice," and in the autumn of 1916 he began to plan it: he would have a marble tablet depicting Leonardo da Vinci's *Last Supper* placed in Trinity Methodist Church. He was willing to import Italian sculptors, skilled artists who could reproduce, in stone, the famous painting that hung in the Cathedral at Milan. "This painting has been reproduced before in marble, but not quite as well as I am hoping to have it copied," Carr told his daughter Lida. "I believe this will be one of the most beautiful pieces in the world when it is finished." He also wanted to place several large sculptures by Nannie's grave in Maplewood Cemetery, and he assured Lida: "This with the landscaping . . . will be very beautiful, nothing as beautiful in any cemetery which I have ever visited, but your dear sweet mother deserves all, and more."[36]

As it happened, plans for Nannie's memorial came to a temporary halt when the American Trade Commission invited Carr to accompany several other prominent businessmen on a fact-finding tour of the Orient. The group would study conditions in Japan, China, and the Philippines in order to assess commercial opportunities for American business. There would be ample time for sightseeing, and, in Carr's case, an opportunity to visit his old friend Charlie Soong. Carr accepted the invitation immediately, with great enthusiasm. When he left Durham on 14 January 1917, "many friends and relatives were at the station to bid him farewell and to hope for him health on the long tour."[37]

13. A Time to Mourn

CARR stopped over in Kansas City for a brief visit with his daughters en route to the west coast, so it took him eight days to reach Seattle. From there he sailed on the *Princess Victoria* to Vancouver, and after a side trip to Victoria, where he was "astonished to find such a Splendid Capital Building," he boarded the *Empress of Russia*, which set sail for Yokahama on 27 January 1917. The ship was "continually running into Squalls, Snow Storms and the like," and the voyage was very rough. Most passengers were too seasick to leave their staterooms, but Carr boasted, in his diary, that he never felt better and usually was "the first one at my table in the Dining Room."[1]

Landing in Yokahama on 6 February, he stayed at the Grand Hotel, "said to be the best Hotel in the Orient and that ain't saying much." His next stop was Tokyo, where he found the Temple of the Shoguns a "Very Wonderful Sight," but his hotel, the Imperial, "very indifferent." Twenty-four hours of sleet, snow, and rain in Nagasaki, plus a hotel that was sleazy and uncomfortable, prompted him to observe: "Don't think much of Nagasaki." Once he was back on board the *Empress of Russia*, his outlook changed and he surrendered himself to the pleasures of the moment. "At a dinner tonight the Wa Wa Touring Club was founded," he noted in his diary on 11 February, "the purpose being to write to each member on the Birthday of said member . . . and herein fail not." As secretary of the twelve-member organization, Carr had its brief history and the minutes of its only meeting printed in a small booklet. His record of that gala occasion concluded with: "Having drunken and eaten most delightfully to the 'full,' the Song Birds having sung the 'Gang's All Here,' the Secretary having disturbed the harmony of the evening with a solo . . . the 'Bunch' adjourned, promising Never Again."[2]

Favorably impressed by Manila, Hong Kong, and Canton, Carr noted that in Canton he "dined at the Palace with the Governor, the Chief Justice of the Supreme Court and his Wife & other members of the Governor's Council. Quite a distinguished body of Chinese Gentlemen." He was part of another distinguished body when he "lunched with the President at the Palace" in Peking; he also met with a group of Peking bankers and attended a joint session of Parliament "with some 600 members present." He then inspected the North China Language School and saw the Great Wall of China before sailing on the *S.S. Siberia* for Shanghai on 20 March.[3]

Carr's long-awaited reunion with Charlie Soong took place at Shanghai's Burlington Hotel, where he was Soong's guest for five days of sightseeing, visits with Soong's family and friends, and meetings with various missionaries and educators. On his first Sunday in Shanghai, he placed wreaths of flowers on the graves of five American missionaries, and after a tour of Soochow University and its Bible school, he donated fifty dollars to the school kindergarten. Charlie was his constant guide and companion. Soong took him where he wanted to go, showed him what he wanted to see, and, on the last day of March, honored him at "a great reception attended by a great crowd." There he was officially welcomed to China by the commissioner of education, the commissioner of agriculture, a member of the board of trade, and a high-ranking officer of the Bank of China.[4]

Carr noted that he made three speeches in Shanghai, but he did not identify his audiences; nor did he record his farewell to Charlie Soong, which took place on 5 April 1917, just before he "embarked on the Tender at 5 P.M. at Shanghai for the Ship Shingo Maru." He made no reference to the fact that when the *Shingo Maru* steamed out of harbor, bound for Nagasaki, Kobe, Yokohama, and San Francisco, three exquisite hand-painted porcelain vases, carefully packed and bearing Carr's Durham address, lay in her hold. They were gifts from Charlie Soong, "in appreciation for all kindnesses."[5]

Still at sea two weeks later, Carr noted "One of the most perfect days I ever saw. Never saw the water bluer. The Ocean smooth as a Mill Pond. Hard to imagine a day more beautiful. The Sky, the Water, the Atmosphere perfect." On that especially beautiful day he began to keep his own private log of the latitude and longitude, the gradually changing face of the clock, the course and average speed of the ship, the distance it covered each day, and the number of miles yet to go before it reached the United States. Apparently eager to plant his feet on American soil, his elation over the *Shingo Maru's* safe arrival in San Francisco was cut short by a wire from Julian Junior informing him that his butler, John O'Daniel, was mortally ill and not expected to live through the night. The next day, after reading a second telegram from his son—"John Daniels [sic] died this morning / Funeral Tuesday of necessity"—Carr wrote in his diary, "John was an honest, faithful servant & a Christian Gentleman. Lived with me 42 years."[6]

According to the Durham *Morning Herald*, O'Daniel's funeral was "in the hands of the colored Masons" and took place at St. Joseph's African Methodist Episcopal Church, "of which he was a consistent member." His three sons, John, Julian, and Will O'Daniel, with Julian, Claiborn, and Austin Carr, were his pallbearers; "at the request of the Carr family, Mr. C. J. Harrell, pastor of Trinity Church, the church of the Carr family, made one of the prayers at the service."[7]

Perhaps because neither his wife nor his faithful servant would be there to welcome him home, Julian Carr did not hurry back to Somerset Villa. After three days in San Francisco and a second visit to Ed Carr's ranch in Santa Fe Springs, he made two- and three-day stopovers in El Paso, Kansas City, Chicago, Louisville, and Asheville before arriving in Durham on 27 May. The *Morning Herald*, reporting his safe return, quoted him as saying that the so-called Yellow Peril was a myth; that the Japanese and Chinese people had received the American Trade Commission "with the utmost cordiality and great honor"; and that America had "tremendous commercial opportunities . . . in both China and Japan."[8]

Carr was equally enthusiastic about what missionaries were accomplishing in China, in spite of a pressing need for more and better equipment. "It is somewhat similar to hiring a man to do a day's plowing, and failing to provide him with horse or plow, or providing a carpenter with a cross-cut saw, and directing him to build a house," he said. Then he added, "I serve notice here and now that I shall not hold my peace until there is some improvement."[9]

But Carr forgot his concern for American missionaries to China while he was in Washington, D.C., attending the annual Confederate reunion during the first week in June. After several days of celebrating the fact that they were still alive and able to congregate, the veterans voted unanimously to promote their comrade, Julian Carr, to Lieutenant General commanding the Army of Northern Virginia, and there was "general rejoicing among North Carolinians."

Being an honorary general did not prevent Carr from volunteering to go to France "as a plain soldier" shortly after the first Americans reached there on 26 June 1917. When President Woodrow Wilson's request for a declaration of war against Germany had been granted by Congress on 6 April, Carr had been aboard the *Shingo*

Maru, but now that he was back home he, too, wanted to make the world safe for democracy. The State Department demurred, however. When it refused to issue a passport to Julian Carr after granting one to Kermit Roosevelt, Carr's angry reaction caught the attention of the North Carolina press: "Why, haven't I fought through as many bloody battles and seen as much war as Roosevelt and his family?" he demanded of an Asheville reporter. "I will not propose to go as a highbrow like Colonel Roosevelt, but I am entirely willing to go as a subaltern. I do not ask to be the whole show. My only desire is to serve where duty calls."[10]

Carr realized his desire after Congress passed an act designed to control domestic industry and consumption and Herbert Hoover became head of the United States Food Administration. Hoover, a former mining engineer, described the Lever Food and Fuel Control Act as "an adventure in democracy" and asked all Americans to reduce their daily intake of butter by three ounces and to eat one wheatless meal a day, as well as two meatless meals a week. This sacrifice would enable the government to "feed Europe in our defense," Hoover asserted. When he warned, "If we fail . . . the soldiers cannot fight,"[11] Julian Carr saw where his personal duty lay.

With four hundred Durham men already in the armed forces and his son, Austin, about to enlist, Carr decided to help the food administration avoid failure, if possible. On 31 August 1917 he noted in his diary that he had "spent the day in Washington conferring with Mr. Hoover." Less than a week later, having booked rooms at the Stoneleigh Court Hotel and hired a valet to attend to his needs, he went to work for the government.[12]

That work consisted, for the most part, of delivering addresses prepared by Hoover's writers for the purpose of gaining support for voluntary rationing. Although Carr kept no record of his speaking engagements, he did save a few samples of the propaganda disseminated by the United States Food Administration during the fall of 1917. One of these pamphlets stated, in part, "Some are called to bear arms and no one doubts that they will give a good account of themselves. Others provide the sinews of war, ships and munitions and money. They will not fail. This service to make the Nation's food resources effective is the one that is universal, enlisting every man, woman, and child. As we succeed in this, we shall make the world safe for democracy, prove democracy safe for the world."[13]

For Carr, the old warrior, fanning the fires of patriotism was a pleasant duty, and he was happy to discover that he could still do his bit for his country while his sons were doing theirs. Julian, Marvin, and Claiborn were manufacturing socks for the military and growing rich in the process; Austin had joined the Army Ordnance Corps and was stationed at Springfield, Massachusetts, where he was safe from bullets and poison gas—but not, as it happened, from germs.

If Austin Carr's courtship of the brown-eyed, auburn-haired Laura Williamson Noell had not culminated in marriage, he might have died in the influenza epidemic that spread from Europe to the United States in September 1918. Luckily Sergeant Carr was spending the weekend with his bride of four months when he came down with influenza, and being allowed to remain at Springfield's Oak Inn, instead of returning to camp, probably saved his life. Laura Carr, a resourceful young woman, was able to persuade a retired trained nurse and a "crusty old town doctor" to help care for her husband, and the combined around-the-clock attention of these three individuals pulled Austin Carr through both a crisis and a relapse of the disease that killed half a million Americans. Austin Carr's recovery was slow, and by the time he was able to take his wife home to Durham, the war had been over for six months.[14]

Julian Carr was grateful not only to God for sparing his son's life, but also to his youngest daughter-in-law for assisting the Almighty in His healing work. Carr soon discovered that the Danville, Virginia, belle who had married Austin possessed brains as well as beauty. Part of her charm was a flashing wit that made him laugh, and he was delighted when she and Austin agreed to move into the house that Julian Junior and his family had vacated, just down the street from Somerset Villa. "Laura and Austin are leading two perfectly sweet lives and seem very happy," Carr told Lalla Ruth. While he thought they "lived too much to themselves and don't get out among their family connections enough," it was a comfort to have them nearby.[15]

The spring and summer of 1919 might have been a happy interlude, except that something was terribly wrong with Marvin. When he had come to Durham the previous fall for a meeting of the Durham Hosiery Mills' board of directors, "the poor fellow didn't have strength then to walk 500 yards without having to sit down and rest." Because Marvin had been converted, by Aurelia, to Christian Science, he had not consulted a doctor. Carr's reaction to this state of affairs was one of extreme consternation, and he began to voice his fears outside the family. Early in January 1919 he told a close friend,

Austin and Laura Noell Carr on their wedding day
(courtesy of Austin Heaton Carr, Jr.)

"Marvin's condition does not grow any better and I am very much alarmed about him. The truth is, unless he gets better before very long, I don't see how the poor boy can live. . . . It is Christian Science or nothing in that household, unless the family on our side rebel, and between you and I we have about arrived at that point."[16]

To gain support for his rebellion against the teachings of Mary Baker Eddy and her Church of Christ, Scientist, Carr appealed to his daughters. In a letter to Lalla Ruth he said:

> Unless there is a change for the better, I don't believe Marvin will live through the spring. I am aware that you and dear Lida consider me an alarmist in such matters, but you remember, my dear Lalla Ruth, that I considered your dear mother's condition very grave before she died, and both of you were a thousand miles away when she passed away. I was no alarmist then, and I am no alarmist now with reference to dear Marvin. You may think so, and when the poor fellow dies, you will say I didn't know, but if you don't it won't be my fault, for I am going to do my duty toward keeping you informed, as I did in the instance of our dear mother.[17]

Marvin's steadily worsening symptoms, combined with pressure from his side of the family, eventually resulted in his admission to a New York hospital on 13 January 1919. Carr reported to Lida and Lalla Ruth that, although their brother was under the care of "the celebrated Dr. Rogers" and finally "out of the hands of the Christian Scientists," his illness had been diagnosed as pernicious anemia and the prognosis was not good. "I believe we may expect the worst," Carr said, "and at almost any time." The next day, reiterating his expectation of the worst to a friend, he added: "I don't want you ever, if you please, to mention Christian Science to me anymore, for I have had my fill of it. . . . I am afraid my dear boy is close to the shore. I feel he was kept too long in the hands of the Scientists, and they are largely responsible, in my judgment, for his condition."[18]

Five days after Marvin entered the hospital, he was given the first of a series of blood transfusions. Within a week he was better, and in February he was well enough to go for an automobile ride with his brother Julian, who had taken over his work as sales manager of the Durham Hosiery Mills and was living temporarily at the Gotham Hotel. When his father came to see him later in the month, Julian arranged another ride for all three of them; Carr reported that fact to his daughters, along with the news that dear Marvin was "up and around his room" more frequently. In May, a red letter month, Marvin acquired his own car and chauffeur and was taking rides "more or less every day." In June the frequent transfusions began to lose their efficacy, however, and on 19 September 1919 he died, at the age of thirty-nine, in New York's Mount Sinai Hospital.[19]

Marvin Carr's father, brothers, and sisters were "at the bedside" with his wife, according to a Durham newspaper, which further reported that the Trinity Methodist Church bell tolled for ten minutes while a brief funeral service was taking place in New York.[20] Because his grieving widow could not decide whether to bury him in New York or in Durham, his body was placed temporarily in a receiving vault. Four months later it was still there despite Carr's repeated attempts to persuade Aurelia to let Marvin's final resting place be "by dear Mother."[21]

Immediately after reaching home from the funeral in New York, Carr had gone to Maplewood Cemetery and "spent about an hour with my wife, telling her about Marvin." For weeks his sorrow spilled over into much of his personal correspondence. "The death of my dear boy Marvin was a great blow to me because he was so well-fitted to live, and had so much to live for, and wanted so much to live," he wrote to a friend in Richmond. "I try through my tears to look up and say, Thy will be done, but take it from me, it is a hard job. It is indeed hard for me to say it and mean it."[22]

Around the middle of October he wrote to Lalla Ruth, "I told Aurelia we realized dear Marvin's body belonged to she and the two dear children, but if I was allowed to have a voice in the matter, I would be very happy if I might be permitted to bring the body to Durham and bury it by dear Mother. I don't know what she will say to that, however, I will send you her reply." When Aurelia's reply finally came, almost three months later, it was to say that she had decided to remove her husband's body to Woodlawn Cemetery in New York. Carr was forced to accept the fact that he would not be able to bury Marvin "next to his dear Mother, where I know he would love to rest, and where I would love to have him rest."[23]

He was still mourning Marvin's death when Lalla Ruth wrote that she was not feeling well. She was tired, she said, and thought she needed a rest from the civic work in which she had immersed herself after Will Patton died; she was planning to take a vacation with young Ruth in San Antonio, Texas. Carr answered by return mail, chastising her about her lifestyle and warning her against overwork:

> You ought to take heed to what I say to you before conditions get too bad with you. My advice to you would be this: to pay more attention to your church life and give less time to civics. I think you are overloading the one and suffering for lack of the other. I have thought this for some time. . . . You won't listen to me; I have tried to talk to you about the unwisdom of your course, and after you have paid for it very dearly then you can understand that Father was right years ago.[24]

Father continued to press his point early in January 1920, after Lalla Ruth returned to Kansas City from San Antonio:

> You haven't been to Durham in two or three years. If I had my way about it you would have spent Christmas in Durham. And very near all those who are near and dear to you live in Durham. . . . I feel about the situation very much like your dear Mother did before she passed away. More than one hundred times, I reckon, she and I talked over the puzzling situation, why it was that her two daughters chose to go elsewhere, sometimes to Europe, and nearly always fail to put Durham on their itinerary. This is one of the questions your dear Mother went to Heaven undecided about . . . if only you could be persuaded to come and live among us . . . we would be very glad.[25]

But Lalla Ruth Patton apparently was disenchanted with the idea of making Durham her permanent home. Fortunately for Carr, his three remaining sons and his nephew Will were not of the same mind. Living within sight of Somerset Villa, these four young men were giving him the attention and affection he craved, and because they had turned the family business into the largest hosiery mill in the world, he was intensely proud of them. "It's a mighty strong one-man team that can beat the four Carr boys, Julian, Claiborn, Austin, and Will," he boasted to Lalla Ruth when the Durham Hosiery Mills increased its capital stock to over $9.5 million. "The man who thinks he is game enough to tackle this combination has a great deal more nerve than brain."[26]

By the time summer arrived, Carr's spirits had regained their normal buoyancy. He told Lida, "Life is pretty nearly what we make it, and I try to get out of it all that is coming to me." As if to prove his point, he left Durham shortly thereafter for a leisurely trip across the continent and another visit to Carrancho.[27] It was while he was on this trip that some of his friends conceived the idea of a citywide celebration of his upcoming seventy-fifth birthday, and soon the chamber of commerce and two civic clubs, the Rotary and Kiwanis, were involved in plans for a Somerset Villa lawn party to which the whole town would be invited.

Governor Thomas Walter Bickett accepted an invitation to speak at Carr's "surprise" birthday party, and both the University of North Carolina and Trinity College agreed to send delegations to the affair. Durham's business and educational institutions promised to close at 3:30 P.M. on Friday, 15 October 1920, so their employees could attend. It was doubtless by design, rather than by accident, that Carr remained out of town until Thursday evening, and he was probably not too surprised to see his picture on the front page of Friday's *Durham Morning Herald*. But he must have been strongly affected by the paper's lead editorial:

> Communities have from ages as far back as history records at suitable occasions honored their leading dead and paid homage to high military and civil officials alive. But it remains for Durham to single out a leading citizen in private life to honor. He is to be honored not for great military or political victory or for any unusual act of heroism, but because he is a true citizen in every sense of that word.
>
> Durham honors General Carr because he has honored Durham, the state, the south, and the nation. It honors and loves him because of his great value to the community and for what he has done for its progress. It is a fitting recognition of service rendered. Durham today will try to let the grand old gentleman know that he has wrought well for the city and that it is duly appreciated. Every class—the manufacturer, the banker, the merchant, the educator, the church worker, the school official, the laborer—every man in every walk of life, every element that makes up this prosperous city at some time or other has either directly or indirectly come in contact with General Carr's influence and has been benefitted thereby. In war and in peace he

has proved himself loyal and constructive. In industry and art he has been a genius and a valuable patron. In politics and society he has been an asset.

Every community has one or more men who have been and still are a power for good in some particular line. There are bankers, manufacturers, financiers, politicians, public spirited men, philanthropists, educators, church workers, and others interested in lines of public endeavor in which they have specialized, but a man in whom is combined all of these is rare indeed. It is not an exaggeration to say that General Carr comes more near embodying all of these characteristics than any man living in North Carolina, probably in the entire south.

No worthy cause or person fails to find a friend in General Carr. His heart and his purse have always been open to the appeal of an honest purpose. Three quarters of a century has he lived, and it is the sincere wish and prayer of people everywhere that he may be spared many more years. And when he has finished his work here, the world can say in all truthfulness that he was a friend to man.[28]

The morning paper also carried a full-page announcement, in extra-large print, that said: "To the People of Durham: *You* are invited to attend a Lawn Party to be given in honor of the 75th birthday of Gen. Julian S. Carr at Somerset Villa, his home, Friday afternoon, October 15, from 3:30 to 5:30 o'clock. This means everybody."

And very nearly everybody went, or so it seemed on that bright autumn day in 1920. Many followed a procession of Confederate veterans and schoolchildren that formed at the courthouse and marched down Main Street, led by the Durham Hosiery Mill band. At Somerset Villa they moved through the crowd that had already gathered, a crowd in which "there were a great many Negroes, because the Negroes in Durham loved General Carr. He had been good to so many of them, and they appreciated him."[29]

When a carefully rehearsed group of schoolchildren had sung the last note of "Carolina, Carolina, Heaven's Blessings Attend Thee," the black community's appreciation of Julian Carr was expressed, in what the *Durham Morning Herald* described as "a beautiful manner, with deep sincerity," by William Gaston Pearson, a prominent businessman and educator who had been a small boy when Carr first befriended him. "I knew General Carr when he made the Bull Durham so strong that he drank water from the far northern lakes and graveled his tail in the sands of New Mexico," Pearson said. Then he recounted his own early struggles and the help he had received from Carr, who financed his education at Shaw University. Asserting that the members of his race wanted to add their "good feeling" to the occasion and show their appreciation for what Carr had done for them, Pearson told the crowd that "no one knows what his life has been to the poor, and especially to the colored people, in giving them a chance." When he finished speaking, he presented Carr with a handsome walking cane "in behalf of the colored people of Durham."

Each speaker had much to say, and because three bands took turns playing between orations, the program was lengthy. It was comprised of greetings by representatives from neighboring cities, towns, and institutions; intermittent remarks by a master of ceremonies; speeches by the mayor and the governor; and the presentation of a gift from Durham's white citizens, a silver loving cup three feet high and at least eighteen inches at its widest point.

Durham's mayor, Marion Eugene Newsom, reminded the crowd that never before had they seen a community "rise up as one man and thus honor a citizen as we are today honoring General Julian S. Carr," and that, "if a vote were taken on it he would be our best beloved citizen." Newsom continued to comment at length on Carr's business genius and his worth to the city before introducing the state's chief executive, who began his own remarks by praising the progressive city of Durham for turning out during business hours "to celebrate the birthday of a distinguished son while that son is still living." Thomas Bickett, who was acquiring a reputation as one of the state's most humanitarian and progressive governors, said, "I interpret the feeling of the people of North Carolina when I say they look upon General Carr as the Good Samaritan." In recounting Carr's achievements, he described them as "inseparable from the old commonwealth he loves so well." Bickett's wish, that Carr would "live 75 more birthdays in this world and have an eternal summer in another," drew prolonged applause.

When that applause had subsided, Dr. John Manning, spokesman for the townspeople, came forward with the silver cup. "In behalf of the great citizenship of Durham," the doctor said to Carr, "we recognize the strength and beauty of your life, its influence for good, and your business acumen and success. I am proud to present you with this loving cup as a token of our appreciation and a tribute to your worth." After more applause, Dr. Manning read aloud the engraving on the cup: "Presented to General Julian Shakespeare Carr from the citizens of Durham on his seventy-fifth birthday, as a token of their love and esteem and appreciation of his life of usefulness in this community."

Carr was so deeply moved that several minutes passed before he could control his voice enough to admit that the occasion was "so unusual and my heart is so full, I don't know what to say." He had been a public speaker for too long not to be able to rise to the occasion, however, and in the next breath he was saying, "Fellow-citizens of the good old town of Durham . . . the sweetest and dearest part of my life has been spent here with you. . . . You have proven the falsity of the old proverb that a man is not without honor save in his own country and among his own people. Me and my boys have made our stuff here, and we are staying right here with you." The closing remark in what may have been his shortest speech on record was, "Thy people shall be my people." Carr shook hands with his guests until darkness sent them back to their homes. If he could have retired that night and died peacefully in his sleep, it would have been a happy ending to a long and eventful life.

But he was not to be so fortunate. Nine months after that splendid birthday gala, he was called to Philadelphia, where he watched his youngest daughter die in the same hospital that had sheltered Will Patton during his last days. A Kansas City newspaper reported that Mrs. William Foley Patton "died at the Pennsylvania Hospital, Philadelphia, Sunday morning July 17, mainly because of overwork in patriotic activities during the war." Ineradicable sadness over her husband's death probably had as much to do with Lalla Ruth's physical collapse as did the means she used to escape from that sadness.[30]

Will Patton had left his wife with an imposing home, a considerable fortune, and a nine-year-old daughter to raise. Although she tried to make young Ruth the focal point of her existence, Lalla Ruth found that being an exemplary mother could not absorb all her lonely hours. She also realized, after the customary period of mourning was over, that the parties and country club functions and yearly trips to Europe she had enjoyed with her companionable husband were boring without him. In her search for a new way of life she ventured first into education and later into volunteer service.[31]

In what may have been unconscious imitation of her father, Lalla

Ruth Patton became one of three founders of the Sunset Hill School, a private school for girls that opened in Kansas City in 1912. She also became chairman of the school's board of trustees, and when a teacher was needed for a course in domestic science, she joined the faculty. Although she had never prepared a meal in her life, she learned at home, from her own excellent cook, what she taught at school on the following day, and the students warmed to her easy-going methods and the contagious laughter that triggered their own schoolgirl giggles. In a very short time, most of them were calling the ingenious Mrs. Patton "Auntie Pat."[32]

As soon as Julian Carr learned that Lalla Ruth had become a schoolteacher, he succumbed to the sin of pride, as he had done back in 1897 when, over his objections, she went from door to door in Durham, begging for money to start a public library. Even though he thought teaching was not "socially right" for his daughter, when she expressed a need for playground equipment for the Sunset Hill girls (of which his granddaughter, Ruth, was one) he sent her a check for $625, "for your outfit for your playground at your school."[33]

Lalla Ruth's organizational skill and willingness to work inevitably came to the attention of many would-be instigators of good deeds, and she soon found herself drawn into a wide range of community projects. She was persuaded to establish and run the Mercy Hospital Auxiliary and the Children's Relief, an adjunct of the auxiliary; she also became president of the Consumers' League and vice-president of the Women's City Club. Under her leadership, the Consumers' League made it mandatory for dairies and retail food stores to sell only milk that had passed a sanitation test; any milk dealer who failed to make the league's "White List" was boycotted.

Teaching, and later working for civic betterment, kept Lalla Ruth Patton as busy as she chose to be after her husband's death. Because she would not forget him and never stopped missing him, she chose to be too busy for her own good, especially after America entered World War I and she became executive director of the Kansas City Red Cross. Her daughter, Ruth, believed the long hours and intense physical effort she put into that job "sapped her strength and brought on the anemia she died of"; doctors at the University of Pennsylvania Hospital also felt that prolonged strain and too much responsibility "overtaxed her condition and hastened her death," which occurred on 17 July 1921, three months before her forty-fifth birthday.[34]

By then death was no stranger to Julian Carr. It had taken Nannie in 1915 and Marvin in 1919, and now, just two years later, it robbed him of one of his beloved daughters. But he was not prepared when death struck again in 1922, eight months after Lalla Ruth was buried in Curwensville, Pennsylvania, beside her husband and infant daughter Nancy. Carr had been ill for several weeks and was slowly recovering from influenza when his nephew Will came to his bedside and told him that Julian Junior had died of heart failure. He had been at the Pennsylvania Hotel in New York City, where he had been staying while he tried desperately to save the Durham Hosiery Mills from bankruptcy.

Carr had not been unaware of his son's financial dilemma, or of its source, a general business recession that had followed the wartime boom. A declining market, coupled with increased interest rates and banks' reluctance to lend money, had forced the Durham Hosiery Mills to suspend operations except for two days a week, and Julian Junior had been grieving over the fact that hundreds of his employees were without jobs. Having seen his dream of true cooperation between management and labor become a reality in 1919, and having watched "industrial democracy" function smoothly for two years, it was heartbreaking for him to see it destroyed by forces beyond his control.[35]

Young Julian never recovered from the loss of his dream. Although he was only forty-four in 1921, his health began to decline as a result of worry and overwork. He refused to abandon, or even to slow down, his efforts to save the Durham Hosiery Mills from financial collapse. Shortly before he left Durham in February 1922 on what was to be his last trip to New York, he said to his father, "Don't worry about me. God will take care of me." Five weeks later he was dead, the victim, perhaps, of an overactive conscience and a compulsive sense of duty. His pastor at Trinity Methodist Church said that God had indeed taken care of him by taking him home to rest, and his father had to cling to that thought for comfort.[36]

The father and son were alike in many ways, probably as much through the son's own efforts as from inherited traits. The elder Carr was an impressive role model; handsome, popular, and highly successful, he was enough to dazzle any boy's eyes, and because his strict parenting was tempered with kindness, there is little doubt that his namesake tried to emulate him. That Julian Carr, Junior, succeeded in that effort can be seen in the record of his accomplishments, which remain impressive, despite his early death. Like his father, he turned a small company into a major industry; gained a national reputation as an astute businessman; and was known for his good works, his generosity to needy causes, and his "indomitable energy." Before he was forty years old, his reputation as "king" of the hosiery business was well established, and his genuine concern for the welfare of his employees made him "perhaps the most popular man among his mill help in the entire country."[37]

His marriage to Margaret Cannon was an unusually happy one. On 18 December 1941 she wrote to a sister-in-law, "This is Dec. 18, 1902 to me. Thirty-nine years ago Julian and I married. Austin was such a little boy, about seven. Granny, Pa Pa, Marvin, my Mother and Father were all there, and it seems my life began then."[38] The children of that marriage, three girls and a boy, saw their father as "loving, sympathetic, handsome, poised, graceful . . . a man of character and gentle strength." According to his son,

Behind Somerset Villa, facing along Elizabeth Street, there was a long, eight-foot-high whitewashed fence with, about midway, an obscure opening I called a cubby-hole. When Father returned from his office at the Durham Hosiery Mill, he came along East Main and then turned into Elizabeth Street, where I would be waiting at the cubby-hole, and we would come in together across the barnyard, past the smoke house, the greenhouse, the grape arbor, and the back yard of Somerset.

One Christmas, when I was about eight, my Uncle Austin gave me a BB gun, which my mother put away on a closet shelf in her room and told me to leave it alone, but Father took my side and showed me how to use it, carefully taught me how to treat it with circumspection. He loved to hunt, and in his early years he played tennis, had the first tennis court in Durham there on the lawn at Somerset. Later he took up golf, and he loved to ride horseback, too. Frequently he rose quite early in order to ride before work, and he usually ate raw eggs beforehand.

When his father-in-law, James W. Cannon, moved the Cannon Mills main plant from Concord, N.C. to its permanent home thirty miles away, this same Mr. Cannon called several

Julian S. Carr, Jr. (courtesy of Julian S. Carr III)

learned men and professors to name the new town. My father named it, in Greek, the *City of Looms*, or the name it still bears, which is "Kannapolis."

He was a very good dresser. He dressed in the English fashion except that he did not wear sports coats or ascots. His tastes were for colors of the same shades, but different tones. For example, he liked two or even three shades of blue, or brown, or gray. For many years he dressed for dinner, putting on a dinner coat to dine with his wife and family. This was not any part of "copying the aristocrat," but it was a part of his concept of relaxing after a day's work.[39]

That concept of relaxation did not include alcohol. Julian Junior told his son that he had no use for whiskey: "I simply do not trust it," he said, "I have no faith in it." He did have faith in people, however, and believed that all of them, regardless of their station in life, should be treated with dignity. "He was firm, but gained the respect of others by fair play," his son said of him. "My father was free of spite, meanness, hypocrisy, and egotism."

Front-page stories and editorial eulogies appeared in every major newspaper in North Carolina following the death of Julian Carr, Junior. Members of the fourth estate agreed that the instigator of industrial democracy, who was "idolized by the thousands of people in his employ," more than deserved his royal status in the realm of hosiery manufacturing. The assumption that he had inherited his strong personality and keen business judgment from his father must have comforted the ailing Carr, as did the messages and telegrams of condolence that came to Somerset Villa.[40] According to Chapel Hill's weekly newspaper, over four hundred such communications "greatly strengthened General Carr in his hour of grief." Although he was still weak from his bout with influenza, he "rose from his sickbed and followed the remains of his son to their last resting place," riding through a steady rain that was "symbolic of the tears of a grief-stricken populace." The funeral procession was reported to be the longest ever seen in Durham, and the people who watched with Julian Carr as his son's body was lowered into the grave formed the largest crowd that ever had assembled at Maplewood Cemetery.[41]

14. From Somerset to Maplewood

LOSING his wife and three of his children within a span of seven years was a crushing blow to Julian Carr, and although he kept a tight rein on his emotions, his secretary, Thomas Gorman, was well aware of his suffering. "Poor soul, it looks like the General has his cup full, but he is brave and keeps a brave front. There is none like him," Gorman said on one occasion.[1] He knew, as many did not, that, in addition to grieving, Carr also was worrying about the steady erosion of what once had been a considerable fortune. Periodic economic recessions were partly responsible, but Carr's impulsive generosity also had been a contributing factor for many years, as Gorman knew only too well.

Carr had supported his parents in their later years, had insured the lives of his sisters and their children, had regularly clothed some of his nieces and sent others to summer camps, and had seldom refused any young person who asked him for help with an education. At Christmas he gave money to the needy, both black and white, in Chapel Hill; on many occasions, when heavy snow and subzero temperatures had threatened the lives of Durham's poor, he had provided them with food to eat and coal and wood to burn in their stoves and fireplaces.[2]

Tom Gorman also knew that the man who had warned his sons against endorsing loans had frequently ignored his own warning. Banks throughout the state were pressing Carr, in 1922, for money that his signature had secured for kinsmen, friends, and business associates who could not pay back what they had borrowed. Repairs and maintenance at Somerset Villa were being neglected, Occonee-chee Farm had been losing money for years, and the Durham Hosiery Mills could not forestall indefinitely the closing of some of its plants. The wartime boom was over, and the Carrs, like many other American businessmen, were in severe financial difficulty.[3]

So, despite his brave front, Julian Carr was troubled about many things in 1922, a disastrous year that was blighted by the death of his oldest son and scarred by severe unemployment, nationwide strikes, agricultural depression, increased bankruptcies and foreclosures,

Julian S. Carr (courtesy of Austin Heaton Carr, Jr.)

bootlegging, a renewal of race hatred, and a revival of the Ku Klux Klan. Women, liberated by their newly acquired right to vote, were bobbing their hair up to their ears and hemming their skirts up to their knees. Nor was that the full extent of their bizarre behavior: many were smoking cigarettes and drinking bathtub gin. One group of feminists had even succeeded in pressuring a committee that was revising the Book of Common Prayer into deleting the promise "to obey" from the sacrament of holy matrimony.[4]

Carr, a product of the antebellum South who had married and raised his children in the Victorian age, must have wondered what the world was coming to, but because he would not live through the decade that was to go down in history as the Roaring Twenties, he would be spared some of its more alarming elements. He would not witness a widespread rebellion against religion and the established moral code, or the general acceptance of Sigmund Freud's theories on sex. And although he would see the first stages of a binge of materialism that would end in the stock market crash of 1929, he would not experience that crash, or the Great Depression that followed it, or another world war.[5]

But Julian Carr would live long enough to receive one more gratifying tribute and suffer one more heartbreaking loss. The tribute came in June 1923, when the University of North Carolina, acknowledging his generosity to alma mater, awarded him an honorary doctor of laws degree. Carr's gifts, beginning in 1875 with a $500 contribution toward the university's reopening after the Civil War, had continued over the years and enriched the school's coffers by more than $60,000, and the 1923 administration, under Dr. Harry Woodburn Chase, was grateful for past favors. Part of Carr's largesse had helped to rebuild Person Hall, destroyed by fire in 1877. Another part had comprised the largest single donation to Alumni Hall, the first building erected on campus by popular subscription. Generous sums also went to the library, the gymnasium, and various scholarship funds; in 1890, for example, his pledge of $10,000 toward a chair of history inspired the alumni association to thank him "in behalf of the University, the alumni, and the unborn children of the State."[6]

Carr had been thanked again, with more fanfare, during commencement week in 1900, when his gift of a new dormitory was formally presented by William Hyslop Sumner Burgwyn, who was, like Carr, a Confederate soldier, banker, alumnus, trustee, and popular public speaker. Carr, seated with his wife and sons on a bunting-bedecked platform fronting the dormitory, heard Burgwyn tell a sizable audience about the day when the University of North Carolina opened, in 1795, with nine students, one professor, one two-story building, one unpainted wooden house, and one red hole in the ground marking the site of the future chapel. "Compare that day to this one," said Burgwyn. Indicating the spacious three-and-a-half-story building that bore Carr's name, he pronounced it the most modern edifice on campus and the largest individual gift ever made to the university. "And there are no strings attached to it," he continued. "It comes with clean hands. The money that built it was made through honest methods, and the donor did not wait to make it by his last will and testament."

Seemingly bent on upholding his reputation as an orator, Burgwyn spoke at some length before relinquishing the podium to Richard Henry Battle, another Confederate soldier of distinction as well as a lawyer, university trustee, outstanding politician and equally outstanding churchman. Himself a practiced speaker, Battle matched Burgwyn in praising Carr. In accepting Carr's gift on behalf of the university, he informed his listeners that, as secretary and treasurer of the board of trustees, he knew exactly how much the beautiful building that would house eighty-four lucky students had cost, because he received from Carr the checks that paid the bills. Construction of the Carr Building had cost $18,841.20, Battle said, and he added, "May the sight of it and the memory of it inspire other loving sons to do a like part by their old mother."[7]

University officials, commencement visitors, friends and kinsmen from Durham, and most of the people of Chapel Hill had been present to hear Carr cited for his accomplishments as "a soldier, a citizen, a farmer, a manufacturer, a banker, a philanthropist, and above all, a North Carolinian." Given such an audience, Carr probably regarded that June day in 1900 as one of his most memorable, for he never lost his childlike pleasure in being the center of attention.

That pleasure was still with him twenty-three years later when, capped and gowned as a doctor of laws, he marched in the academic procession. The good front that he managed to maintain despite sorrow and trouble was with him, too. Spectators at the 1923 commencement could not see that the short, portly gentleman whose strutting walk and ready smile exuded confidence and well-being was, in fact, nostalgic for the past and apprehensive about the future.

Nothing in Carr's demeanor suggested that he was facing the loss of one of his most prized possessions.

He must have known, at the time, that he would have to part with Occoneechee Farm. Legally, the property belonged to his three remaining children, for he had long since deeded it to his wife and her heirs, never dreaming that he would outlive any of them. But as far as the public knew, General Julian S. Carr owned Occoneechee. And he loved every inch of it, even in its present state.

Each time he drove through the gates and down the avenue to the big house, it must have sickened him to see what toll the lack of ready cash was exacting. The effects of a tornado that had ripped through the area in 1919 were still visible, since money had been too scarce to eradicate all of the damage. The big house had miraculously survived the fierce wind, but two of the three elegant barns had not. The roof of the third barn, which had collapsed on ten pure-bred cows, still sagged into the empty stalls. The horses, mules, sheep, pigs, and cows that were killed had to be dragged to one of the largest fields and dumped into a common grave; nobody knew how many chickens, geese, ducks, and guineas had blown away in a whirl of feathers and flying wood. Cleaning up the debris had taken months. In addition to the outbuildings that were demolished, several large oaks were uprooted and many cedars and fruit trees were twisted off and flung aside, as if by a giant hand.[8]

When Carr came up from Durham and saw what the twister had done to his farm, one of Charlie Brown's daughters heard him say that he knew the Lord was supposed to be in the wind, but he was sure the devil was in that one.[9] Nevertheless, he seemed to take the catastrophe in stride, and he told Lida that "only the fellow who's got it can lose it." But by 1923, when he knew that Occoneechee had to be sold because the Durham Hosiery Mills had to be saved, he may have found it hard to be philosophical—especially when advertisements of the coming auction began to appear in the *Durham Morning Herald.*

The first announcement, authorized by the Carver Real Estate Company two weeks after Carr's seventy-eighth birthday, read: "General J. S. Carr has placed in our hands the sale of Occoneechee Farm. The farm is disposed of for division among the heirs of Mrs. J. S. Carr. Watch this paper for date and sale and more details of this splendid property."[10]

During the next five weeks, eight additional advertisements, paid for by the Atlantic Coast Realty Company with Carver as its representative, appeared in the *Herald*. The last notice, which ran on 22 November 1923 and covered an entire page, stated:

Thursday Nov. 22nd at 10:30 a.m.
Gen. J.S. Carr's Famous Occoneechee Farm
This beautiful farm, located on the Durham-Greensboro Highway one mile from Hillsboro, has been sub-divided into a number of small farms and will be offered on the above day and date. All the personal property, including cows, sheep, hogs, farming utensils, etc., will be offered at the same time. Thousands know it as the showplace of the state. Big barbeque dinner will be served on the grounds free.

Carr's former water boy, Clarence Walker, never forgot the day Occoneechee was sold. Over fifty years later he remembered:

When they had the auction, when Occoneechee was sold, that was the most food we ever had. The General, he had fourteen shoats barbecued; they had to cook all night to feed everybody. They even had a band playing, and they sold the livestock. The sorriest horse on the place brought the most money. Her name was Molly, and she was no 'count, but she sold high.

And the General, he was there that day, him and his boys, Claiborn and Austin. Julian and Marvin, they were dead by then. It was just a little before Thanksgiving, in 1923, but it was a sad day. Sad for everybody.[11]

Lida Carr Flower did not attend the sale of Occoneechee; she was in Zurich, Switzerland, studying psychology under Dr. Carl Gustav Jung. By the next spring she had returned to America—to Chicago. Having come for an indefinite stay, to visit her friend Edith Rockefeller McCormick, Lida had taken a suite of rooms at the Hotel Webster. She and Mrs. McCormick, another enthusiastic follower of Jung, were continuing their examination of psychology when Julian Carr decided he needed a change of scenery and a visit with his daughter.[12]

He had no idea, when he left Somerset Villa during the last week in April, that he would never see it again.

In death, as in life, Julian Carr created a tremendous stir. His was not the peaceful demise of an old man who experienced a gradual lessening of physical strength; nor did it occur in familiar surroundings, among family and friends. Instead, Carr died unexpectedly in a Chicago hotel on 29 April 1924.

The story made headlines across the country. An Associated Press bulletin called him "a splendid citizen and a good Confederate soldier," and President Calvin Coolidge telegraphed condolences to Carr's children. Departing from his usual brevity, Coolidge said: "I have learned with deep regret of the death of your distinguished father, General Julian S. Carr. I had grown to have a high admiration for him and remember well speaking with him at the dedication of the Grant Monument in Washington, D.C. Mrs. Coolidge joins me in expressions of sincerest sympathy in your great loss."[13]

Banner headlines in the *Durham Morning Herald* on 30 April 1924 announced "General Julian S. Carr Dies At Daughter's Home In Chicago." In the story that followed, the reporter called Carr "Durham's grand old man." The people of the city began to mourn. Men walking to work stopped on street corners to talk about the General and his untimely death. Children spoke of it on the way to school. Women left their household duties and went next door, or across the street, or down the block, to discuss it with the neighbors. They spoke in hushed tones, and their eyes were shocked, unbelieving. Only last week they had seen him downtown, they said to each other. Seen him in the bank, seen him standing on his favorite corner, at Main and Corcoran, talking to his cronies, smiling and tipping his hat to ladies as they passed, bending down to speak to little children. And he had looked so well, they said, in spite of that operation he'd had a month ago. Tonsils, at his age! Almost seventy-nine years old, and he'd had his tonsils taken out . . .

If only he hadn't done that, they said to each other, he might still be alive.[14]

What most Durham residents did not know was that, while Carr was not a hypochondriac in the true sense, the state of his health became extremely important to him as he grew older. At seventy-two he was reading, and apparently practicing, "The Art of Getting Younger Again," a treatise that gave instructions on how to strengthen the eyes, reduce the abdomen, massage the liver, avoid dyspepsia, cure headaches, and generally tone up the system with a series of exercises "to be done every morning under cover of the bedclothes." He also was reading medical columns, which he cut from newspapers and pasted into his personal diary.[15] His severe bout with influenza in 1922 left him fearful of respiratory infections, and he may have thought that a tonsillectomy would reduce the risk of such infections. At any rate, he decided to have the surgery performed by a throat specialist in Washington, D.C. He traveled there during the latter part of March 1924 and returned to Somerset Villa about a week later. His throat was slow in healing, but confinement made him so restless that Austin and Laura, who were living with him, were not surprised when he announced that he was going to visit Lida. Swallowing was still painful for him when he left Durham on Saturday, 26 April, but Laura Carr, who helped him into his topcoat before he went to board the train at Union Station, thought he looked well and seemed in good spirits.[16]

By the time he reached Chicago, however, he was ill and feverish and complained of having caught cold on the train. Lida immediately called a doctor, who pronounced the ailment influenza and ordered Carr to bed. He did not improve. Two days later he was so much worse that his daughter called in several other physicians for consultation. This time the diagnosis was pneumonia, with heart complications, and Lida Flower was told that her father might not live through the night. Frantic calls to her brothers, Claiborn and Austin, were too late: Carr died at ten-fifteen that evening, a thousand miles from the home he loved and with only one of his children at his bedside.

On 30 April 1924, the *Durham Morning Herald*'s front-page story and lead editorial spoke of Carr's business career, his influence on the cultural growth of the town, his membership in numerous organizations, and his considerable philanthropies. Mention was made of his strong support of the Democratic party, his record as a delegate to the conventions of 1884, 1888, and 1890, and the fact that he had received fourteen votes as a Democratic nominee for vice-president of the United States in 1900. Nothing was said about his unsuccessful Senate race against Furnifold Simmons, or about the bitter campaign that preceded it; but readers were reminded that he had been a member of the North Carolina General Assembly, and that he had worked, without pay, as a federal food administrator in Washington during World War I.[17] On 1 May, the day when Carr's body was due to arrive from Chicago, a second editorial in the *Durham Morning Herald* admitted that "he had his faults, it is true, because he was human; but they were due to the weakness of the flesh and not of the heart, and it is the heart that really counts in forming the true estimate of a man. The city, the county, the state and the nation have profited because Julian Carr lived and labored here on earth. No greater tribute can be paid to any man."

Tributes continued to pour in, nevertheless, and Calvin Coolidge's telegram became one of many that accumulated on a table in the great hall of Somerset Villa. Governor Cameron Morrison and General W. B. Halderman, the acting commander of the United Confederate Veterans, were among those who wired their sympathies. Morrison called Carr a true patriot whose death was a loss to "the state, the south, and the whole country." Halderman, who was ill, promised to send a delegate to the funeral and said that all of Julian Carr's Confederate comrades would mourn his loss.[18]

Those comrades, many in veterans' homes that Carr had helped to establish and finance, did indeed mourn the loss of one of the best friends they would ever have. Since the end of the Civil War he had championed their cause, working for higher pensions, homes for their widows and orphans, and monuments to their bravery. They loved him for all of that, but they loved him, too, because he truly believed that the whole South was "sanctified by the precious memory of Robert E. Lee."[19] And so they grieved, not only in private, but openly. A group from Durham joined another from the Old Soldiers' Home in Raleigh when the train carrying Carr's body arrived in the Raleigh station at five-fifteen on the afternoon of May Day 1924. They walked in pairs behind the casket as it was carried from the train to a waiting hearse, and they would march again three days later when, with members of the R. F. Webb Camp, in Durham, they formed a guard of honor at the funeral.

This delegation from Durham, which filled twelve automobiles, arrived back at Somerset Villa as the skies were beginning to darken. Inside the house, Carr's family and some of his intimate friends waited; outside, on the sidewalk beyond the iron fence, people crowded together and watched the hearse drive through the gates. The next day, and the day after, they would come by the hundreds for a last look at the General, lying in the north parlor of Somerset, with a white carnation pinned to his resplendent gray uniform and with two Confederate flags draped over his casket.[20]

Although he had asked that books be given to the public library when he died, instead of flowers for his grave, most people either forgot Carr's wish or chose to ignore it. Relatively few books were received by the library, while the largest floral offering in Durham's history was made in his memory. Vases of cut flowers, potted plants, and intricate designs filled the downstairs rooms of Somerset Villa, overflowed onto the porch, and lined either side of the front walk leading to the gates.

From Wednesday to Sunday, flags on all of the city's public buildings flew at half mast, and the Durham Hosiery Mills shut down. A wreath of white carnations hung on the door of the First National Bank; people lowered their voices as they passed it, and some wept unashamedly. Their grand old man, the most glamorous figure many of them had ever known, was gone.

That they were not apt to see his like again was reiterated in all of North Carolina's leading newspapers. Editors eulogized Carr in the *News and Observer, High Point Enterprise, Hickory Record, Henderson Dispatch, Greensboro News, Raleigh Times, Greensboro Record, Winston-Salem Journal, Charlotte Observer, Asheville Citizen, Wilmington Star,* and both the *Durham Morning Herald* and the *Durham Sun*. It surprised no one that Carr commanded such attention from the press, for in death, as in life, he was good copy. A general without an army, a politician who had failed in his one attempt to gain high office, and a world-acclaimed businessman who had been forced to sell out to a younger, stronger rival, he was, nevertheless, the most outstanding man in the state—and by far the most picturesque. No one had Jule Carr's flair. No one did things the way he did them, with such exuberance, such passionate intensity.

As a writer for the *Greensboro News* stated:

> The thing above and beyond all the virtues that rush to mind, the thing that made him peculiarly himself, the thing that was not shared by any of his contemporaries, not even the greatest, in any thing like the same degree to which he possessed it, was the grand manner. . . . Whatever Julian Shakespeare Carr did, he did it with an air. Less gifted men, trying to imitate him, became merely pompous, but Carr was not that because it was no affectation with him, but the natural, unstudied expression of his personality.[21]

During the four days preceding Carr's funeral, the press continued to recount his contributions to industry, religion, education, and agriculture. "No other man exerted such powerful influence in so many constructive lines," the *Durham Morning Herald* declared. The

Wilmington Star, calling Carr "an extraordinary man who won great popularity," said the state of North Carolina deplored "the passing of one of her greatest and most beloved sons."[22]

The *Hickory Record* accorded Carr his rightful place as a pioneer in the tobacco industry by saying, "Long before Mr. Buck Duke, another Durham man . . . took over the Blackwell plant, Mr. Carr had become a wealthy man and was noted over the state for his liberality." The *High Point Enterprise* reminded its readers that Carr also had pioneered in the field of billboard advertising, and that "the spirit that carried the 16-year-old boy into the heat of war abided in him throughout his long and useful life, and helped give tone to the state."

Josephus Daniels, inspired by the spirit of the man who had helped him become the editor of the Raleigh *News and Observer*, said, "You do not associate General Julian Shakespeare Carr with age, nor with death. . . . To the last he radiated enthusiasm and keen interest. . . . He had never grown old in spirit or in bearing or in temperament. To the last he was the buoyant and optimistic young man whose arteries and affections seemed to have no relation to the all but four score years he had lived." Daniels saw Carr as the embodiment of optimism and cheerfulness, one who attracted men and women alike by his vitality and contagious enthusiasm. "Life had been to him joyous, and remained so to the end," the Raleigh editor said. "He loved folks, he loved action, he loved flowers, he loved to live and be part of things that touched his fellowmen. He never knew what *ennui* was."

Each day the accolades continued. The *Asheville Citizen* viewed Carr as one of the builders of the state "whose initiative as a tobacco manufacturer made Durham and North Carolina known all over the world"; the *Winston-Salem Journal* claimed that "North Carolina has had few men of his ability, energy, character and achievement. Indeed, he stands out prominently in the entire south and even in the nation . . . and his work counted mightily in bringing North Carolina to that point of progress which she now occupies."

The *Charlotte Observer*, recalling one of Carr's grand gestures, said, "At the close of the Spanish American War the North State troops were stranded in Havana. The state had no money available to bring them home and the prospect was for an indefinite stay. General Carr was quick to come to the rescue. Out of his own pocket he advanced the money necessary for the return."

In Greensboro, the general's personality again took precedence over his accomplishments. "As to how Carr will appear to posterity we do not pretend to know," said an editor at the *Greensboro News*, "but we think that he will linger in the memory of his contemporaries not as the manufacturer, the soldier, the philanthropist nor even as the patriot, notwithstanding that he was all of these things; but by reason of his peculiarly striking quality as the courtliest southern gentleman of his day."

That particular compliment would have pleased Carr, for he set great store by good manners and often boasted that "nobody will ever be more polite to me than I to him." His unfailing courtesy, like the carnation in his lapel, was a hallmark of sorts. Wherever he went, he was constantly bowing, smiling, tipping his hat, equally Chesterfieldian to black and white, and especially to children.[23]

On the Sunday morning five days after Carr's death, the people of Durham awoke to find Main Street draped with black streamers from Somerset Villa through the business district to Five Points, a distance of seven blocks; there were also black wreaths on many store fronts. Such an act of public mourning had never occurred in the city before, nor was it likely to be repeated. Visitors continued to call at Somerset Villa until three o'clock, when the casket was closed. A Methodist bishop, three ministers, and a choir of twenty began the first part of a service that would end at Maplewood Cemetery, one of Carr's first gifts to Durham. There was room in the house only for Carr's family, his Confederate guard of honor, and representatives from three organizations that were dear to him: the United Daughters of the Confederacy, the Royal Arch Masons, and the Benevolent Protective Order of Elks. Hundreds of people, including many relatives and close friends, stood on the porch and in the yard while the Right Reverend James Cannon, the Reverend W. W. Peele, the Reverend G. T. Adams, and the Reverend Reuben Hibberd read scriptures and prayed. The choir sang "Rock of Ages" and "How Firm a Foundation," two of Carr's favorite hymns.[24]

Local reporters claimed the funeral was the largest ever held in Durham, with 20,000 people lining the streets and "sorrow on every face." One hundred and fifty cars were in the cortege that wound from Dillard Street to Main, up Main to Milton Avenue, from Milton to Chapel Hill Street, and, finally, to the cemetery. Many streets along the way were closed to traffic, and the Southern Railway Company ordered its trains to cease running between three and four

*Julian S. Carr with infant from Children's Home Society
(courtesy of Austin Heaton Carr, Jr.)*

o'clock, so that the automobiles could cross the tracks at Milton Avenue without a holdup. Only the hearse and those cars carrying the immediate family were allowed inside the cemetery grounds, but a large crowd had already gathered at the Carr plot, where the stone angels the general had ordered from Italy stood watch over his wife's grave. Many in that crowd were black people, whose leaders had organized a mass meeting the day after Carr's death for the purpose of adopting a resolution to be presented to his family. That resolution, duly adopted and formally presented to Claiborn Carr, had read:

> Be it resolved that we, the colored citizens of this community, do give sincere thanks to Almighty God for the kindness and help that have come to us through the life of General Julian S. Carr;
>
> That we offer our services and our scant means to be used along with that of other citizens of the community to perpetuate his wonderful life;
>
> And we do herewith tender his bereaved family heartfelt sympathy and sincere gratitude, such gratitude as can come only from those who, in the midst of their greatest suffering, have lost a true friend.[25]

A large part of Durham's black population watched the white preachers perform last rites for their true friend. Some of these spectators had worked for him at the Bull Factory, or at Mill Number Two, or at Somerset Villa. John Daniels, who had succeeded John O'Daniel as butler, was there; so was Aurelia Burnett, the cook; and so was Tom Charleston, who had driven Miss Nannie's funeral coach to Maplewood nine years earlier. Fieldhands who had worked at Occoneechee when it was the finest and fanciest farm in North Carolina were there, standing alongside Negro teachers and doctors and lawyers and businessmen whose careers had been furthered by Carr's generosity. All of them were there to pay their respects to Julian Carr. Even though he had fought on the wrong side in the Civil War, when that war was over he had said, for everybody to hear, that he was the black man's friend. And he meant it. He had proved it not once, but many times, and they were there to tell him goodbye.

After the choir from Trinity Church sang "Sleep in Jesus," one of the ministers began to pray. Sunlight, filtering through the trees, dappled the marble faces of the angels and warmed the bowed heads of the mourners. Some wept into white linen handkerchiefs; others let the tears slide down their cheeks. Soon the funeral would end and they would go home, leaving Julian Carr to "sleep quietly in Maplewood, roofed by the blue dome of heaven, guarded by the stars, and lulled by the music of the breeze."[26]

Afterword

THE people of Durham were not ready to forget the man who had infused so much of his own vigor into their town, and twenty-one years later many of them would return to Maplewood Cemetery, ready to begin a day-long celebration of the centenary of his birth on 12 October 1845. In the fall of 1944, J. M. Templeton, a Confederate veteran from Cary, North Carolina, conceived the idea of the centenary celebration; he passed the suggestion along to Josephus Daniels, the editor of the Raleigh *News and Observer*. After Daniels voiced his approval of Templeton's idea in print and the *Durham Morning Herald* also looked with favor upon it, the Durham Chamber of Commerce appointed a committee to plan and execute a program recognizing Carr's achievements on the hundredth anniversary of his birth.

Headed by Arnold Briggs, the president of the Austin Heaton Company, the committee did its work well. The North Carolina General Assembly adopted a resolution endorsing the movement to honor Carr, one which stated, in part, "At the peak of his career, General Carr was the state's greatest business man, measured by the past and those of his day. He was president or a leading spirit in nearly forty corporations promoting business, civic and cultural interests of the community, centering around Durham and extending throughout the state." Following ratification of the resolution on 20 March 1945, Governor R. Gregg Cherry proclaimed 12 October "General Julian S. Carr Day" in North Carolina "in the hope that proper and adequate recognition may be accorded to this great-hearted citizen and his honored career by commemorative exercises in his home city of Durham and by the press and radio throughout the state."

Both press and radio responded to the governor's wish by giving Carr's upcoming birthday party maximum coverage. Broadcasters announced the occasion frequently prior to its occurrence, and from 8 February through 16 October 1945, nine North Carolina newspapers carried editorial comments about Carr that clearly indicated his importance to both the state and the nation. The commemorative exercises included a graveside memorial service at Maplewood Cemetery sponsored by the United Daughters of the Confederacy (one of whom characterized him as "a cavalier, heroic and romantic,"[1] and another of whom laid a wreath on his grave); dedication of a local school, which was renamed the "Julian S. Carr Junior High School"; a luncheon at the Washington Duke Hotel honoring members of the Carr family and visiting dignitaries; a memorial worship service at Trinity Methodist Church; and a banquet in the city armory, at which Dr. Bangnee Lui, a noted Chinese educator and member of the United Nations advisory staff, was the speaker.

The audience included North Carolina's governor, representatives from the state legislature, many local and state politicians, and a large segment of Durham's population. Carr's only living children, Lida Flower and Claiborn Carr; his nephew, Durham mayor Will Carr; five grandsons (Claiborn, Julian, Boylan, Rufus, and Noell Carr); and a grandnephew (Albert Carr) heard four prayers, eleven musical renditions, and nine speeches during the long day. Although it was one that none of them was likely to forget, in order to remind them of all that had gone into the making of "General Julian S. Carr Day," Claiborn Carr commissioned C. Sylvester Green, the editor of the *Durham Morning Herald*, to compile all speeches, resolutions, congratulatory telegrams, editorials, and photographs into a hardcover volume. Entitled *General Julian S. Carr, Greathearted Citizen*, and dedicated by Claiborn Carr "with admiration and deep affection to my father," several hundred copies of the book were distributed to Julian Shakespeare Carr's kinsmen and friends and to many of the state's libraries.

In 1945, when the centennial of Carr's birth took place, fewer than a thousand Confederate veterans were living. Fourteen years later, when Walter Williams died in Houston, Texas, on 19 December 1959, at the age of one hundred and seventeen, Carr's army, which had inspired him to so much impassioned rhetoric during his lifetime, ceased to exist.

Notes

CHAPTER ONE

1. Green, *Greathearted Citizen*, 79–82.
2. Ibid., 8.
3. Boyd, *Story of Durham*, 75.
4. Chamberlain, *Old Days in Chapel Hill*, 30; *Durham Morning Herald*, 30 Apr. 1924.
5. Carr Family Bible, in possession of Kate Lee Hundley Harris, Durham, N.C.; A. H. Carr, Jr. Papers, on loan to author from Austin Heaton Carr, Jr., Winston-Salem, N.C. An unnamed, undated newspaper clipping pasted in Julian Carr's personal diary for 1907 states that when Carr's boyhood home on Franklin Street in Chapel Hill was sold early in 1907, he had the remains of his brothers, William, Joseph, and John, brought from their resting place under a large oak tree in the back yard to his plot in Durham's Maplewood Cemetery. The graves of Joseph and John, who were five months and fourteen months old, respectively, when they died, yielded only a few pieces of two small wooden coffins; but the body of William Green Carr was "natural looking after being in the ground for over 44 years." William died, possibly of typhoid fever, at the age of twenty, while he was a student at the University of North Carolina, and his body's remarkable state of preservation was due to the fact that it had been placed in a casket made of metal (probably iron) and glass. It astonished a number of people "who viewed the remains through the glass. The white collar and tie had not faded and there was a bunch of green looking flowers, perhaps artificial, on the lappel of his coat."
6. A. H. Carr, Jr. Papers.
7. Ibid.
8. Ray, *Colonial Granville County*, copy in North Carolina Collection, Wilson Library, University of North Carolina at Chapel Hill (hereafter cited as NCC/UNC/CH).
9. A. H. Carr, Jr. Papers; Winston, "John Wesley Carr."
10. A. H. Carr, Jr. Papers.
11. Ibid.
12. Ibid.; interview with J. Claiborne Carr. (Mr. Carr spells his middle name with an *e*.)
13. Ibid.
14. Winston, "John Wesley Carr," 210.
15. Johnson, *Antebellum North Carolina*, 248, gives an account of what was for sale in many North Carolina stores before the Civil War. I assume that Carr's store was more or less typical.
16. Winston, "John Wesley Carr," 213.
17. Russell, *Rare Pattern*, 23, describes cooking in a Chapel Hill kitchen of that era.

18. Winston, "John Wesley Carr," 213.

19. Battle, *History of the University of North Carolina* 1:608; Vickers et al., *Chapel Hill, an Illustrated History*, 58–59, 64–65. John and Eliza Carr lived with Eliza's mother, Martha Bullock, in 1841; John bought his mother-in-law's house in 1843, and a few years later he purchased, from the University of North Carolina, Lot #7, on the northwest corner of Franklin and Columbia streets, where he build a store and, just beyond it, a home large enough to accommodate student roomers, sometimes as many as nine. Between 1835 and 1889 he engaged in over one hundred real estate transactions and owned, from time to time, a brickyard, a sawmill, a cotton gin, and a blacksmith shop.

20. Register of Deeds Office, Orange County Court House, Hillsborough, N.C.

21. *Durham Morning Herald*, 18 Mar. 1945.

22. Winston, "John Wesley Carr," 213.

23. Green, *Greathearted Citizen*, 8–10, 56.

24. Chamberlain, *Old Days in Chapel Hill*. From writings of Cornelia Phillips Spencer, a long-time resident of Chapel Hill and a friend of the Carrs, one can picture the life Julian Carr may have led before the war and for a short time afterward. Mrs. Spencer was a keen-eyed observer of the village and its people; she mentioned John, Eliza, and Julian Carr with some frequency in various letters to friends and in her diaries.

25. Battle, *History of the University of North Carolina* 1:612.

26. Powell, *First State University*, 66.

27. Battle, *History of the University of North Carolina* 1:569–72.

28. Wheeler, *Reminiscences and Memoirs*, 358.

29. Battle, *History of the University of North Carolina* 1:569–72. For details on President Buchanan's commencement visit, described in the following paragraphs of this chapter, see ibid., 698–706.

CHAPTER TWO

1. Battle, *History of the University of North Carolina* 1:719–21.

2. Ibid., 726–29.

3. *Morehead Family*, 111, on loan to author from Julia Manning Wily, Durham, N.C.; "Memorial Address on the Life and Character of Col. Eugene Morehead. Delivered Before the Commonwealth Club, Durham, N.C., March 18, 1889 by His Friend, Julian S. Carr," pamphlet in NCC/UNC/CH.

4. University Student Records, University Archives, UNC; Battle, *History of the University of North Carolina* 1:730.

5. Powell, *First State University*, 89.

6. Battle, *History of the University of North Carolina* 1:731.

7. Ibid., 740.

8. Ibid., 732.

9. Quoted in ibid., 751.

10. Quoted in Chamberlain, *Old Days in Chapel Hill*, 89.

11. Battle, *History of the University of North Carolina* 1:733.

12. Manarin, *North Carolina Troops* 2:255.

13. Clark, *Histories of the Several Regiments* 3:635; also two artifacts related to Carr's military record, both in possession of Laura Noell Carr Chapman, Spartanburg, S.C. As founder and president of the First National Bank in Durham, Carr placed at the bank's front entrance a cannonball and a block of wood, each with a silver plaque. The plaque on the cannonball was inscribed: "Thrown on the evening of the raid the Yanks made upon the little town of Bellefield, Virginia, at which time much property was destroyed and the Railroad Station was burned. February, 1865." The plaque on the wood proclaimed that it was "Cut from the body of a tree that sheltered the person of General Julian S. Carr during the fight of Hatcher's Run, fought on October 27th, 1864. It contains eight Minnie Balls and one Grape Cannister."

14. Davis, *Sherman's March*, 131, 301.

15. Chamberlain, *Old Days in Chapel Hill*, 84.

16. Ibid., 82–85.

17. Powell, *First State University*, 89; Vickers et al., *Chapel Hill, an Illustrated History*, 71; Chamberlain, *Old Days in Chapel Hill*, 85.

18. Russell, *Rare Pattern*, 3. Historians disagree as to the number of Union soldiers sent to occupy Chapel Hill immediately after the surrender at Bennett Place. Some believe 400, rather than 4,000, would be a more accurate count.

19. Chamberlain, *Old Days in Chapel Hill*, 95.

20. Ibid., 86.

21. Ibid., 42, 95; Henderson, *Campus of the First State University*, 186.

22. Quoted in Chamberlain, *Old Days in Chapel Hill*, 87.

23. J. S. Carr Papers, the Southern Historical Collection, Wilson Library, University of North Carolina at Chapel Hill (hereafter cited as SHC/UNC/CH).

24. Henderson, *Campus of the First State University*, 186.

25. Spencer quoted in Chamberlain, *Old Days in Chapel Hill*, 99; Powell, *First State University*, 89.

26. Henderson, *Campus of the First State University*, 186.

27. Lefler and Newsome, *North Carolina*, 460.

28. Russell, *Rare Pattern*, 40; Battle, *History of the University of North Carolina* 1:746, 747; Spencer quoted in Chamberlain, *Old Days in Chapel Hill*, 88.

29. Lefler and Newsome, *North Carolina*, 479; Chamberlain, *Old Days in Chapel Hill*, 125.

30. Chamberlain, *Old Days in Chapel Hill*, 117; address by J. S. Carr at the unveiling of a monument to the Confederacy in Chapel Hill, 2 June 1913, J. S. Carr Papers, SHC/UNC/CH.

31. Lefler and Newsome, *North Carolina*, 479; Battle, *History of the University of North Carolina* 1:754.

32. Henderson, *Campus of the First State University*, 187.

33. Ibid., 188.

34. Spencer quoted in Chamberlain, *Old Days in Chapel Hill*, 143.

35. R. P. Baker (Archivist, Arkansas Historical Commission) to author, 5

Feb. 1980: "According to the 1870 U.S. Census of Little Rock Mr. [James M.] Carr was a merchant born in North Carolina and 57 years of age."

36. Russell, *Rare Pattern*, 46.

37. Chamberlain, *Old Days in Chapel Hill*, 174; Henderson, *Campus of the First State University*, 195.

38. Russell, *Rare Pattern*, 46.

39. Ibid., 48.

40. Powell, *First State University*, 92.

41. Russell, *Rare Pattern*, 49; Henderson, *Campus of the First State University*, 189.

42. Henderson, *Campus of the First State University*, 192; Russell, *Rare Pattern*, 49.

43. Green, *Greathearted Citizen*, 7.

CHAPTER THREE

1. Wheeler, *Reminiscences and Memoirs*, 359.

2. Paul, *History of the Town of Durham*, 25.

3. *Durham Sun*, 14 Nov. 1916.

4. Boyd, *Story of Durham*, 59.

5. *Durham Sun*, 14 Nov. 1916; Boyd, *Story of Durham*, 58.

6. Wheeler, *Reminiscences and Memoirs*, 359.

7. Boyd, *Story of Durham*, 59; Paul, *History of the Town of Durham*, 26.

8. Boyd, *Story of Durham*, 60.

9. Ibid.; Wheeler, *Reminiscences and Memoirs*, 360.

10. Boyd, *Story of Durham*, 61.

11. Wheeler, *Reminiscences and Memoirs*, 360.

12. *Durham Sun*, 14 Nov. 1916; Wheeler, *Reminiscences and Memoirs*, 361.

13. A. H. Carr, Jr. Papers.

14. Ibid.

15. Wheeler, *Reminiscences and Memoirs*, 361.

16. Tilley, *Bright Tobacco Industry*, 51–54.

17. Ibid., 59–62.

18. Ibid., 498–99.

19. Boyd, *Story of Durham*, 69.

20. Paul, *History of the Town of Durham*, 144–45; Tilley, *Bright Tobacco Industry*, 206–9.

21. Tilley, *Bright Tobacco Industry*, 207, 238–40.

22. Minutes of the Board of Aldermen, Durham, N.C., 6 Jan. 1873.

23. Eliza Morehead Carr [Flower] Papers, on loan to author from Ruth Flower Lester, Kansas City, Mo. Subsequent information on the Ward and Parrish families is from this source.

24. Boyd, *Story of Durham*, 19.

25. Eliza Morehead Carr [Flower] Papers. Quotations in subsequent paragraphs are also from this source.

26. J. S. Carr to W. T. Blackwell, n.d., W. T. Blackwell Papers, on loan to author from Mary Blackwell Pridgen Martin, Durham, N.C.

27. Minutes of the Board of Aldermen, Durham, N.C., 6 Mar. 1873.

28. Raleigh *Daily Sentinel*, 6 Oct. 1875; Catherine W. Bishir to author, 6 Aug. 1982.

29. Photograph in A. H. Carr, Jr. Papers.

30. Ibid.

CHAPTER FOUR

1. J. S. Carr to W. T. Blackwell, n.d. [1877], in W. T. Blackwell Papers; Tilley, *Bright Tobacco Industry*, 550. Washington Duke, founder of W. Duke Sons and Company, moved with his family to Durham from a farm in Orange County in 1874. His eldest son, Brodie Duke, had preceded him there in 1869.

2. Tilley, *Bright Tobacco Industry*, 551.

3. Boyd, *Story of Durham*, 62.

4. Ibid., 67.

5. Paul, *History of the Town of Durham*, 61; Boyd, *Story of Durham*, 62.

6. Paul, *History of the Town of Durham*, 51.

7. Ibid., 61–64, 70.

8. Robert, *Story of Tobacco*, 124.

9. Tilley, *Bright Tobacco Industry*, 524.

10. Paul, *History of the Town of Durham*, 76–77.

11. "Big Smoker: An exact reproduction of an advertisement issued by W. T. Blackwell & Co. . . . January, 1878," [July 1908], pamphlet in NCC/UNC/CH.

12. Tilley, *Bright Tobacco Industry*, 525.

13. J. S. Carr to W. T. Blackwell, n.d. [1877], W. T. Blackwell Papers.

14. Tilley, *Bright Tobacco Industry*, 550.

15. J. S. Carr to W. T. Blackwell, n.d. [1877], W. T. Blackwell Papers.

16. Boyd, *Story of Durham*, 65.

17. Battle, *History of the University of North Carolina* 1:426, 703.

18. Boyd, *Story of Durham*, 67–68.

19. J. S. Carr to W. T. Blackwell, 3 May 1877, W. T. Blackwell Papers.

20. Boyd, *Story of Durham*, 67.

21. Tilley, *Bright Tobacco Industry*, 549–55.

22. Ibid., 549–50.

23. Ibid., 550.

24. J. S. Carr to W. T. Blackwell, 4 May 1877, W. T. Blackwell Papers.

25. Ibid., 5 Nov. 1877.

26. Ibid., 2 Nov. 1877.

27. Ibid.

28. Ibid., 8 Feb. 1877.

29. Tilley, *Bright Tobacco Industry*, 208.

30. J. S. Carr to W. T. Blackwell, 21 Mar. 1877, W. T. Blackwell Papers.
31. Ibid., 30 Mar. 1877.
32. Ibid., n.d.
33. *Durham Morning Herald*, 26 Apr. 1953.
34. Tilley, *Bright Tobacco Industry*, 549.
35. Boyd, *Story of Durham*, 71; Tilley, *Bright Tobacco Industry*, 500.
36. Tilley, *Bright Tobacco Industry*, 499.
37. Ibid., 500–502.
38. J. S. Carr to W. T. Blackwell, 26 Apr. 1877, W. T. Blackwell Papers.
39. Ibid., n.d. [Sept. 1877].
40. Ibid.
41. Boyd, *Story of Durham*, 75; *United States Tobacco Journal Directory, 1881–82*.
42. J. S. Carr to W. T. Blackwell, n.d. [Dec. 1877], W. T. Blackwell Papers.
43. Cameron, *Sketch of the Tobacco Interests*, 52–55.
44. Paul, *History of the Town of Durham*, 104–5.
45. Tilley, *Bright Tobacco Industry*, 502, 517.
46. Ibid., 500–502.
47. Boyd, *Story of Durham*, 72–73; Paul, *History of the Town of Durham*, 105.
48. Tilley, *Bright Tobacco Industry*, 577.

CHAPTER FIVE

1. Paul, *History of the Town of Durham*, 80.
2. Webb, "Birth of a County."
3. Tilley, *Bright Tobacco Industry*, 549.
4. Webb, "Birth of a County." Samuel A'C. Ashe withdrew from the firm of Merrimon, Fuller, and Ashe in 1879.
5. *United States Tobacco Journal Directory, 1881–82*; Boyd, *Story of Durham*, 75; Tilley, *Bright Tobacco Industry*, 551.
6. Boyd, *Story of Durham*, 75; A. H. Carr, Jr. Papers.
7. A. H. Carr, Jr. Papers.
8. Boyd, *Story of Durham*, 75; Tilley, *Bright Tobacco Industry*, 532–35.
9. Tilley, *Bright Tobacco Industry*, 532; A. H. Carr, Jr. Papers.
10. Korner, *Joseph of Kernersville*, 86, 88, 89; Paul, *History of the Town of Durham*, 109.
11. *United States Tobacco Journal*, 17 Nov. 1883.
12. *Tobacco Leaf*, 20 Oct. 1883.
13. Tilley, *Bright Tobacco Industry*, 550, 577–78.
14. Boyd, *Story of Durham*, 72–73.
15. R. L. Patterson Papers, SHC/UNC/CH.
16. Ibid.
17. Tilley, *Bright Tobacco Industry*, 577–78.
18. Ibid., 578–79.
19. Ibid., 577.

20. J. S. Carr to the Piedmont Poultry Association and the United Daughters of the Confederacy, J. S. Carr Papers, SHC/UNC/CH.

21. Robert, *Story of Tobacco*, 152.

22. Tilley, *Bright Tobacco Industry*, 595.

23. Hobson, *South-Watching*, 66–70.

24. Tilley, *Bright Tobacco Industry*, 634–35.

25. Cash, *Mind of the South*, 198–200.

26. Durden, *Dukes of Durham*, 123–24.

27. *Inventory of Early Textile Mill Villages*; Boyd, *Story of Durham*, 121–22; Tilley, *Bright Tobacco Industry*, 634–35.

28. A. H. Carr, Jr. Papers.

29. Ibid. In 1885, Julian Carr was the father of two daughters and three sons. A fourth son, Austin Heaton Carr, was born in 1894.

30. Ibid.

31. Ibid.; see also John Franklin Heitman Papers, University Archives, Duke University.

32. A. H. Carr, Jr. Papers; Vickers et al., *Chapel Hill, an Illustrated History*, 109. While John Wesley Carr was serving as magistrate of police in 1874, his fellow commissioners expelled him "in consequence of mental derangement," but four months later "he led the balloting . . . and returned to his seat again in 1875." Julian Carr's "statement" to his family, and George Tayloe Winston's reference to John Carr's illness in his later years, seem to indicate that he suffered from periodic depressions. Nevertheless, he continued to function as a leading merchant of Chapel Hill until his death in 1889.

CHAPTER SIX

1. Boyd, *Story of Durham*, 136–37.

2. Tilley, *Bright Tobacco Industry*, 565.

3. Boyd, *Story of Durham*, 138–39; Tilley, *Bright Tobacco Industry*, 213.

4. Morehead Journal, 25, 26; photocopy on loan to author from Julia Manning Wily, Durham, N.C.

5. Ibid., 11–12.

6. "Memorial Address on the Life and Character of Col. Eugene Morehead. Delivered Before the Commonwealth Club, Durham, N.C., March 18, 1889 by His Friend, Julian S. Carr," pamphlet in NCC/UNC/CH.

7. Morehead Journal, 17.

8. Ibid., 3, 35.

9. Boyd, *Story of Durham*, 117, 115.

10. Tilley, *Bright Tobacco Industry*, 541; Boyd, *Story of Durham*, 117.

11. *Morehead Family*, 81.

12. Boyd, *Story of Durham*, 138–39; Tilley, *Bright Tobacco Industry*, 213.

13. Tilley, *Bright Tobacco Industry*, 565; Boyd, *Story of Durham*, 139.

14. Boyd, *Story of Durham*, 141–42.

15. Ibid., 142–45.

16. Ibid., 149; Tilley, *Bright Tobacco Industry*, 566.

17. Boyd, *Story of Durham*, 233–35.

18. *Tobacco Plant*, 14 Feb. 1872.

19. Boyd, *Story of Durham*, 235.

20. *Tobacco Plant*, 15 Sept., 22 Sept., 29 Sept. 1886. Quotations in the next four paragraphs are also from these issues.

21. Ibid., 29 Sept. 1886.

22. *Daily Tobacco Plant*, 2 June 1888.

23. Ibid., 5 June 1888.

24. Boyd, *Story of Durham*, 241–42.

25. Ibid.; *Durham Daily Globe*, 20 Jan. 1892.

26. Daniels, *Tar Heel Editor*, 255.

27. Ibid., 247.

28. Green, *Greathearted Citizen*, 37–38.

29. Boyd, *Story of Durham*, 150–51.

30. Ibid., 152; *Daily Tobacco Plant*, 1 Jan., 10 Mar. 1887.

31. *Daily Tobacco Plant*, 10 Mar. 1887.

32. Boyd, *Story of Durham*, 152–54.

33. *Forty Years*, 9.

34. Ibid., 15.

35. Ibid., 14–15.

36. Ibid., 11–14.

37. Ibid., 11–14, 18.

38. Ibid., 24.

39. *Morehead Family*, 82, 83.

40. J. S. Carr to Cornelia P. Spencer, 15 Mar. 1889, Cornelia Phillips Spencer Papers, North Carolina State Archives.

CHAPTER SEVEN

1. "History of Construction of Somerset Villa."

2. Ibid., 1.

3. "Somerset Villa."

4. "History of Construction of Somerset Villa"; "Somerset Villa."

5. "Somerset Villa"; Rose Hartwick Thorpe, "Curfew Must Not Ring Tonight," first two lines of stanza seven. Entire poem was printed in the *Tobacco Plant*, 15 Dec. 1886. Also found in Hazel Feldman, ed., *The Best Loved Poems of the American People* (New York: Doubleday & Company, 1936), 159.

6. "Somerset Villa."

7. "History of Construction of Somerset Villa," 2, 6.

8. Six years after the cornerstone-laying and dedication, Carr became the father of a fourth son, Austin Heaton, named for two of his business associates.

9. Green, *Greathearted Citizen*, 62.

10. Mike Bradshaw, "Chinese Lad Left Trinity College to Found Own Dynasty," *News and Observer*, 28 June 1936.

11. Tourtellot, "C. J. Soong," 202.

12. Ibid., 203; Green, *Greathearted Citizen*, 64.

13. Green, *Greathearted Citizen*, 64–65.

14. Ibid., 62–63.

15. Ibid., 19.

16. Seagrave, *Soong Dynasty*, 13–16, 20, 25–27; Green, *Greathearted Citizen*, 66.

17. Green, *Greathearted Citizen*, 66.

18. *News and Observer*, 28 June 1936.

19. Ibid., 28 Feb. 1943.

20. Ibid., 28 June 1936.

21. Chaffin, *Trinity College*, 274.

22. Ibid., 274–75.

23. Ibid., 275; Seagrave, *Soong Dynasty*, 34–36.

24. Mims, *History of Vanderbilt University*, 175.

25. Ibid., 176.

26. Kathy Stone (Special Collections, Vanderbilt University Archives) to author, 5 Mar. 1982: "The Vanderbilt University Archives has a small folder of information on Mr. Soon(g). Enclosed are copies of some relevant material in that file." Soong's entry in Margaret Baskette's autograph album "has been reproduced photographically." Miss Baskette also "preserved newspaper articles about him and Madame Chiang Kai Shek in her autograph album."

27. Mims, *History of Vanderbilt University*, 175.

28. Chaffin, *Trinity College*, 311, 326.

29. Ibid., 341–43; J. S. Carr to J. F. Heitman, n.d. [May 1884], John Franklin Heitman Papers.

30. Chaffin, *Trinity College*, 347–57.

31. Ibid., 362.

32. John Franklin Heitman Papers. Much of the correspondence between Carr and Heitman indicates that Heitman acted as president of Trinity College between Marquis L. Wood and John Franklin Crowell, although he did not have the title.

33. J. S. Carr to J. F. Heitman, 10 Oct. 1885, ibid.

34. 16 Dec. 1885, ibid.

35. *News and Observer*, 28 Feb. 1943.

36. Mims, *History of Vanderbilt University*, 177.

37. Seagrave, *Soong Dynasty*, 41.

38. Ibid.; Hahn, *The Soong Sisters*, 24.

39. *News and Observer*, 28 June 1936; Seagrave, *Soong Dynasty*, 69–70.

40. *News and Observer*, 28 June 1936, 28 Feb. 1943.

41. Ibid., 28 June 1936. Information in the following paragraphs is also from this source.

42. Seagrave, *Soong Dynasty*, 87.

CHAPTER EIGHT

1. Durham Chamber of Commerce, *Durham, North Carolina.*
2. *News and Observer*, 28 June 1936.
3. Chaffin, *Trinity College*, 370–71.
4. Ibid., 387–88.
5. Porter, *Trinity and Duke*, 21.
6. Chaffin, *Trinity College*, 391–92, 387–88.
7. Porter, *Trinity and Duke*, 19.
8. Ibid., 21.
9. Durden, *Dukes of Durham*, 91–92.
10. Boyd, *Story of Durham*, 159–60.
11. Ibid., 166.
12. Durden, *Dukes of Durham*, 92; Powell, *Dictionary of North Carolina Biography* 1:466. In 1925, after James B. Duke endowed Trinity College with $40 million, its name was changed to Duke University; thus Crowell's dream was realized thirty-one years after he resigned the presidency of the college, and six years before his death in 1931.
13. Tilley, *Bright Tobacco Industry*, 594.
14. Ibid., 271.
15. Durden, *Dukes of Durham*, 68.
16. Ibid.
17. Claiborn McD. Carr, Jr. to author, 5 Jan. 1982.
18. Tilley, *Bright Tobacco Industry*, 594; Durden, *Dukes of Durham*, 68.
19. Gray, "'Jule' Carr, the Man."
20. Tilley, *Bright Tobacco Industry*, 550, 594.
21. Ibid., 635.
22. Letterhead of Occoneechee Farm, 31 Mar. 1921; *Hillsboro Observer*, 3 June 1965.
23. McLaurin, "Nineteenth-Century N.C. State Fair," 213.
24. Ibid., 217.
25. North Carolina Agricultural Society, *Rules and Regulations and Schedule of Premiums for the Seventeenth Annual Exposition of the North Carolina Agricultural Society, at Raleigh, N.C., October, 1877,* (Raleigh: John Nichols, Book and Job Printer, 1877), NCC/UNC/CH.
26. Ibid., Oct. 1878, 1879, 1880, 1881, 1882; *News and Observer*, 21 Oct. 1880.
27. *News of Orange County*, 20 Mar. 1980.
28. Gray, "'Jule' Carr, the Man." The Easter Monday picnics were a custom Carr established and maintained for many years.
29. Advertisement for the sale of Occoneechee Farm by the Atlantic Coast Realty Company, Winston-Salem, N.C., and Petersburg, Va., 22 Nov. 1923; on loan to author from A. H. Carr, Jr.
30. Interview with Mary Leigh Webb.
31. *Durham Daily Globe*, 5 July 1893.
32. Advertisement for sale of Occoneechee Farm, 22 Nov. 1923.

33. Korner, *Joseph of Kernersville*, 92; advertisement for sale of Occoneechee Farm, 22 Nov. 1923.

34. *News and Observer*, 23 Oct. 1894.

35. Ibid., 27 Oct. 1894.

36. Ibid., 23 Oct. 1895.

37. McLaurin, "Nineteenth-Century N.C. State Fair," 225–26; *News and Observer*, 2 Oct. 1895.

38. J. S. Carr to Cornelia P. Spencer, 15 Mar. 1889.

39. *News and Observer*, 24 Oct. 1895; McLaurin, "Nineteenth-Century N.C. State Fair," 219.

40. *News and Observer*, 1 Nov. 1895.

41. Paul, *History of the Town of Durham*, 81–83.

42. Ibid.; Ruth Flower Lester to author, 25 Aug. 1977.

43. Unidentified newspaper clipping, datelined Durham, Dec. 18 [1895], pasted in Eliza Morehead Carr's Bride Book, on loan to author from Ruth Flower Lester, Kansas City, Mo.

44. Ibid.; *Durham Daily Globe*, 13 Oct. 1893.

45. *Handbook of Durham*.

46. *Durham Daily Globe*, 13 Oct. 1893.

47. Eliza Morehead Carr's Bride Book.

48. Ibid.

49. Ibid.

50. J. S. Carr to Eliza Carr Flower, 18 Dec. 1895, in Eliza Morehead Carr's Bride Book.

51. Eliza Morehead Carr's Bride Book.

52. Ibid.

53. Boyd, *Story of Durham*, 166, 263.

54. *Durham Sun*, 26 Feb. 1976.

55. Ibid.

56. Lalla Ruth Carr to Eliza Carr Flower, 7 Sept. 1899, in Eliza Morehead Carr's Bride Book.

57. *Commemorative Biographical Record of Central Pennsylvania*.

58. Webb, "The House Bull Durham Built," 28.

59. Interview with Gertrude Winston Webb.

CHAPTER NINE

1. Powell, *Dictionary of North Carolina Biography* 1:291.

2. Ibid.; Albright, "Simmons Machine," 11.

3. Albright, "Simmons Machine," 10.

4. *Durham Daily Globe*, 16 Mar. 1892.

5. Ibid., 17 Mar.; *Raleigh Signal*, 19 Mar. 1892.

6. *Durham Daily Globe*, 13 Apr. 1892.

7. Powell, *Dictionary of North Carolina Biography* 1:329.

8. *Durham Daily Globe*, 18 May 1892.

9. Ibid.

10. Ibid., 19 May 1892; Daniels, *Tar Heel Editor*, 499.

11. Faulkner, "North Carolina Democrats," 230–31.

12. *News and Observer*, 11 Aug. 1895.

13. Daniels, *Editor in Politics*, 154–55; Crow and Durden, *Maverick Republican*, 43–45.

14. *Cyclopedia of Eminent and Representative Men* 1:571–74; Daniels, *Editor in Politics*, 154–55.

15. Daniels, *Editor in Politics*, 155.

16. Ibid., 191–93.

17. Ibid., 201.

18. Crow and Durden, *Maverick Republican*, 73, 140.

19. "The Issues of the Campaign Stated: An Open Letter to Van B. Sparrow, Patterson Township, Durham County, from J. S. Carr, Chairman, Durham County Democratic Executive Committee, October 24, 1898," Campaign Literature, 1898, NCC/UNC/CH.

20. Albright, "Simmons Machine," 10.

21. Daniels, *Editor in Politics*, 295.

22. Ibid., 295–302; Crow and Durden, *Maverick Republican*, 127–31.

23. Albright, "Simmons Machine," 11.

24. Reprinted in *News and Observer*, 1 Oct. 1899.

25. Ibid., 3 Oct. 1899.

26. Ibid., 8 Apr. 1900.

27. "Announcement of Gen. Julian S. Carr for U.S. Senator to the Democratic Electors of North Carolina, Durham, N.C., August 25, 1900." Broadside in NCC/UNC/CH.

28. Moye, "N.C. Senatorial Primary."

29. Daniels, *Editor in Politics*, 372.

30. Moye, "N.C. Senatorial Primary."

31. *Carr Building Presented*; *News and Observer*, 26 Sept. 1900.

32. Daniels, *Editor in Politics*, 420.

33. Ibid., 321, 364, 371.

34. *News and Observer*, 7 Nov. 1900.

35. Ibid., 8 Nov. 1900.

36. Moye, "N.C. Senatorial Primary."

37. Morrison, *Josephus Daniels Says* . . . , 277.

CHAPTER TEN

1. Boyd, *Story of Durham*, 124; Minutes of the Golden Belt Hosiery Company's organizational meeting, 13 Dec. 1895, Golden Belt Hosiery Company Papers, North Carolina State Archives.

2. GBHC Minutes, 4 Dec. 1895.

3. Ibid., 13 Mar. 1896.

4. Ibid., 17 Feb. 1898; Boyd, *Story of Durham*, 124.

5. Boyd, *Story of Durham*, 124.

6. Address by J. S. Carr to the Chapel Hill High School Class of 1920, J. S. Carr Papers, SHC/UNC/CH.

7. J. S. Carr to the Julian S. Carr Bible Class, Trinity Methodist Church, Durham, N.C., n.d. Carr used the International Sunday School Lessons (still being used in the Carr Bible Class today), which he frequently edited, as the basis for his teaching; J. S. Carr Papers, ibid.

8. J. S. Carr, Jr. to J. S. Carr, Sr., 16 Sept. 1897, ibid.

9. Ibid.

10. Alumni Records of the University of North Carolina at Chapel Hill; *The Hellenian*, 1898.

11. Student Records and Faculty Reports, Vol. S-6, University Archives, UNC/CH; *The Hellenian*, 1898–99.

12. *The Hellenian*, 1898–99.

13. Battle, *History of the University of North Carolina* 2:564.

14. *Inventory of Early Textile Mill Villages*, H-4 through H-6.

15. Ibid., H-5.

16. Quinney, "Mill Village Memories," 105.

17. Ibid., 98–109.

18. *Durham Morning Herald*, 7 Mar. 1982; Mary Evelyn Carr Quisenberry to author, 4 Sept. 1977.

19. *The Yackety Yack*, 1902.

20. Mary Evelyn Carr Quisenberry to author, 4 Sept. 1977.

21. Powell, *Dictionary of North Carolina Biography* 1:320; Margaret Carr Levings to author, 27 July 1983.

22. Boyd, *Story of Durham*, 125–26.

23. Ibid.

24. Minutes of the Durham Hosiery Mill directors, 10 Apr. 1907; interview with Albert G. Carr.

25. *The Yackety Yack*, 1905; University Student Records, 1905, University Archives, UNC/CH.

26. DHM Minutes, 9 Mar. 1909; Shetley and Bonds, *A Place to Live*.

27. DHM Minutes, 10 Jan., 7 May 1910.

28. Boyd, *Story of Durham*, 132.

29. Ibid.

30. DHM Minutes, 10 Jan., 15 Apr., 27 Aug., 19 Sept., 14 Dec. 1914; 29 Jan., 28 Sept. 1915.

31. *The Yackety Yack*, 1915; A. H. Carr, Jr. to author, 7 Sept. 1981.

32. Laura Noell Carr Chapman to author, 22 Aug. 1975; A. H. Carr, Jr. to author, 7 Sept. 1981.

33. *The Yackety Yack*, 1915; University Student Records, 1915, University Archives, UNC/CH.

34. J. S. Carr Papers, SHC/UNC/CH; J. S. Carr's personal diary for 1911, on loan to author from A. H. Carr, Jr.; A. H. Carr, Jr. to author, 7 Sept. 1981.

35. J. S. Carr to his four sons, 18 Aug. 1916, courtesy of Albert G. Carr, Durham, N.C.

36. *United States Tobacco Journal*, 17 Nov. 1883.

37. Webb, "Confederate Veterans Associations."

CHAPTER ELEVEN

1. Webb, "Confederate Veterans Associations."

2. "To the Confederate Soldier of the Rank and File and to Henry L. Wyatt, the First Hero Who Fell in Defense of the South. By one who sympathized with their successes, mourned their losses, admired their heroism, and shared their hardships. J. S. Carr, Private," speech given by Carr at the Confederate Veterans Reunion, Wilmington, N.C., 1894. Pamphlet loaned to author by O. L. "Bugs" Barringer, Rocky Mount, N.C.; also found in J. S. Carr Papers, SHC/UNC/CH.

3. Scott, *The Southern Lady*, 48.

4. *News and Observer*, 26 May 1899.

5. Russell, *Rare Pattern*, 8.

6. "To the Confederate Soldier." Quotations in ensuing paragraphs are also from this source.

7. J. S. Carr Papers, SHC/UNC/CH.

8. Battle, *History of the University of North Carolina* 2:719–22.

9. J. S. Carr Papers, SHC/UNC/CH.

10. Ibid.

11. J. S. Carr to the Julian S. Carr Bible Class, ibid.

12. Interview with Arthur M. Harris.

13. Childs, *Trinity Methodist Church*, 15; undated newspaper clipping in A. H. Carr, Jr. Papers.

14. *Gen. Julian S. Carr*, 3–6; copy ibid.

15. Childs, *Trinity Methodist Church*, 15; *Durham Daily Globe*, 6 Oct. 1889.

16. J. S. Carr to J. F. Heitman, 10 Oct. 1885, John Franklin Heitman Papers.

17. Ibid., 25 Sept. 1886.

18. *Durham Daily Globe*, 6 Oct. 1889.

19. Occoneechee Farm Diary kept by J. S. Carr, C. S. Brown, and B. S. Skinner; Julian S. Carr Papers, Perkins Library, Duke University.

20. Federal Writers' Project, *North Carolina*, 420. A letter from Charlotte Brown Tyner to Aycock Brown, dated 18 Mar. 1975 and later given to author by Aycock Brown, a son of Charles Spurgeon Brown, states: "After Rufus Patterson and John Motley Morehead gave the Bell Tower to the University of North Carolina, Mr. Patterson told Papa that any time he wanted to, to go over and play whatever he wanted to hear."

21. Occoneechee Diary, 25 Sept. 1910.

22. Ibid., 10 Oct. 1910.

23. Ibid., 15 Oct. 1910.

24. Ibid., 22, 26 Nov. 1910.

25. Ibid., 8–25 Mar. 1911.

26. Letter to author from M. L. Toler, University Archivist, North Carolina State University, Raleigh, containing a photocopied excerpt from David A. Lockmiller's *History of the N.C. State College*.

27. Occoneechee Diary, 11 Apr. 1911.

28. Ibid., 9 Aug. 1911.

29. Ibid., 16 Sept.–30 Dec. 1911.

CHAPTER TWELVE

1. J. S. Carr Diary, Jan.–Feb. 1911, A. H. Carr, Jr. Papers.

2. J. S. Carr Diary, 20 June 1911, ibid.

3. Powell, *Dictionary of North Carolina Biography* 1:205.

4. *News and Observer*, 16 Nov. 1911.

5. Ruth Patton Kline to author, 18 Aug. 1979; J. S. Carr Diary, 1912, J. S. Carr Papers, SHC/UNC/CH.

6. Mary Evelyn Carr Quisenberry to author, 4 Sept. 1977; A. M. Carr to J. S. Carr and N. G. Carr, 12 Apr. 1912, J. S. Carr Papers, SHC/UNC/CH.

7. Aurelia B. Fitzpatrick to J. S. and N. G. Carr, 12 Apr. 1912, ibid.

8. J. S. Carr Diary, 27 Feb.–1 Aug. 1912, ibid.

9. Western Union Telegram from A. M. and A. F. Carr to J. S. and N. G. Carr; J. S. Carr to A. M. and A. F. Carr; both 12 Oct. 1912, ibid.

10. J. S. Carr Diary, 10 Oct. 1912, ibid.

11. Durden, *Dukes of Durham*, 138.

12. J. S. Carr Diary, 1 Jan., 4 Feb. 1913; A. H. Carr, Jr. Papers.

13. Ibid., 22 Aug. 1913; J. S. Carr to A. F. Carr, 6 Feb. 1914, courtesy of Mary Evelyn Carr Quisenberry.

14. J. S. Carr to A. F. Carr, 6 Feb. 1914; J. S. Carr to Mary Evelyn Carr, 24 Dec. 1919, both courtesy of Mary Evelyn Carr Quisenberry.

15. J. S. Carr to L. R. C. Patton, 18 July 1919; J. S. Carr Papers, SHC/UNC/CH.

16. Interview with Clarence Walker.

17. *Durham Sun*, 26 Apr. 1939; interview with Arnold Briggs (past president of Austin Heaton Company).

18. *Durham Sun*, 26 Apr. 1939.

19. Ibid., 25 Oct. 1967; letter to author from Nita M. Brock, former secretary to Arnold Briggs, 28 July 1983. Austin Heaton Carr eventually became chairman of the board of directors of the Austin Heaton Company, which was sold to the Harris Milling Company of Owassa, Michigan, in 1961, but continued to operate as a subsidiary of that firm until it was acquired, in 1966, by the Nebraska Consolidated Mill Company of Omaha. In 1967, Nebraska Consolidated sold the Durham Plant to the Durham Redevelopment Commission, which tore down the mill building and the grain elevators in 1970.

20. *Durham Sun*, 18 Aug. 1915; J. S. Carr Diary, 10 May–14 June 1914, J. S. Carr Papers, SHC/UNC/CH.

21. J. S. Carr Diary, 10 May–14 June 1914, ibid.

22. *Durham Morning Herald*, 19 Aug. 1915.

23. Ibid.

24. Copy of undated clipping from *Durham Morning Herald*, A. H. Carr, Jr. Papers.

25. *Durham Morning Herald*, 19 Aug. 1915.

26. Interview with Kate Lee Hundley Harris.

27. Selected Up-To-Date Club Minutes, courtesy of Julia Manning Wily, Durham, N.C.; A. H. Carr, Jr. to author, 4 Sept. 1984.

28. Green, *Greathearted Citizen*, 111–13.

29. Nannie G. Carr to J. S. Carr, n.d.; on loan to author from Rufus T. Carr, Lawrence, N.Y.

30. J. S. Carr Diary for 1916, J. S. Carr Papers, SHC/UNC/CH.

31. DHM Minutes, 16 Jan. 1912; J. S. Carr Diary, 21 Feb. 1916.

32. Edward Parrish Carr to Claiborn McD. Carr, 18 Jan. 1947; on loan to author from Rufus T. Carr.

33. J. S. Carr Diary, 23 Apr.–23 June 1916.

34. J. S. Carr to "My Four Dear Good Boys," 18 Aug. 1916, on loan to author from Albert G. Carr, Durham, N.C.

35. Undated clipping in J. S. Carr Diary, 1917, A. H. Carr, Jr. Papers.

36. J. S. Carr to Martha Boynton Craige, Atlanta, Ga., n.d.; J. S. Carr to E. M. C. Flower, n.d. [1919]; both in J. S. Carr Papers, SHC/UNC/CH.

37. *Morning Herald*, 15 Jan. 1917. This paper later became the *Durham Morning Herald*.

CHAPTER THIRTEEN

1. J. S. Carr Diary, 14–17 Jan. 1917, A. H. Carr, Jr. Papers.

2. Ibid., 6–11 Feb. 1917; Wa Wa Touring Club Minutes, printed aboard ship and placed in diary by Carr.

3. J. S. Carr Diary, 22 Feb., 26 Feb.–20 Mar. 1917.

4. Ibid., 21–31 Mar. 1917.

5. Ibid., 1–6 Apr. 1917; C. McD. Carr, Jr. to author, 19 Oct. 1976: "These vases were given to C. M. Carr, Sr. and would be worth a considerable amount today, but alas—they were broken by CMC's boys playing ball in the library [at Somerset Villa]. On JSC's return from China, he tried to send Soong an appropriate gift to offset the three vases. His choice was a fire siren for the town in which Soong lived." Actually, only two of the vases were broken, and only one beyond repair; the other was skillfully mended. After the pair came into the possession of A. H. Carr, Jr., they were presented to Morehead house, part of the Morehead Planetarium at the University of North Carolina. The mended vase was stolen from Morehead House and has not been recovered; the remaining vase is at the entrance to the hall leading

to the parlor. The top opening is fifteen inches across; it is approximately twenty-five inches wide at its widest middle curve, and it stands three feet high. The design is in royal blue, Chinese red, and gold, on a creamy white background. An impressive artifact.

6. J. S. Carr Diary, 19–28 Apr. 1917; Postal Telegraph-Cable Company Night Letter, 28 Apr. 1917, pasted in diary.

7. *Durham Morning Herald*, 1 May 1917.

8. Ibid., n.d.; also pasted in diary.

9. Raleigh *Christian Advocate*, 17 May 1917.

10. Newspaper clipping pasted in J. S. Carr diary for 1917.

11. *Food Administration Bulletin No. 6* (Washington, D.C.: Government Printing Office, 1917), 2.

12. J. S. Carr Diary, 31 Aug., 5 Sept. 1917.

13. *Food Administration Bulletin No. 6*, 4.

14. Laura Noell Carr Chapman to author, 30 Oct. 1975.

15. J. S. Carr to L. R. C. Patton, 1 Dec. 1919, 1 Jan. 1920, J. S. Carr Papers, SHC/UNC/CH.

16. J. S. Carr to Mrs. W. J. Conzelman, Pekin, Ill., 4 Jan. 1919, ibid.

17. J. S. Carr to L. R. C. Patton, 10 Jan. 1919, ibid.

18. J. S. Carr to E. M. C. Flower, 16 Jan. 1919; J. S. Carr to L. R. C. Patton, 16 Jan. 1919; J. S. Carr to Mrs. R. U. Lyons, Washington, D.C., 17 Jan. 1919, ibid.

19. J. S. Carr to L. R. C. Patton, n.d. [May 1919], ibid.; *Durham Morning Herald*, 23 Sept. 1919.

20. *Durham Morning Herald*, 23 Sept. 1919.

21. J. S. Carr to L. R. C. Patton, 15 Oct., 20 Jan. 1919, J. S. Carr Papers, SHC/UNC/CH.

22. J. S. Carr Diary, 25 Sept. 1919; J. S. Carr to Mrs. E. M. Moffatt, Richmond, Va., 16 Oct. 1919, J. S. Carr Papers, SHC/UNC/CH.

23. J. S. Carr to L. R. C. Patton, 15 Oct. 1919, J. S. Carr Papers, SHC/UNC/CH.

24. Ibid., 1 Dec. 1919.

25. Ibid., 20 Jan. 1920.

26. Ibid.

27. J. S. Carr to E. M. C. Flower, 18 July 1919, ibid.

28. *Durham Morning Herald*, 15 Oct. 1920.

29. Webb, "Columbus Day Big in Durham"; interview with Laura Noell Carr Chapman.

30. Two clippings from unnamed, undated newspapers sent by Ruth Patton Kline to author, 5 June 1982.

31. Ruth Patton Kline to author, 18 Aug. 1977.

32. Ibid., 5 June 1982.

33. Ibid.; J. S. Carr to L. R. C. Patton, 14 July 1914, J. S. Carr Papers, SHC/UNC/CH.

34. Ruth Patton Kline to author, 5 June 1982.

35. Boyd, *Story of Durham*, 134–35.

36. "Tribute to the Memory of Julian S. Carr, Jr. by his Pastor, Rev. A. D. Wilcox, Upon the Occasion of His Funeral, Sunday, March 19th, 1922," undated clipping on loan to author from Julian S. Carr III, Atlanta.

37. *Greensboro Daily News* and *Charlotte Observer*, 18 Mar. 1922.

38. Margaret Cannon Carr to Laura Noell Carr, 18 Dec. 1941, A. H. Carr, Jr. Papers.

39. J. S. Carr III to author, 5 Oct. 1977.

40. *Chapel Hill News*, 25 Mar. 1922.

41. Ibid.; *Greensboro Daily News*, 20 Mar. 1922.

CHAPTER FOURTEEN

1. Thomas M. Gorman to C. L. Blomberg, 24 Aug. 1921, J. S. Carr Papers, SHC/UNC/CH.

2. J. S. Carr to Lizzie Carr Harris, 13 Dec. 1919, ibid.

3. T. M. Gorman to Bank of Cooleemee, Bank of Roxboro, Bank of Alamance, Bank of Chapel Hill et al.; 18 July, 6, 17, 29 Aug., 5, 8 Sept. 1921, ibid.

4. Webb, "Columbus Day Big in Durham"; *Durham Morning Herald*, 1, 2, 6 Apr. 1922.

5. *Durham Morning Herald*, 12 Oct. 1976.

6. Battle, *History of the University of North Carolina* 2:104, 127, 448, 552, 272, 245, 589, 444.

7. *Carr Building Presented.*

8. Interview with Aycock Brown; Charlotte Brown Tyner to Aycock Brown, 26 Feb. 1975, copy in author's possession.

9. Charlotte Brown Tyner to Aycock Brown, 26 Feb. 1975; J. S. Carr to E. M. C. Flower, n.d. [1919], J. S. Carr Papers, SHC/UNC/CH.

10. *Durham Morning Herald*, 26 Oct. 1923.

11. Interview with Clarence Walker.

12. *Chicago Tribune*, 25 May 1924.

13. *Durham Morning Herald*, 4 May 1924.

14. This account of Durham's public reaction to Carr's death was told to the author by Caro Bacon Fuller (deceased), Durham, N.C., and enhanced in an interview with Laura Noell Carr Chapman.

15. J. S. Carr Papers, SHC/UNC/CH.

16. Interview with Laura Noell Carr Chapman.

17. *Durham Morning Herald*, 30 Apr. 1924.

18. Ibid., 4 May 1924.

19. J. S. Carr Papers, SHC/UNC/CH.

20. *Durham Morning Herald*, 30 Apr., 1 May 1924.

21. Reprinted in *Durham Morning Herald*, 4 May 1924.

22. Ibid. The *Wilmington Star* editorial and others from the *Hickory Record, High Point Enterprise, News and Observer, Asheville Citizen, Winston-Salem Journal, Charlotte Observer*, and *Greensboro News*, were reprinted in the 4 May 1924 edition of the *Durham Morning Herald*, along with telegrams received by

Carr's family from the president of the United States, the governor of North Carolina, and the commanding general of the United Confederate Veterans of America.

23. Accounts of Carr's consistent good manners were forthcoming after the *Durham Morning Herald* requested, on 4 September 1945, that readers send in "anecdotes, illustrative stories, personal experiences, and other personal and interesting data about General Carr." An interview in the *United States Tobacco Journal,* 17 Nov. 1883, also referred to Carr's politeness, especially to his employees.

24. *Durham Morning Herald,* 5 May 1924.

25. *News and Observer,* 2 May 1924.

26. *Durham Morning Herald,* 5 May 1924.

AFTERWORD

1. Green, *Greathearted Citizen,* 84.

Bibliography

ARCHIVAL MANUSCRIPT COLLECTIONS

In Durham County (N.C.) Court House:
  Minutes of the Board of Aldermen, 1872–73.
In Orange County (N.C.) Court House:
  Orange County Deed Books
In Perkins Library, Duke University, Durham:
  Julian S. Carr Papers, Manuscript Department
  John Franklin Heitman Papers, University Archives
In North Carolina State Department of Archives and History, Raleigh:
  Julian S. Carr Papers
  Golden Belt Hosiery Company Papers
  Cornelia Phillips Spencer Papers
In Wilson Library, University of North Carolina, Chapel Hill:
  Julian S. Carr Papers, North Carolina Collection
  Julian S. Carr Papers, Southern Historical Collection
  R. L. Patterson Papers, Southern Historical Collection
  Student Records and Faculty Reports, University Archives
  University Student Records, University Archives

PRIVATE COLLECTIONS

W. T. Blackwell Papers. In possession of Mary Blackwell Pridgen Martin, Durham, N.C.
Carr Family Bible. In possession of Kate Lee Hundley Harris, Durham, N.C.
Carr Family Papers. In possession of Austin Heaton Carr, Jr., Winston-Salem, N.C.
———. In possession of Rufus Tucker Carr, Lawrence, N.Y.
Eliza Morehead Carr's Bride Book. In possession of Ruth Flower Lester, Kansas City, Mo.
Eliza Morehead Carr [Flower] Papers. In possession of Ruth Flower Lester, Kansas City, Mo.
Artifacts re: Julian S. Carr's military record. In possession of Laura Noell Carr Chapman, Spartanburg, S.C.
"Tribute to the Memory of Julian S. Carr, Jr., by His Pastor, Rev. A. D. Wilcox, Upon the Occasion of His Funeral, Sunday, March 19th, 1922." Clipping (n.d.) in possession of Julian S. Carr III, Atlanta, Ga.
John B. Halcott's handwritten "History of the Construction of Somerset Villa, the Residence of Mr. J. S. Carr, Durham, N.C." In possession of Austin Heaton Carr, Jr., Winston-Salem, N.C.

Eugene Morehead Journal, 1869–71. In possession of Julia Manning Wily, Durham, N.C.

PERSONAL COMMUNICATIONS

Charlotte Brown Tyner to Aycock Brown, 18 Mar. 1975. (Copies of this and all subsequently cited correspondence are in the author's possession.)
R. P. Baker to author, 5 Feb. 1980.
Catherine W. Bishir to author, 6 Aug. 1982.
Nita M. Brock to author, 28 July 1983.
A. H. Carr, Jr. to author, 7 Sept. 1981, 4 Sept. 1984.
Claiborn McD. Carr, Jr. to author, 19 Oct. 1976, 5 Jan. 1982.
J. S. Carr III to author, 5 Oct. 1977.
Laura Noell Carr Chapman to author, 30 Oct. 1975.
Ruth Patton Kline to author, 18 Aug. 1977, 18 Aug. 1979.
Ruth Flower Lester to author, 25 Aug. 1977.
Margaret Carr Levings to author, 27 July 1983.
Mary Evelyn Carr Quisenberry to author, 4 Sept. 1977.
Kathy Stone to author, 5 Mar. 1982.
M. L. Toler to author, 27 July 1982.

INTERVIEWS

Briggs, Arnold. Interview with author. Durham, N.C. 10 May 1978. (Transcripts of this and all other interviews are in author's possession.)
Brown, Aycock. Interview with author. Manteo, N.C. 12 Aug. 1977.
Carr, Albert G. Interview with author. Durham, N.C. 1 June 1983.
Carr, J. Claiborne. Interview with author. Hillsborough, N.C. 20 Sept. 1982.
Chapman, Laura Noell Carr. Interview with author. Spartanburg, S.C. 27 Nov. 1977.
Harris, Arthur M. Interview with author. Durham, N.C. 7 May 1975.
Harris, Kate Lee Hundley. Interview with author. Durham, N.C. 10 May 1979.
Walker, Clarence. Interview with author. Hillsborough, N.C. 10 May 1978.
Webb, Gertrude Winston. Interview with author. Durham, N.C. 14 Apr. 1975.
Webb, Mary Leigh. Interview with author. Hillsborough, N.C. 9 June 1979.

NEWSPAPERS

Asheville Citizen, Asheville, N.C.
Charlotte Observer, Charlotte, N.C.
Daily Sentinel, Raleigh, N.C.
Daily Tobacco Plant, Durham, N.C.

Durham Daily Globe, Durham, N.C.
Durham Morning Herald, Durham, N.C.
Durham Sun, Durham, N.C.
Greensboro Daily News, Greensboro, N.C.
Hickory Record, Hickory, N.C.
High Point Enterprise, High Point, N.C.
Hillsboro Observer, Hillsboro, N.C. (Spelling of the name of the town of
   Hillsboro changed to Hillsborough within the past decade.)
News and Observer, Raleigh, N.C.
News of Orange County, Hillsborough, N.C.
Tobacco Leaf, New York, N.Y.
Tobacco Plant, Durham, N.C.
United States Tobacco Journal, New York, N.Y.
Wilmington Star, Wilmington, N.C.
Winston-Salem Journal, Winston-Salem, N.C.

BOOKS, ARTICLES, THESES

Albright, R. Mayne. "The Senator and the Simmons Machine." *The State*
   50:6 (Nov. 1982): 8–12–31.
Battle, Kemp Plummer. *History of the University of North Carolina*. 2 vols. Ra-
   leigh: Edwards and Broughton Printing Company, 1907 and 1912.
Boyd, William Kenneth. *The Story of Durham: The City of the New South*. Dur-
   ham: Duke University Press, 1927.
Cameron, J. D. *A Sketch of the Tobacco Interests in North Carolina*. Oxford,
   N.C.: W. A. Davis Company, 1881.
*The Carr Building Presented: A Handsome Gift Worthily Presented and Received on
   Commencement Day at Chapel Hill, N.C., June 8, 1900*. Philadelphia: George
   H. Buchanan and Company, 1900.
Cash, W. J. *The Mind of the South*. New York: Alfred A. Knopf, 1941.
Chaffin, Nora C. *Trinity College, 1839–1892: The Beginnings of Duke Univer-
   sity*. Durham: Duke University Press, 1950.
Chamberlain, Hope Summerell. *Old Days in Chapel Hill: Being the Life and
   Letters of Cornelia Phillips Spencer*. Chapel Hill: University of North Caro-
   lina Press, 1926.
Childs, Benjamin G. *Trinity Methodist Church, 1861–1936: 75 Years of Meth-
   odism*. Durham: Trinity Methodist Church, on the occasion of its Dia-
   mond Jubilee [1936].
Clark, Walter, ed. *Histories of the Several Regiments and Battalions from North
   Carolina*. 5 vols. Raleigh: E. M. Ussell, 1901.
Commemorative Biographical Record of Central Pennsylvania. Chicago: J. H.
   Beers and Company, 1898.
Crow, Jeffrey J., and Durden, Robert F. *Maverick Republican in the Old North
   State: A Political Biography of Daniel L. Russell*. Baton Rouge: Louisiana
   State University Press, 1977.

Cyclopedia of Eminent and Representative Men of the Carolinas of the Nineteenth Century. 3 vols. Madison, Wis.: Brant and Fuller, 1892.

Daniels, Josephus. *Editor in Politics.* Chapel Hill: University of North Carolina Press, 1941.

———. *Tar Heel Editor.* Chapel Hill: University of North Carolina Press, 1939.

Davis, Burke. *Sherman's March.* New York: Random House, 1980.

Durden, Robert F. *The Dukes of Durham.* Durham: Duke University Press, 1975.

Durham Chamber of Commerce. *Durham, North Carolina: A Young, Prosperous and Progressive City of the New South.* Durham: Seeman Printery, 1906.

Durham Trinity Methodist Church Diamond Jubilee, 1861–1936. Durham: Trinity Methodist Church, 1936.

Faulkner, Ronnie W. "North Carolina Democrats and Silver Fusion Politics, 1892–1896." *North Carolina Historical Review* 59:3 (July 1982): 230–51.

Federal Writers' Project. *North Carolina: A Guide to the Old North State.* Chapel Hill: University of North Carolina Press, 1939.

Feldman, Hazel, ed. *Best Loved Poems of the American People.* New York: Doubleday & Company, 1936.

Food Administration Bulletin No. 6. Washington, D.C.: Government Printing Office, 1917.

Forty Years, 1887–1927. Durham: First National Bank, 1927. (Privately printed by Claiborn McD. Carr, Sr. Copy in possession of author.)

Gen. Julian S. Carr: An Appreciation. Durham: Trinity Methodist Church, 1922.

Gray, Robert Lilly. "'Jule' Carr, the Man: A Pen Picture." Raleigh *News and Observer* pamphlet, n.d., n.p. (Copy in Austin Heaton Carr, Jr., Papers.)

Green, C. Sylvester, ed. *General Julian S. Carr, Greathearted Citizen: Addresses and Addenda of the Centennial Observance of His Birth, Durham, North Carolina, October 12, 1945.* Durham: Seeman Printery, 1946. (Privately printed by Claiborn McD. Carr, Sr.)

Hahn, Emily. *The Soong Sisters.* New York: Doubleday, Doran and Company, 1941.

Handbook of Durham. Durham: The Educator Company, 1895.

The Hellenian. 1898. (Early yearbook published by the fraternities at the University of North Carolina.)

Henderson, Archibald. *The Campus of the First State University.* Chapel Hill: University of North Carolina Press, 1949.

Hobson, Fred, ed. *South-Watching: Selected Essays by Gerald W. Johnson.* Chapel Hill: University of North Carolina Press, 1983.

An Inventory of Early Textile Mill Villages. Durham: Durham Technical Institute, 1980.

Johnson, Guion Griffis. *Antebellum North Carolina: A Social History.* Chapel Hill: University of North Carolina Press, 1937.

Korner, Jule Gilmer, Jr. *Joseph of Kernersville.* Durham: Seeman Printery, 1958.

Lefler, Hugh Talmage, and Newsome, Albert Ray. *North Carolina: The His-*

tory of a Southern State. Chapel Hill: University of North Carolina Press, 1973.

McLaurin, Melton A. "The Nineteenth-Century North Carolina State Fair as a Social Institution." *North Carolina Historical Review* 59:3 (July 1982): 213–29.

Manarin, Louis H. *North Carolina Troops, 1861–1865.* 3 vols. Raleigh: North Carolina Department of Archives and History, 1966.

Mims, Edwin. *History of Vanderbilt University.* Nashville: Vanderbilt University Press, 1946.

The Morehead Family of North Carolina and Virginia. New York: Privately printed by John Motley Morehead, 1921.

Morrison, Joseph L. *Josephus Daniels Says. . . .* Chapel Hill: University of North Carolina Press, 1962.

Moye, William Transou. "The North Carolina Senatorial Primary of 1900 between Furnifold M. Simmons and Julian S. Carr." Master's thesis, University of North Carolina, 1964.

Paul, Hiram Voss. *History of the Town of Durham, North Carolina, Embracing Biographical Sketches and Engravings of Leading Business Men and a Carefully Compiled Business Directory of Durham.* Raleigh: Edwards and Broughton & Company, 1884.

Porter, Earl W. *Trinity and Duke, 1892–1924.* Durham: Duke University Press, 1964.

Powell, William S. *The First State University: A Pictorial History of the University of North Carolina.* Chapel Hill: University of North Carolina Press, 1972.

_____. , ed. *Dictionary of North Carolina Biography*, I. Chapel Hill: University of North Carolina Press, 1979.

Quinney, Valerie. "Mill Village Memories." *Southern Exposure* 8:3 (Fall 1980): 98–109.

Ray, W. S. *Colonial Granville County and Its People.* Baltimore: Southern Book Company, 1956.

Robert, Joseph C. *The Story of Tobacco in America.* New York: Alfred A. Knopf, 1949.

Russell, Lucy Phillips. *A Rare Pattern.* Chapel Hill: University of North Carolina Press, 1957.

Scott, Anne Firor. *The Southern Lady: From Pedestal to Politics, 1830–1930.* Chicago: University of Chicago Press, 1970.

Seagrave, Sterling. *The Soong Dynasty.* New York: Harper and Row, 1985.

Shetley, Frances L., and Bonds, Lou. *A Place to Live: Carrboro, North Carolina.* N.p. Privately printed by the authors, 1978.

"Somerset Villa, the Home of Mr. Julian S. Carr, Durham, North Carolina." *The Southern Building Record* (Richmond, Va.) 1:1 (Mar. 1890): 4.

Tilley, Nannie May. *The Bright Tobacco Industry, 1860–1929.* Chapel Hill: University of North Carolina Press, 1948.

Tourtellot, Arthur. "C. J. Soong and the United States Coast Guard." *U.S. Naval Institute Proceedings* 75 (Feb. 1949): 201–3.

Vickers, James; Scism, Thomas; and Qualls, Dixon. *Chapel Hill, an Illustrated History.* Chapel Hill: Barclay Publishers, 1985.

Webb, Mena. "Birth of a County." *Durham Morning Herald*, 26 Apr. 1981.
———. "Columbus Day Big in Durham Because of Birth of Julian Carr."
Durham Sun, 12 Oct. 1976.
———. "The House Bull Durham Built." *Tar Heel* 7:1 (Jan.–Feb. 1979): 27–
28, 61.
Webb, William E. "A History of Confederate Veterans Associations and Re-
lated Societies." Master's thesis, Duke University, 1947.
Wheeler, John Hill. *Reminiscences and Memoirs of North Carolina and Eminent
North Carolinians*. Columbus, Ohio: Columbus Printing Works, 1884.
Winston, George Tayloe. "John Wesley Carr." *University Magazine* 9:5 (1889–
90): 209–14.
The Yackety Yack. 1902, 1905, 1915. (University of North Carolina student
yearbook.)

Index

as JSC's company, 74–80, 82, 102, 104, 144; bought out by American Tobacco Company, 138–39, 163. *See also* W. T. Blackwell Company

Blackwell v. *Dibrell*, 55

Blanche Hosiery Mill Company, 185

Blandwood (Morehead estate), 88–90

Bloomer, A. T., 177

Bon Ton Flour, 226

Booth, Nash, 53

Borglum, Gutzon, 231

Bottled water business, Austin's, 188

Bowles, W. H., 30

Boyd, William Kenneth, xi

Boylan, Margaret Jordan (Mrs. Claiborn Carr), 213, 217

Boylan, William, 213

Bradsher, Jones, 223

Brady, Anthony N., 139

Branson, William H., 81, 97

Brewster, J. C., 107

Briggs, Arnold, 267

Brown, Charles Spurgeon, 200–206, 209, 211, 223, 229, 256

Brown, Maggie (Mrs. Charles S.), 201–3, 205, 206

Bryan, Charles Shepard, 101, 102

Bryan, James Augustus, 101

Bryan, William Jennings, 165, 167–68, 171

Buchanan, James (President), 14–16

Bull Durham tobacco. *See* "Genuine Durham Smoking Tobacco"; Trademark

Bull Factory. *See* Blackwell's Durham Tobacco Company; W. T. Blackwell and Company

Bullock, Eliza. *See* Carr, Eliza Bullock

Bullock family history, 5

Burgwyn, William Hyslop Sumner, 254–55

Burke, Carl, 224

Burke, Lorena (Mrs. Carl), 224

Burkhead, W. G., 93–96

Burnett, Aurelia, 265

Butler (Senator), 57

Butler, Marion, 161, 164, 165, 168, 171, 172

Cameron, Bennehan, 71, 148, 150

Cameron, Paul, 71

Campbell, Mary, 89

Cannon, James (Reverend), 263

Cannon, James William (Margaret's father), 183, 249

Cannon, Margaret (Mrs. Julian Carr, Jr.), 183, 222, 249

Canterbury Club, 157

Carlyle, Thomas, 57, 222

Carolina Hosiery Commission, 177

Carr, Albert (JSC's grandnephew), 268

Carr, Albert Gallatin (JSC's brother), 4, 25, 104, 221, 230

Carr, Albert Marvin (JSC's son), 114, 124, 213, 232, 249; as businessman, 140, 182–85, 238; illness and death of, 238, 240–41, 248, 257

Carr, Albert Marvin, Jr., 222

Carr, Anderson Beaufort, 6

Carr, Annie Parrish, 220–21, 227, 230

Carr, Austin Heaton, 157, 213, 220, 226, 232, 236, 237, 249, 257, 259; as businessman, 140, 185, 242; birth, 148; as student, 185, 187–88, 229; in World War I, 237, 238; marries, 238

Carr, Boylan, 268

Carr, Burroughs Cheek, 6

Carr, Claiborn McDowell (JSC's son), 114, 230, 232, 236, 257, 259, 268; as businessman, 140, 184–85, 238, 242; marries, 213; his first son's birth, 217, 220

Carr, Claiborn McDowell, Jr., 220, 223, 224

Carr, Edward Parrish (JSC's nephew), 230, 236

Carr, Elias (Governor), 147, 157, 162–65, 168

Durham, Dr. Bartlett, 9
Durham (N.C.): John Wesley Carr's
    business in, 9; growth of, 29–32,
    34, 62, 70, 85, 135; holds party
    for JSC, 243–46
Durham and Clarksville Railroad,
    91
Durham and Northern Railroad,
    91–92
Durham and Roxboro Railroad, 86,
    91
Durham and Southern Railroad, 91
Durham Chamber of Commerce,
    267
Durham Consolidated Land and
    Improvement Company, 100
Durham Cotton Manufacturing
    Company, 80–82, 97, 98, 137, 145
Durham County (N.C.): creation of,
    70–72
Durham Daily Globe, 162, 163
Durham Electric Lighting Company,
    99, 100, 104
Durham Hosiery Company, 176–77
Durham Hosiery Mill, 228, 248,
    249, 261; JSC establishes, for his
    sons, 140, 175–77, 181–88, 222,
    229, 238, 240, 242; company
    housing for workers, 181; child la-
    bor, 181–82; black workers, 183–
    84; profit sharing at, 186–87; JSC
    retires from, 200, 212; financial
    difficulties of, 252, 256
Durham Manufacturers' Home Fur-
    nishing Agency, 144
Durham Morning Herald, 228, 236,
    243–44, 256–59, 261, 267, 268
Durham Street Railway, 99–100
Durham Sun, 261
Durham Traction Company, 100
Durhamville (N.C.). *See* Durham
    (N.C.)
Duty, Martha, 45

Eagle Hotel (Chapel Hill), 12, 13
Early, Jubal, 194
Eddy, Mary Baker, 240

Edgemont (N.C.): company housing
    in, 181–82, 187
Electricity: and JSC, 98–100
Emancipation Proclamation, 26, 193
Erwin, Mrs. (J. Harper), 229
Essner, Carl G., 153–54
Exum, Wyatt, 163

F. S. Kinney Company (New York
    and Richmond), 79
Fairbrother, Al, 96–97, 162
Farmer and Mechanic (newspaper), 97
Farmers Alliance, 161, 163, 168
Farming. *See* North Carolina State
    Agricultural Society; Occoneechee
    Farm
Ferribault, George, 223
Fetter, Manuel, 9, 19
Fidelity Trust Company, 186
Fifth Street Methodist Church (Wil-
    mington), 122, 130
First National Bank of Durham,
    104, 112, 176, 197, 226, 227, 229,
    261; establishment of, 101–3; as
    JSC's main interest, 103, 188
Fitzpatrick, Aurelia Blassingame
    (Mrs. Albert Marvin Carr), 217,
    220–22, 238, 241
Fitzpatrick, Benjamin, 217
Flour, 225–26
Flower, Henry Corwin, 148, 152–54,
    157, 160, 186, 213
Flower, Henry Corwin, Jr., 158
Flower, Lida Carr (Mrs. Henry C.).
    See Carr, Eliza Morehead ("Lida")
Flower, Ruth (JSC's granddaugh-
    ter), 158, 231
Fou Foong Flour Mill, 132, 140
Freedmen's Bureau, 26, 193
Freeland, J. F., 8, 94–95
Freud, Sigmund, 254
Fuller, Annie Staples, 73
Fuller, Thomas B. (accountant), 78
Fuller, Thomas C. (lawyer), 62, 71
Fuller, Williamson Whitehead, 71–
    74, 91, 100, 102
Furches, David, 163

U.S.S. *Maine*, 177
Union Tobacco Company, 139
United Confederate Veterans of America, 97, 188–98, 212–13, 260; reunions of, 191, 195–98, 226, 231, 236
United Daughters of the Confederacy, 79, 263, 268
United States Department of Revenue, 89
United States Food Administration, 237
United States Tobacco Journal, 55, 75
University of North Carolina: JSC's father and, 9; as influence on JSC, 12, 57, 127; commencements at, 13–18, 25–26, 28, 58–59, 254–55; effects of Civil War on, 16–29; and JSC's sons, 178–79, 182–85, 187–88; honors JSC, 243, 254–56
Up-to-Date Club, 228, 229

Vance, Zebulon B., 164–65, 179, 231
Vanderbilt University: Charlie Soon attends, 125–27
Vickers, Riley, 53
Villa, Pancho, 231
Virginia: tobacco production in, 70
Voting requirements: for blacks, 170–71

W. Duke Sons and Company, 55, 79, 91–92, 101, 102
W. E. Dibrell and Company, 54–55, 62
W. S. Kimball and Company, 79
W. T. Blackwell Company, 68, 69, 73, 93, 141, 144; JSC's father buys into, 3, 9, 35–37; origins of, 30–34; legal conflicts involving, 51–56; and rivals, 51–61, 79–80, 138–39; and ads, 57–60, 94; its effect on Durham, 63, 70–71; and railroads, 86, 91–93. *See also* Advertising; Blackwell's Durham Tobacco Company; Inventions

Waddell, Alfred M., 169, 172, 173
Waddell, John A., 47
Waitt, Kendal, 22
Wake Forest College, 138
Walker, Clarence, 223–25, 231, 257
Walker, J. W., 102
Walker, Mildred, 5
Walker, Solomon, 4–5
Ward, Edward, 42
Ward, Enoch, 42
Ward, Marmaduke, 42
Ward, N. A., 32
Ward, Ruth Ann. *See* Parrish, Ruth
Ward, W. A., 30
Washington, George, 4–5, 194
Watson, Cyrus B., 168
Watson, Jones, 8
Watts, George Washington, 98–99, 101
Watts, Gerrard S., 60, 101
Watts and Company, 62
Waverly Honor, 47, 50, 82, 90, 104, 124–26, 132–33
Wesley, John, 6
Wetherill Corless Co., 94
Wheeler, Joseph (General), 22, 46
Whitaker, J. B., 95, 96
Whitelaw, John, 107
White supremacy: as campaign issue, 168–74
Whitney, William C., 139
Whitted, John Y., 32–33
Widener, Peter A. B., 139
Wier, William John, 107
Wilbur, Mr. (poultryman), 203, 204
Williams, Horace, 129, 136
Williams, Julia R., 150
Williams, Walter, 268
Wilmington Messenger, 162
Wilmington *Star*, 122, 261–62
Wilson, J. A., 107
Wilson, John M., 47
Wilson, Peter M., 91
Wilson, Woodrow (President), 232, 236
Windsor Ledger, 172
Winston-Salem Journal, 261–62